Tales from Topographic Oceans

Yes album
Listening Guide

This book is dedicated to all Yes fans

Tales from Topographic Oceans

Yes album Listening Guide

Kevin Mulryne

Five Per Cent For Something Publishing
yesmusicbooks.com
Email: show@yesmusicpodcast.com

First Published in the United Kingdom 2025
First Published in the United States 2025
British Library Cataloguing in Publication Data: A Catalogue record for this book is available from the British Library

Copyright © Kevin Mulryne 2025

ISBN 9781739213343

The right of Kevin Mulryne to be identified as the author of this work has been asserted by him in accordance with the Copyright, Designs and Patents Act 1988

All rights reserved. No part of this publication may be reproduced, stored in a retrieval system or transmitted in any form or by any means, electronic, mechanical, photocopying, recording or otherwise, without prior permission in writing from Five Per Cent For Something Publishing

Typesetting and production management: Bob Carling
Cover Design: Paul Laue

Paintings, logos and design for Tales from Topographic Oceans and other incidental works are painted by and © Roger Dean 1973 and later, used by kind permission
www.rogerdean.com

By the same author:

Tales from Topographic Oceans – Yes album Listening Guide Full-Colour Supplement

Yes – The Tormato Story

Yes – The Tormato Story Full-Colour Supplement

https://yesmusicbooks.com

CONTENTS

PREFACE	1
PART 1 – INTRODUCTION	**3**
1 THE CONTEXT	5
2 THE CONCEPT	15
PART 2 – PREPARING AND RECORDING THE ALBUM	**29**
3 REHEARSALS AT MANTICORE	31
4 RECORDING AT MORGAN STUDIOS	43
PART 3 – THE INSTRUMENTS AND TECHNICALITIES	**67**
5 RICK WAKEMAN'S KEYBOARDS	69
6 ALAN WHITE'S DRUMS AND PERCUSSION	95
7 STEVE HOWE'S GUITARS	101
8 CHRIS SQUIRE'S BASSES	113
PART 4 – THE MOVEMENTS	**125**
9 MY MOVEMENT REVIEWS	127
10 THE LYRICS	137
11 TALES LISTENING GUIDES	145
12 MOVEMENT GUIDE 1 – THE REVEALING SCIENCE OF GOD – DANCE OF THE DAWN	155
13 MOVEMENT GUIDE 2 – THE REMEMBERING – HIGH THE MEMORY	165
14 MOVEMENT GUIDE 3 – THE ANCIENT – GIANTS UNDER THE SUN	175
15 MOVEMENT GUIDE 4 – RITUAL – NOUS SOMME DU SOLEIL	183
PART 5 – ALBUMS AND SINGLES	**193**
16 ALBUM ARTWORK AND RELEASE FORMATS	195
17 STEVEN WILSON REMIX	235
PART 6 – PROMOTION AND RECEPTION	**255**
18 ALBUM AND TOUR PROMOTION	257
19 ALBUM RECEPTION	263
PART 7 – TALES LIVE	**269**
20 TALES ON TOUR IN 1973 AND 1974	271
21 THE SCENERY	297

22	TALES LIVE – A FAN'S VIEW	309
23	TALES ON TOUR IN LATER YEARS	315
24	LIVE TALES BY GEOFF BAILIE	319
25	LIVE REVIEWS	331
26	TOUR BOOKS/PROGRAMMES	337
27	CONCERT MEMORABILIA	347

PART 8 – EPILOGUE — **351**

| 28 | EPILOGUE | 353 |
| | ACKNOWLEDGEMENTS | 357 |

EXECUTIVE PRODUCERS
who made this book possible

John Thomson
Rachel Hadaway
Phil Rathe
Paul Jeynes
Simon Stopher
Al Dell'Angelo
Paul Tomei
Sean McCarthy
Doug Curran
Steven English
Keith Winters
Marc Troyan
James McQuinn
Michael OConnor
Thomas Perkins
Emma Leach
Jeffrey Crecelius
Paulina Mennen
Timothy Landers
Bob Vandiver
Raymond Riethmeier
Stewart Munro
Preston Michael Frazier
Frank Natale
Michael Handerhan

Thank you
Kevin Mulryne 2025

PREFACE

" ... probably progressive rock's biggest and most difficult work."

Bill Martin, Music of Yes – Structure and
Vision in Progressive Rock, 1996

"It could have been Yes' Titanic. Would it sink or not? I think that was the real challenge. If Yes did not have a challenge, then we would slip into a place we did not want to go. Topographic was a quest, a mission that Jon and I conceived. Was it viable? Was it doable? Was it reasonable? Was it musical? Was it going to strangle the audience or was it going to enlighten them? I think that vastness was one of the wonderful things about it, because during that time, we had tremendous scope, and the freedom to dabble with all sorts of music."

Steve Howe quoted in the Gottleib Bros. official tour book
for The Classic Tales of Yes Tour, 2023

When I completed *Yes – The Tormato Story*, I had learned many lessons about researching, writing and publishing a book about the world's greatest progressive rock band. However, this did not give me much comfort when embarking on my next project – the book you are now reading. *Tales from Topographic Oceans* was not exactly the easy choice for that 'difficult second book'. The scale of this record is daunting. Not only is it a double album but it also has significant musical, thematic and even visual complexity. The story that surrounds its creation, challenging reception and troublesome but ground-breaking tour deserves careful and painstaking attention. Fortunately, I have had the help of innumerable knowledgeable and generous fans, musicians, technical crew, researchers and collectors. Without them, I could never have completed this listening guide. I have attempted to thank all these people in the acknowledgements section at the end of the book and I hope I haven't missed any out. I am deeply grateful to everyone who has helped in any way.

Initially, the idea for this book was to create a simple – and fairly short – guide to help listeners enjoy the album. Unfortunately, or fortunately, depending on your viewpoint, once I started researching *Tales*, I kept discovering fascinating 'rabbit holes' to explore. From feedback I received about my first book and from listeners to the Yes Music Podcast, I knew that a lot of fans share my love of delving as deeply as possible into the stories around the edges of Yes music. In my experience, this always provides greater understanding of the music, the musicians and the context of their creative processes. As you will see, I have decided to make it clear where these 'side-quests' appear by marking them as RABBIT HOLE TALES. I hope you enjoy reading these as much as I have enjoyed uncovering them.

There is still a listening guide at the heart of this book, which I hope you will find useful and entertaining, but what has evolved could be called sleeve notes on steroids. So this book is for those of us who remember the delight of listening to a Yes album while poring over whatever text we could find on the sleeve – and losing ourselves in the wonderous stories conjured up by Roger Dean's (and occasionally others') artwork.

So let us awaken our musical sensibilities and leap onward ...

Kevin Mulryne, February 2025

PART 1 – INTRODUCTION

1

THE CONTEXT

" ... hearing the music ... was baffling.
It was ... exhilarating.
It was astonishing.
It was exciting.
It was head-scratching.
But in a sense, you just kind of trusted the band, as you did in those days ... that somehow it would all be alright."

Sid Smith, Yes Music Podcast, 2023

Sid Smith is a prolific sleeve note writer and music journalist whose book, *In the Court of King Crimson*, is the definitive study of the band often (if not necessarily accurately) credited with inventing progressive rock. The links between King Crimson and Yes are, as we shall see, numerous and complex, but another reason we wanted Sid to come and talk to us about *Tales* on the Yes Music Podcast was that he wrote the sleeve notes for the Steven Wilson remix of the album.

Sid's view of *Tales* is that it was something Yes had to go through, regardless of its success as an album. As always, there were factions within Yes in 1973 with some members who simply wanted to create *Close to the Edge* Part 2 and others who wanted to keep progressing, to keep pushing the boundaries even further. Steve Howe and Jon Anderson were certainly in the second camp. Sid saw two shows on the *Tales* tour at Newcastle City Hall, so is able to give first-hand testimony about the reaction of fans to hearing the four sides of *Tales* live, the day after the album had been released. Many, if not all, of the audience had not yet heard the record.

A list of selected other albums released in 1973, the year *Tales* emerged, is packed full of influential progressive rock studio albums:

- The Mahavishnu Orchestra – *Birds of Fire*
- Rick Wakeman – *The Six Wives of Henry VIII*
- King Crimson – *Lark's Tongues in Aspic* (featuring the recently acquired former Yes drummer, Bill Bruford)
- Jethro Tull – *A Passion Play*
- Genesis – *Selling England by the Pound*
- ELP – *Brain Salad Surgery*

Sid mentions in his sleeve notes that Yes were perhaps less prone to interference from their record company at this time than other bands. Some of their contemporaries were under pressure to keep doing the same thing but Yes were freer to progress. This was due to a lack of reliance on hit singles and having less of a definable formula than other acts. As Sid stresses, the 1970s was a very different time for record companies – and music – compared to today, or to the decades before then. Music in the 70s was central to popular culture amongst young people. Fortunately for a lot of bands, however, there was a tier of record company executives at the time who had no idea what was going on in popular culture. They appeared simply to trust that the artists on their books would come up with something that would sell. Bands tended to be given time to come up with a formula and produce something people would go out and buy in their droves but for Yes, that period was coming to an end after their second album, *Time and a Word*. It was essential to have not only the songs but also the musicians to enable bands to succeed. Certain members of Yes started to realise that firstly guitarist Peter Banks and then keyboardist Tony Kaye might not be able to provide what they needed to achieve the kind of success they thought they deserved. These concerns were compounded by personality clashes.

When Steve Howe replaced Peter Banks, Sid describes the band as 'going into another gear' with *The Yes Album*. Subsequently, Rick Wakeman replaced Tony Kaye for *Fragile* and *Close to the Edge* and Yes appeared to have solved both its musical and personnel puzzles.

However, there was to follow a surprising and seismic event for the band – the departure of Bill Bruford, just after the completion of *Close to the Edge*. The remaining members have recorded their sense of shock at the time and Sid makes it clear in his book that the leader of King Crimson, Robert Fripp, had planned to try and persuade Bruford to join his band for some time prior to his exit from Yes.

Crimson had themselves undergone a period of massive change between 1969 and 1973 and Fripp had developed a very clear vision for the direction in which he intended to take the band. In 1972, he had lost confidence in King Crimson and was looking to establish something radically different. For example, he had floated ideas back in 1971 for songs which eventually became part of 1973's *Lark's Tongues in Aspic* album and 'Lament' from 1974's *Starless and Bible Black*, but the band as it existed couldn't get to grips with what was required. As Sid points out, Fripp was writing music for a band that didn't exist and the lineup that toured the US in 1972 simply fell apart in April of that year.

Around this time, Fripp was involved in a large number of different musical activities outside King Crimson and probably had his eye on Bill Bruford to work with. The Yes connections with King Crimson were longstanding. For example, Jon Anderson provided guest vocals for a song on the Crimson album *Lizard* right back in 1970 and members of Yes visited Robert Fripp in his flat in 1971 to hear the pre-release Crimson album, *In the Wake of Poseidon* or perhaps more likely *Islands*, due to the date. Yes certainly viewed *Poseidon* as a kind of benchmark against which they could measure their own output. Sid believes that Yes and King Crimson didn't see themselves as rivals in the musical world but certainly Jon Anderson viewed Robert Fripp as someone who was constantly pushing forward, much as he wanted to do with Yes. Yes had a sense of being spurred on by other bands such as King Crimson and The Mahavishnu Orchestra. In fact, Jon Anderson once told Sid of the time they were watching Mahavishnu from the wings in a venue and he turned to the rest of the band and said, "Guys, we got to do some more rehearsing!"

Robert knew Bill well, including his musical strengths. While developing ideas and playing with various different musicians, Robert found himself homeless and Bill Bruford invited him to stay at his flat, during the time Yes were working on *Close to the Edge*. Bill was becoming jaded by the process of recording Yes' masterpiece so maybe conversations between him and Robert Fripp touched on the possibility of working together. In fact, Sid says from talking to both Bill and Robert about the situation, there don't seem to have been any extended late-night conversations chez Bruford and the change was quick when it happened.

Bill has always maintained that he is immensely proud of what he achieved with Yes, and particularly on *Close to the Edge*, but he was also convinced that he had reached the end of what he could with his first major band and wanted to explore more diverse musical landscapes, something he believed was on offer from Robert Fripp. In one of those odd twists of history, Bill was to be complemented in King Crimson's rhythm section by Jamie Muir, the percussionist who was to introduce Jon Anderson to *Autobiography of a Yogi* by Paramahansa Yogananda, a footnote in which became the main inspiration for Anderson's *Tales* vision (see chapter 2).

The departure of Bill Bruford and the arrival of Alan White provide crucial context to how *Tales* ended up sounding. Sid is very impressed with what

White achieved on *Tales*. As we will return to later in this book, Alan not only played his part on the drums but also contributed musical ideas and even played some piano. In an interview for Sounds magazine in 1976, Alan sheds some light on joining Yes:

> "I didn't really know whether I wanted to join a band like that – a progressive band, I mean. I'd always been happy just playing the way I was, with musicians I enjoyed playing with. And the music I was playing was usually a funky kinda thing. But it was a challenge, playing with Yes.
>
> It took me about a year to learn to play with the band, like something always moving forward with your instrument, learning to develop the sound in a certain way, and still keeping the basic roots of your instrument in the music. It really works now."

RABBIT HOLE TALES – HEALTHY BROWNIES'

In the interview above, Alan White (who was reportedly dating Errol Flynn's daughter Rory at the time of the *Tales* recording) mentions a somewhat surprising reason why he managed to fit into the band so quickly:

> [Interviewer] "Was it very difficult to fit into such a tight unit? For example, everybody knows, that Yes are ardent vegetarians. Was there any conflict there?"
>
> [Alan White] "None at all, because I was a vegetarian before I ever joined up with Yes. Eddie Offord was the guy who turned Yes onto vegetarianism, and he got me into it at the same time. I feel much better for it as well. Steve Howe's probably going to stop eating dairy foods as well … there's a lot of energy in the band that I think comes out of their vegetarian attitude, the band can communicate on a much higher level because of it."
>
> [Interviewer] "If most people thought about what they were putting into their bodies." (shudders with disgust/distaste)
>
> [Alan White] I agree with you, though, the self-discipline on its own has a lot to do with it. Steve Howe and myself own a health food shop, y'know, in Hampstead High Street, the one with the bear on the front window, Brownies'."

I asked Steve Howe about how important vegetarianism was to the band at the time of *Tales*.

> "I became vegetarian in 1972 and I guess other people were for a while … It wasn't a necessity that you did, but it spread because Eddie Offord was also very hip to world matters, world food, and it was a kind of a shared thing, really, I guess. The vegetarian side interested me because I guess I was always going to do that anyway … "
>
> Steve Howe, Yes Music Podcast, 2025

1 – THE CONTEXT

Alan and Steve frequented and then bought 'Brownies" from its original owners, Terry and Rene Yallop, sometime between May 1973 and February 1974, after financial problems meant the couple couldn't afford to keep it going.

Daily Express article on Terry Yallop, founder of Brownies', licensed from Reach Publishing Services Ltd.

Despite references to Hampstead High Street in various places, the shop was actually located a little way down the same road, at 36 Rosslyn Hill. Named Brownie's (or Brownies') in reference to the supposedly healthy choices of brown bread and brown sugar, the Yallops bought a 21-year lease on the property and quickly built up a thriving business, according to the article above.

> "Brownie's looks not unlike a Victorian shop with brown painted shelves and an old brass weighing machine. Little packets of nutty, flaky cereals are stacked next to an amazing variety of honeys, all with home-made looking labels."
>
> Daily Express article, April 1973

Chris Welch caught up with Steve Howe just before he left for the North American leg of the *Tales Tour*. Writing in Melody Maker on 16th February 1974, Welch mentions twice that Alan and Steve own and run the health food shop. The pair certainly wanted to make the Yes-Brownies' connection clear to customers. Roger Dean was commissioned to create at least 2 large panels or screens for display in the shop. There was a painted screen in the front window featuring a bear in a similar style to Dean's cover for *One Live Badger* (with original Yes keyboardist Tony Kaye) and was mentioned by Dean in his book *Views*. The other was a version of his *Tales* cover, presumably the current Yes album at the time.

From an unidentified newspaper article – Steve Howe pictured in Brownies' in front of a panel of the cover of *Tales*, photo courtesy of David Watkinson Collection

I understand that either one or both panels in the photos above are still in Roger Dean's possession. Yes and Roger Dean fan, Paul Denham (see chapter 16), spoke to Roger about the *Tales* one and Roger said, " ... the silkscreen print ... was started from scratch and comprised of forty hand drawn separations and was much more detailed than the original painting ... "

Alongside the health food retailing, Steve wanted to develop the business in a different direction as well. He explains in August 1974:

> "When we heard [the shop] was going to close down, we decided to buy it, just to keep it open, not really as a money-making thing. Some space above the shop was vacant and I originally thought that I might just start a guitar repair workshop there."
>
> Steve Howe, quoted in *Beat Instrumental Magazine*, August 1974

Guitars were definitely imported from the US to be sold above Brownies', as mentioned by Howe, but the Beat International article is a little vague on the details. The situation was clarified to me by Steve Howe:

> "The local council said,' no, you can't do that' ... it was kind of silly because, why not? But ... they have those rulings about things, there's supposed to be a doctor's surgery or treatment centre or something. So I didn't push it ... And I was already ready. I had a stock of 20 guitars or something ... So when I was out in Nashville and other

place, New York, I was buying up guitars I didn't actually want, but I thought would sell ... I mean, I suppose I might have sold or gifted a couple. But in a way, I adopted some of those guitars in my collection and then eventually found no, I didn't need them. So I sold them on. But that was kind of enjoyable. But the idea of the shop was kind of unique ... Brownies' was a very funky environment ... it had atmosphere, you know ... But anyway, in the end, it became very useful because it became a workshop for a guitar repairer called Sam Li. So basically we did make use of it in a guitar sense, you know, but not my shop."

Steve's soon to be wife Janet looked after Brownies' from day to day:

> ■ **What things have changed since I last saw you six months ago?**
>
> Well we've bought a Health Food Shop and we've also bought a house. We bought the shop because we're both health food addicts and the idea appealed to us. In fact there were many wiser investments we could have made with our money but we wanted to get satisfaction out of what we do and we thought we'd enjoy it. Jan goes down to the shop every day and keeps an eye on things and in a couple of years I might use the top part of the shop to open a little guitar studio, I'd really enjoy that.

Newspaper interview from the mid-1970s, photo courtesy of David Watkinson Collection

In the 1974 *Beat International* article, Steve mentions that Brownies' was once again struggling financially. For example, a much-needed new carpet could not be afforded. However, in the 1976 *Sounds* article above, Alan White says Steve and he still own Brownies' and mentions the bear in the front window. More excellent research from Forgotten Yesterdays' Geoffrey Mason revealed this advertisement from the 17th May 1978 edition of *The Field* magazine which seems to confirm that Brownies' was no longer in existence (see image on page 12).

Just when I thought I had reached the end of this particular rabbit hole, I discovered more. Brownies' original owner, Terry (now referred to as Terence) Yallop's name reappears years later in relation to Steve Howe. After selling Brownies' to Howe and White, he seems to have launched a

By this date in 1978, Brownies' had gone to be replaced at 36 Rosslyn Hill with Cane and Table, a furniture and plants shop

music career of his own. In 1980, he set up a record label called Real Music, focussing on the burgeoning genre of New Age music. At some point, he seems to have introduced one of his artists, Paul Sutin, to Howe and they started to talk about collaborating on some music. Sutin had already produced 2 albums for Yallop's label and had started work on a third. Howe was interested in exploring New Age music and agreed to play on it. In the end, an album called *Seraphim* emerged, credited to 'Paul Sutin featuring Steve Howe'. Re-releases of *Seraphim* seem to be credited to Steve Howe and Paul Sutin, presumably to aid marketing. The collaboration must have been rewarding because Howe and Sutin went on to record another album in 1995 called *Voyagers* that also featured Steve's son Dylan on drums.

In his 2020 autobiography *All My Yesterdays*, Steve Howe is effusive about his partnership with Paul Sutin:

> "On 11 May 1988 I met someone very special. ... He asked me to work on his new album, *Seraphim* ... Paul and I hit it off. His music was meditative and soothing, and I got right into it. ... Our friendship has developed and we have become a great team."

Later on in *All My Yesterdays*, Howe also mentions their 1995 album, *Voyagers*, which he describes as, " ... a truly collaborative project," and having, " ...

a celestial sound, melodically and rhythmically."

Health food entrepreneur and subsequently Steve Howe musical matchmaker Terry Yallop's Real Music label is still in operation today and seems to be thriving with many artists and releases:

> "Real Music is home to chart topping, award winning and critically acclaimed artists who create music in support of personal wellbeing. Established in 1980, we are experts in identifying and nurturing the very best talent in the health and wellness space. Our passion is sharing this talent with the world, connecting people to the transformative power of music to help relax, destress, meditate, recover and reconnect."
>
> Real Music website[1]

As pointed out by Chris Welch in his book *Close to the Edge – The Story of Yes*, 1973 was a very busy year for Yes. The live triple album, *Yessongs*, became their best-selling album to date and on 29th September 1973 the influential Melody Maker Readers' Poll was released. The band were putting the finishing touches to *Tales* at this time. Yes won both the British and the International Band categories and individual members were placed highly in their respective charts. *Yessongs* was the only live album to be placed at all (again in both British and International categories) and *Close to the Edge* also appeared in the British Album category, despite being released over a year earlier. Another significant winner was Rick Wakeman for his solo album, *The Six Wives of Henry VIII*, a fact that may have contributed to his dissatisfaction with the process of creating *Tales*. Welch tells us that the band were a little taken aback by this success but managed to present a unified front at the awards ceremony. Atlantic Records' co-founder and Yes champion Ahmet Ertegun was present and Jon Anderson sat with Robert Plant of Led Zeppelin, Yes' stablemates at Atlantic.

Even this success failed to ensure *Tales*' very existence, however. Atlantic Records were more than a little uncertain about how the album would be received:

> "Many at the label were rather paralyzed by the breadth of the collection. The darlings of progressive rock had progressed beyond some at Atlantic's understanding of how to market them. No single was even attempted. But label honchos Ahmet and Neshui Ertegun stepped in and pulled their troops into line in support of the album. 'That was the kind of thing Ahmet was made of,' says Steve with great admiration. 'He was a real music man. He had great ears. He was a producer. He put his stamp of approval on it. That was a solidarity with Yes. He didn't

---
1 https://tormatobook.com/real

want us to just disappear. He knew that there was strength in the band. I think any band releasing a double album was always going to scare labels to some extent, as you can imagine.'"

From the Gottlieb Bros. tour book
for *The Classic Tales of Yes Tour,* 2003

Fans were also concerned about what the follow-up to *Close to the Edge* might be like. Yes author Bill Martin says that Jon Anderson's comments during the creation of the album about the band moving in a more 'earthy' and 'funky' direction caused uneasiness amongst many fans who were hoping for a record continuing in the same vein as the previous, world-beating release.

2

THE CONCEPT

Advertisement from Melody Maker, with Jon Anderson's original spelling of 'TOBERGRAPHIC', 29th September 1973, uploaded to Forgotten Yesterdays by Steven Sullivan[2]

"Jon didn't want to delve too deeply into the religious aspects of the

---

2 https://tormatobook.com/tobergraphic

music because, 'It's too pretentious'.

'This is not a means to an end. It's just entertainment ... You can look into anything and find out things about it. You can find out as much about that [he taps the lamp next to him in the room] as you can about the music we will play tonight. Or you can just accept it and dig it, which I'm more interested in people doing. The fact that they accept it and enjoy themselves is just as important as seeking out any deep meanings.'"

> Jon Anderson talks to Rick Cain about the importance of the concept behind *Tales* in an *Indianapolis Star* interview from 9th March 1973, during the *Tales Tour*

In classical instrumental music there is a centuries-old tradition of using concepts to inspire composition. Well-known examples of this programmatic music include Vivaldi's *Four Seasons*, Debussy's *La Mer*, Respighi's *Pines of Rome* and Richard Strauss' *Also Sprach Zarathustra*, amongst countless others. Opera not only has narrative but also tries to embrace philosophical themes from art and drama.

RABBIT HOLE TALES – CONCEPTUAL INTROS AND OUTROS

One of the most interesting articles Yes author David Watkinson has published on Yesword.com[3] is about Yes concert introduction music. The majority of shows have begun with the end of the final movement of Stravinsky's *The Firebird Suite* but there are many others, both classical and not. For the North American leg of the *Tales Tour*, the band used both 'Spring' and 'Winter' movements from keyboard pioneer Wendy Carlos' (then known professionally as Walter Carlos) album, *Sonic Seasonings*. 'Spring' was used before *The Firebird Suite* music as the crowd gathered and 'Winter' was used following the concert, as the audience departed. Just like Vivaldi, Carlos used the seasons as inspiration for what was to become known as the first 'new age' album. So concerts featuring Yes' performance of its only concept album were 'bookended' by music from another concept album, the first of a completely new genre.

In rock and pop music, as with so many other labels, what we now term the 'concept album' developed gradually, much like the term 'progressive rock'. There are concept albums dating back to the 1940s by artists such as folk singer Woody Guthrie and superstar entertainer Frank Sinatra. What links these albums with progressive rock works like *Tales* is the presence of a unifying

---

3 https://tormatobook.com/opening

idea that ties all the songs together. Progressive rock artists embraced the notion of creating whole albums around a theme or topic in the 1960s and 1970s and today the concept album is most closely associated with this genre and time period.

The Yes member whose solo output has most frequently featured concept albums, perhaps somewhat ironically due to his dislike of *Tales*, is Rick Wakeman. 1970s classics *The Six Wives of Henry VIII*, *Journey to the Centre of the Earth* (although this might not be strictly a concept album – see below) and *The Myths and Legends of King Arthur and the Knights of the Round Table* are only the first three of his many concept albums. 2020's *The Red Planet* is a personal favourite of mine. When Yes embarked on their solo albums following *Relayer* in 1975/6, one of the resulting records was based on a story and is often, perhaps inaccurately regarded as a concept album – Jon Anderson's *Olias of Sunhillow*. Its songs tell the story of the inhabitants of the planet of Sunhillow. They have to leave and travel to a new planet under the direction of Olias in the Moorglade Mover starship. The tale is reminiscent of the theme of Roger Dean's artwork for Fragile and subsequent album covers.

Despite the interest of these band members in concept albums, this is the only Yes release that can truly be said to be in this category. There are other examples of literary and thematic connections in Yes songs such as 'Close to the Edge', inspired by Hermann Hesse's 1922 book *Siddhartha* and 'The Gates of Delirium' on the next record, *Relayer*. This has a programmatic theme based on the novel *War and Peace* by Leo Tolstoy and Jon Anderson originally planned to base the whole album on the work but decided against it. Perhaps his decision had something to do with the difficult reception *Tales* received.

> " … we started somewhere and we ended up in this bigger concept than *Close to the Edge* so that was the kind of challenge really … [a] concept album that was more consuming than *Close to the Edge*, a braver outing, and I guess we never looked back, once we thought, well it's a double album and there are going to be four sides and we had the outlines of all those sides."
>
> Steve Howe, Yes Music Podcast, 2025

Yes book author, academic and journalist Simon Barrow points out that it is impossible to produce music to 'describe' something, but it is possible to evoke feelings, memories and ideas through the way music is constructed and experienced by the listener. Also, many of the records commonly described as concept albums are actually just sets of songs collected together with a common theme. True concepts are abstract – they deal with underlying principles, thoughts and beliefs. However, *Tales* certainly is a concept album. Yes author Bill Martin agrees. In his book, *Music of Yes – Structure and Vision in*

Progressive Rock, he points out that other rock works on a similar scale such as The Who's double albums *Tommy* (1969) and *Quadrophenia* (1973) are collections of interrelated songs. *Tales* differs in that its four movements form a single work. He also suggests that Yes were the only progressive rock band with the ability – and audacity – to create something this vast. He believes King Crimson's proclivity for improvisation prevented them from producing a work on a similar scale while Genesis' theatrical tendencies precluded them from creating anything with 'big philosophical themes'. ELP, says Martin, did come up with large-scale visions but these were always interrupted by 'silly songs'. Other bands were prevented from creating whole concept albums by their record labels. Yes Music co-host Mark Anthony K says this was true of the Canadian prog legends Rush, who may have released more concept albums than the single one they managed at the end of their career had their record label not been nervous of the approach. This led to only one-side concept songs 'The Fountain of Lamenth', side B of *Caress of Steel* (1975) and 1976's *2112* (the title song on side A).

The story of how Jon Anderson chose the concept for Tales is told by Sid Smith on Loudersound.com[4]:

> "Tales From Topographic Oceans began with a single conversation between two characters at very different ends of the musical spectrum. In Bill Bruford's London flat in early March 1973, along with dozens of other friends celebrating the drummer's wedding earlier in the day, Anderson sat perched on an open windowsill talking with Jamie Muir. "He was an unbelievable stage performer," says Anderson of the eccentric King Crimson percussionist, known at the time for wearing bearskins, spitting blood capsules from his mouth and flailing his percussion rig and packing cases with heavy chains. 'I wanted to know what made him do that; what had influenced him.'
>
> Muir enthused about Autobiography Of A Yogi by Paramahansa Yogananda. The late guru was well-known in esoteric circles, and had made a more secular cameo appearance on the cover of The Beatles' Sgt. Pepper's Lonely Hearts Club Band, wedged between HG Wells and James Joyce. Reading Yogananda's words, Muir told the singer, had had a profound impact upon him. "He said to me, 'Here, read it,' and it started me off on the path of becoming aware that there was even a path," says Anderson. 'Jamie was like a messenger for me and came to me at the perfect time in my life… he changed my life.'
>
> It was powerful stuff. Reading the book prompted Muir to quit music and become a Buddhist monk, and while the effect upon Anderson may not have been so extreme, it was the catalyst that took Yes into uncharted waters."

---

4 https://tormatobook.com/sidsmith

Sadly, Jamie Muir died in February 2025. Bill Bruford, his percussion collaborator on King Crimson's *Larks Tongues in Aspic* (also released in 1973 like *Tales*), posted a tribute to the unknowing originator of the *Tales* concept:

> "[Jamie] had a volcanic effect on me, professionally and personally, in the brief time we were together many years ago – an effect which I still remember half a century later ...
>
> He was a lovely, artistic man, childlike in his gentleness. There was probably a dark side underneath. It could be glimpsed as he climbed the PA stacks in a wolf's fur jacket, blood (from a capsule) pouring from his mouth, on a rainy Thursday night in Preston, Lancs., to hurl chains across the stage at his drumkit. One of these Robert Fripp will tell you, only narrowly missed him.
>
> His conversations with Jon Anderson at my 1973 wedding party, in Jon's words, 'changed my life'. Jamie also changed mine.
>
> I consider it a privilege to have known, and benefitted from the company of a man of such quiet power, even briefly. He struck me as one of those about whom one might truthfully say he was a beautiful human being. He will be much missed. Goodbye, Jamie."
>
> Bill Bruford statement, DGM Live website, February 2025

The October 1973 issue of *Beats International* included a preview of *Tales* still using the original spelling, author's collection

'Autobiography of a Yogi' has sold in the region of 4 million copies and has been translated into dozens of languages. Born in India, author Paramahansa Yogananda spent a lot of time in the US and founded a school of meditation that later crossed over into the West. Simon Barrow doubts that Anderson read the whole book but he certainly became fixated on the now-famous footnote he found:

> 10-6: Pertaining to the shastras, literally, "sacred books," comprising four classes of scripture: the shruti, smriti, purana, and tantra. These comprehensive treatises cover every aspect of religious and social life, and the fields of law, medicine, architecture, art, etc. The shrutis are the "directly heard" or "revealed" scriptures, the Vedas. The smritis or "remembered" lore was finally written down in a remote past as the world's longest epic poems, the Mahabharata and the Ramayana. Puranas are literally "ancient" allegories; tantras literally mean "rites" or "rituals"; these treatises convey profound truths under a veil of detailed symbolism.
>
> Gutenburg.org

It might seem like a rather short passage on which to base an entire double-album of music but we can't tell how much additional research the footnote encouraged Anderson to do. Knowing the story of how he found the footnote and the contents of the footnote itself, it is interesting to read Anderson's own explanation on the inside cover of *Tales*:

> "We were in Tokyo on tour and I had a few minutes to myself in the hotel room before the evening's concert. Leafing through Paramahansa Yogananda's 'Autobiography of a Yogi' I got caught up in the lengthy footnote on page 83. It described the four part shastric scriptures which cover all aspects of religion and social life as well as fields like medicine and music, art and architecture. For some time I had been searching for a theme for a large scale composition. So positive in character were the shastras that I could visualise there and then four interlocking pieces of music being structured around them. That was in February. Eight months later the concept was realised in this recording.
>
> While still on tour, first in Australia and then the U.S., I had spelled out the idea to Steve. He liked it and the two of us at once began holding sessions by candlelight in our hotel rooms. By the time we reached Savannah, Georgia, things had come together very clearly. There, during one six-hour session, which carried on until 7 a.m., we worked out the vocal, lyrical and instrumental foundation for the four movements. It was a magical experience which left both of us exhilarated for days. Chris, Rick and Alan made very important contributions of their own as the work evolved during the five months it took to arrange, rehearse and record.

Although Anderson cites only *Autobiography of a Yogi*, he was also immersed in a wide variety of different spiritual, religious and anthropological topics at the time of developing *Tales*, including popular mass media offerings:

> "'I've been watching Professor Bronowski's The Ascent Of Man (BBC 2's Saturday night series), and that's really given me a lot to think about.' ... Our conversation ranged from the mystery of Stonehenge, the ancient ley lines, the significance of St Michael's Mount (draw a line on the map through all the St Michael's churches), and the probability of the human race having 'planet hopped' around the solar system."
>
> Jon Anderson speaking to Chris Welch for *Melody Maker*, 4th August 1973, courtesy of Doug Curran

Simon reminds us that Jon Anderson is essentially an autodidact – someone who hasn't studied formally at a high level but has picked things up himself. This is not meant to be disrespectful. Perhaps the most remarkable example of

2 - THE CONCEPT

Anderson's success in working things out for himself is his masterpiece, *Olias of Sunhillow*. He wrote the story, composed and arranged the music, played all the instruments and sang all the vocal parts. By any measure, this is a staggering creative achievement. This capacity for self-development is combined with his tendency to mix and match. He likes to take aspects of traditions, cultures and belief systems and develop his own ideas by blending everything he has found together.

Autodidact Jon Anderson seeks to get his ideas across to Rick Wakeman (and possibly others out of shot) in Morgan Studio 3 during the recording of *Tales*, photo credit: Laurens Van Houten / Frank White Photo Agency

As pointed out by the Gottlieb Brothers in their tour book for 2023's *The Classic Tales of Yes Tour*, "Yes did not set out to put the four shastras to music. Instead, they launched into lyrics and music that drew inspiration from, and aspired to, higher truths and purposes."

> "Jon had a lot of material he wanted to incorporate and the themes were really interesting to us at the time because we'd seen how *Close to the Edge* had been adopted for a healing aspect, you know, in certain places in America.
>
> And so the whole revitalising or sustaining, if you like, of the hippy era was to come again. We were still fundamentally kind of hippies in our beliefs, but we were developing it ... I'd read Siddhartha [inspiration for *Close to the Edge*] and things like this but Jon was a bit further down in that stuff."
>
> Steve Howe, Yes Music Podcast, 2025

In creating the lyrics for *Tales*, Simon believes Anderson and Howe took the vast scope of the ideas and concepts referred to in the four Shastras and tried to create a kind of journey out of them across the four sides of the album. As Bill Martin points out, this led to music that abandoned the usual rules of writing rock music – or at least stretched them to their limits. He argues that what Rick Wakeman (and many others) has often referred to as 'padding' or 'filler' is precisely what is needed to allow the 4-movement structure to become more than simply a series of interconnected songs. In the classical period of music (roughly 1750 to 1820), structures such as sonata form and the four-movement symphony were used extensively to create a satisfying 'journey' in a piece. These forms would have been known intimately by Rick Wakeman after his classical training at The Royal Academy of Music but grander, larger-scale musical constructions were also enjoyed by Jon Anderson and Steve Howe. Anderson was a self-confessed fan of composers such as Holst, Stravinsky and Sibelius and Howe's guitar idols included the classical virtuoso guitarist Julian Bream and composers such as Vivaldi. Consequently, some of the inspiration for the structure of *Tales* will have come from knowledge and experience of classical forms.

Although the four movements of *Tales* do not neatly coordinate to the four movements of the classical or Romantic symphony, it is arguable that something a little like classical sonata form is attempted in places. Certainly, I think the ideas of exposition (stating the theme), development (working on the theme to explore its possibilities) and recapitulation (repeating the main theme) can be identified. However, the way in which Anderson and Howe worked out the structure of the album could have been the cause of Rick Wakeman's dissatisfaction with the record. As pointed out by Bill Martin, Wakeman possibly thought the construction of *Tales* was 'groundless' – or at least he couldn't follow the logic of its design, blending all sorts of different ideological, musical and philosophical ideas.

In our attempt to understand the concept of *Tales*, a basic version of the plan for the album might be described as follows:

The title of the first movement of *Tales*, 'The Revealing Science of God – Dance of the Dawn' provides a link to the work of Paramahansa Yogananda who was keen on finding ways to unite religion and science. The 'Dance of the Dawn' is conveyed via Anderson's chanted vocals in what could be described as a creation story. Following the chant, the first side begins to 'walk back into memory'. Side 2 picks up this memory idea with 'The Remembering' and then side 3 goes beyond living memory into 'The Ancient', a past which isn't recoverable. Finally all the preceding ideas are integrated in a 'Ritual'. In this way, there is a definite coherence in what Jon Anderson had created. What some might criticise as random music across 4 sides of an album is not random at all. Whether it ends up being based on a definite philosophy is a different question. Simon believes what we have is Jon Anderson's (and to a lesser extent Steve Howe's) own ideas and concepts in *Tales* with a very loose connection back to the stated inspiration of the Shastras.

> "You must not let your life run in the ordinary way. Do something that nobody else has done, something that will dazzle the world."
>
> Paramahansa Yogananda

This quotation encapsulates what Jon Anderson and Steve Howe and the rest of the band, with perhaps a little reluctance, were trying to do with *Tales*. It is probably a mistake to become too caught up in how closely the concept of the album matches or doesn't match the stated sources, particularly as the footnote cited by Anderson has very little to do with the rest of Paramahansa Yogananda's book. In fact, Simon believes that the cover and the name of the album (once it had been corrected from the initial misspelling of 'tobergraphic') tell us more about what is contained within. Oceans do not have topography in the common definition of the word and topographic features are structured rather than watery and flowing. This deliberate paradox perhaps shows what is to come on the record. Roger Dean's artwork (see chapter 16) also points out the paradox and shows elements of earth, sky and sea that are referred to in the music and lyrics of the 4 movements. The blend of different physical elements in the artwork reminds us of the conceptual, thematic elements in their eclectic nature. The cover can almost be seen as a metaphor for the journey of the album.

The album Rick Wakeman nicknamed, in his inimitable style, 'Tales from Toby's Graphic Go-Kart' is a deeply-affecting work for many Yes fans, including Simon Barrow who kindly set out his thoughts even more clearly in the following essay on the concept.

The Oceanic Enigma of Yes: An Appreciation
by
Simon Barrow

The signature clue of Jon Anderson's distinctive alto-tenor voice aside, few listeners unfamiliar with the span of Yes music would be likely to guess that any single portion of *Tales from Topographic Oceans* was part of the same catalogue of recordings as that of the band which released 90125 a decade later. While the latter, with all its artistry, is more oriented towards the physical release of adrenaline, the former is far closer to legendary classical pianist Glenn Gould's central definition of music as art: "the gradual, lifelong construction of a state of wonder." Something that directs us towards exploration, discovery, creativity and beauty in all its shapes and forms.

Tales from Topographic Oceans - Yes album Listening Guide

Jon Anderson was very much 'hands-on' in the process of creating *Tales*, photo credit: Laurens Van Houten / Frank White Photo Agency

That echoes my own experience with *Tales* over five decades of listening. Each visit reveals something new. Here is a sweeping, undulating, 81-minute sound odyssey that ebbs and flows lyrically and texturally across time and space. In so doing, it navigates humanity's subterranean origins, its reconstructed memories, its unrecoverable pre-histories, and its ritual aspirations and destiny. It does this partly by dabbling poetically with many musical and spiritual sources, not least the fragmentary influence of Paramahansa Yogananda's 1946 classic, *Autobiography of a Yogi* – the 1960s self-realisation best seller which landed with Ravi Shankar, George Harrison and others in the '70s. But even more evocatively, it does it through the imaginative deployment of a panoply of different sonic resources (classical, jazz, folk, Eastern, ambient, experimental and more) refracted through the medium of a form of rock music taken to new widths and heights.

2 - THE CONCEPT

The word 'epic' is frequently overused in the lexicon of progressive rock. It is not uncommonly employed as a description for almost any piece of music lasting longer than 10 or 15 minutes. (In classical music, by contrast, that would likely be a short orchestral study or chamber work.) It also commits the common error of comporting depth with length. Whereas, in fact, the term 'epic' is about storifying scope and cultural reach, which is something that can also be achieved with relative economy in music. Yes often did so in a handful of minutes, as well as through their more extended compositions like 'Awaken' (expanded from 16 minutes to around 20 live) which is off-the-scale in its two colourfully intense cycles of fifths surrounding a hypnotic organ, harp and bell-like percussion interlude.

When we come to *Tales From Topographic Oceans*, it is more than reasonable to apply the term 'epic' in every sense: its scale, ambition, structure and scope runs long, deep and wide in both aural and oral terms. Its subject matter is history and pre-history read mythically and condensed into imagination and ritual. As an autodidact, Jon Anderson, aided by Steve Howe, took Yogananda's exploratory memoire as a point of imaginative departure, rather than as a guidebook to be followed. Anderson's was not a close reading. He even managed to spell the author's name incorrectly. But, as Steven Wilson rightly said at the time of the release of his 5.1 Tales remixes, the key thing to understand is that, sonically and narratively, this extraordinary double-album is the fruit of "the band working at the very peak of their powers to create one of the most ambitious, beautiful and eccentric albums in the whole rock music canon."

I could not agree more. Along with pieces precious to me that come from the worlds of jazz, experimental and classical music, the four sides of Tales (which I will always prefer to listen to together, and in order) played a major role in shifting my musical horizons and impacting the way I experienced music as a young person. Even today, an album which has probably produced more controversy – adulation contrasted with opprobrium – than any other in the Yes catalogue, and that of progressive rock as a whole, continues to move me and arrest me in a whole range of unexpected ways.

To understand why some fall deeply in love with this record, while it leaves others cold or frustrated, we need to consider what makes it both special and unusual. The central clue can perhaps be found in its name. Topography is about tracing a landscape according to the key features, commonalities and contrasts etched into its very form. It is about fixed points, certainly, but also change and development over time. Oceans, on the other hand, are by their very nature concerned with fluidity and lack of fixity. The music roars and withdraws, carrying you with it and asking you to leave the safety of dry land. It simply cannot be mapped in the same way as solid earth, or conventional rock – though it has more than trace elements of both.

This helps us to recognise that there is a strong and inherent element of tension in the way the album was conceived, composed, recorded and delivered – musically, lyrically and in the interweaving of these elements. There are strong melodic moments and climaxes (the end of side two is a magnificent example of cumulative tension and release). But there are also tender ballads, and washes of sound which Rick Wakeman has – quite wrongly, in my view – dismissed as "padding", because they feel suspended in time. They destabilise conventional melody, harmony and tonality in a rock context. To listen to this album successfully, therefore, you need to allow yourself to be swept along, and sometimes swept away. Even today, 52 years after its release, Tales defies easy categorisation.

When you hear this album with open ears you will have a sense of it enveloping and propelling you at the same time. As for the words, they are indeed sound sculptures. Don't ask precisely what they mean, as if looking for some simple correspondence between the poetic and the prosaic. Instead, ask how they make you feel, and what areas of thought or expression they point you towards in the widest span of life as you experience it. One way of thinking about the album in terms of both its music and its lyrics is to consider side one ('The Revealing') as pointing towards the unfolding of the natural order; side two ('The Remembering') as being about the shaping of our different thought-worlds; side three ('The Ancient') as constituting a headlong dive into both the wild and calming aspects of our subconscious or unconscious; and side four ('Ritual') as an invitation to the integrate various gifts from the past into a dynamic new rhythm of living in the present, passing through dense shadows and emerging into the light. *Nous sommes du soleil*.

Duke Ellington once declared that there are two kinds of music. Good music and the other kind. The distinction is a matter of personal aesthetic judgement and taste, not just a cold assessment of technical capability or artistic aspirations and limitations. But within such oceans of discrimination, there lie the two other poles of music as advancement ('progress') and music as entertainment. This is the distinction between what turns our lifelong attention to unveiling beauty on the one hand, and what satisfies an often more immediate and physical need (which, as musician and YouTuber Andy Edwards argues, can too readily degenerate into "slavish fake viscerality" in the rock world) on the other.

Yes music slides within, between and across these different sensibilities, without ever losing its own unique, boundary-crossing authenticity. Along with *Relayer* and *Close to the Edge*, *Tales from Topographic Oceans* leans heavily towards art and advancement. This is why it will always be an acquired taste, meriting every degree of effort it demands of the listener in coming to appreciate great music on its own terms and as a whole. Here is an album which sums up the oceanic enigma that is Yes. Long may it flow with, around and beyond us.

Simon Barrow is a writer and poet. His recent books include *Solid Mental Grace: Listening to the Music of Yes* (Cultured Llama, 2018) and *Beyond Our Means: Poems, Prose and Blue Runes* (Siglum, 2025).

PART 2 – PREPARING AND RECORDING THE ALBUM

3
REHEARSALS AT MANTICORE

Jon Anderson and Steve Howe directing operations at
Manticore, photo by Martyn J Adelman

Despite the pressure, the band persevered with its grand design.

"I've a lot of cassettes of Jon and I sitting in places like New York or Cincinnati recording songs," recalls Howe. "Jon would say to me, 'What have you got that's a bit like that...' so I'd play him something and he'd go, 'That's great. Have you got anything else?' and I'd play him another tune. I notice that one of the pieces he turned down early on eventually became part of side three. He heard it later and said, 'That's a good piece,' because we were looking for something different then."

Steve Howe quoted in an article in *Prog Magazine* online by Sid Smith

After the initial writing sessions on tour, the band needed to get together to arrange and rehearse this massive, complex work. They convened at Manticore Studios.

> "Over several weeks in the summer of 1973, occupying the main stage at the rehearsal complex, they got to grips with fragments, sketches and outlines. In some respects, this was business as usual for the group. Countless times in their history, Yes had sewn together different musical elements."
>
> Sid Smith, loudersound.com, 2020

Prog supergroup Emerson, Lake and Palmer (ELP) already had many connections to Yes by the time *Tales* was in development. ELP had recorded their first three albums at Advision Studios with Eddie Offord, the same combination that Yes employed for *Fragile* and *Close to the Edge*. In fact, Offord would have engineered ELP's next studio album, *Brain Salad Surgery*, at Advision Studios if he hadn't been working with Yes on *Tales* at Morgan Studios at the time.

ELP were enjoying their success and decided to launch their own record company, in order to take more control of their business operations and to free themselves from the constrictions of contracts. Often, regular releases were stipulated, whether the musicians felt they were ready or not. The band also wanted to help artists they knew were having difficulty securing record company backing. The resulting records were initially distributed by the band's original label, Island Records, and then Ahmet Ertegun became involved. A passionate supporter of progressive rock including Yes, Ahmet was determined to ensure ELP's Manticore releases were distributed by the Atlantic Records behemoth, providing global reach. Therefore, Yes and ELP were briefly and slightly tenuously stablemates at Atlantic in 1973.

In an unusual move, ELP also decided to purchase an abandoned ABC cinema in Fulham, West London, and convert it into rehearsal space and company offices. They had been using small church halls but problems with neighbours over noise levels and unsociable hours eventually made this impossible. In keeping with their flamboyant musical style, they decided to call the company Manticore Records. The manticore is a mythical Persian animal featured in one part of the title suite of ELP's second album, *Tarkus*, and is depicted inside its gatefold sleeve. The manticore was a creature with a man's head, a lion's body and the tail of a dragon or scorpion.

The Art Deco building they chose had been built by Associated British Cinemas (ABC) and opened in August 1935. Created in the 'golden age' of cinema, it held 1,129 viewers in the stalls and another 800 in the balcony (see facing page).

3 – REHEARSALS AT MANTICORE

Photo uploaded by https://cinematreasures.org/members/jazzlers/photos Attribution 3.0 Unported (CC BY 3.0)

Photo uploaded by https://cinematreasures.org/members/jazzlers/photos Attribution 3.0 Unported (CC BY 3.0)

Originally called 'The Regal' and then re-named 'ABC' in 1962, it was an impressive building and featured a Compton 3-manual theatre organ with an illuminated console, as can be seen in the photograph (see previous page). The cinema closed in February 1972 and ELP moved in the next year, replacing the original marquee (the board that held the names of the films showing) with their own Manticore sign.

A screenshot published on Discogs.com from the YouTube video of ELP's 1973 tour[5]

RABBIT HOLE TALES – ROXY AT MANTICORE

Thanks to the legendary band Roxy Music (not at this time featuring the brief Yes member Eddie Jobson), we can take a glance or two inside the auditorium at the Manticore building. Bryan Ferry and the band recorded a video for their hit single 'Dance Away' at Manticore in 1979, with views of the balcony and the stage appearing (clearly, the seats have been removed):

Screenshots from the Roxy Music video[6] on YouTube (see facing page)

The end of the Roxy Music video is also interesting. Bryan Ferry is seen walking out of the Manticore building and across to Barclay Road. Just before he reaches the corner, a record shop is seen, complete with vinyl records hanging up in the window. No fewer than 3 Yes albums are on display – *Fragile*, *Going for the One* and the recently released *Tormato*. It's a shame that *Tales from Topographic Oceans* isn't amongst them (see page 36).

---

5 https://tormatobook.com/manticoreELP
6 https://tormatobook.com/roxy

3 - REHEARSALS AT MANTICORE

After Manticore left the cinema in the early 1980s, it was partly used as a shop, owned by some of the first discount retailers in the country, Dickie Dirts and (perhaps later) Inverwear, who used to open from 7am – 11pm, 7 days a week, despite the restrictive Sunday trading laws of the time. The fabric of the building deteriorated and it was demolished in December 1984. There is a Waitrose supermarket on the site today.

Photo uploaded by https://cinematreasures.org/members/jazzlers/photos Attribution 3.0 Unported (CC BY 3.0)

3 – REHEARSALS AT MANTICORE

Photo uploaded by https://cinematreasures.org/members/jazzlers/photos Attribution 3.0 Unported (CC BY 3.0)

Rather than signing up with Manticore Records, Yes took advantage of the rehearsal space at 392 North End Road, Fulham, London. I asked Steve Howe if Manticore was a good place to rehearse Tales. His response was categorical – "No". He explained that ELP 'sold them the idea', not in a pressurised way but Yes agreed to use the venue. However, Steve pointed out that Yes tended to persevere, even when they weren't happy with a situation. They, " ... just carried on being unhappy but got on with the work ... " This was in stark contrast to Steve's memories of rehearsing *The Yes Album* at what became his home, Langley Farm in Devon.

ELP themselves originally intended to use the main auditorium of the former cinema for rehearsal but ended up using the foyer area on the first floor most of the time. Apparently, this was at the front of the building in the middle and there were no double-glazed windows in those days, so I assume anyone walking past the building would be able to hear the band! Footage of the band rehearsing in this area of Manticore can be seen on YouTube[7]. This is where they worked on their 1973 album *Brain Salad Surgery*. Other groups who famously used the Manticore rehearsal facilities included Led Zeppelin, who prepared for their 1977 US tour in the venue.

In his autobiography, *All My Yesterdays*, Steve Howe confirms that, unlike ELP, Yes used the main auditorium to rehearse *Tales*:

"The stage didn't seem quite the right place to be working but we did

---

[7] https://tormatobook.com/ELP

manage to get a rough shape of each side before we moved on to Morgan Studios ... "

Jon Anderson hard at work at Manticore – note the ELP logo behind him, photo by Martyn J Adelman

As always with Yes, the process of putting the songs together at Manticore wasn't without its problems. Clearly, Steve Howe and Jon Anderson had to try to instil in the other band members the same enthusiasm they had for the loose collection of conceptual and musical ideas.

" ... I really can't believe how we could have rehearsed so much in preparation, you know, all at one time.
 Somehow we got the gist of it so that we had sufficient mapping, if you like, demoing so that when we got in the studio Jon and I could continue forging with the other guys what the idea was.
 The other guys often showed reluctance, you know, 'are you sure about it?' [But we said] yeah, we're really sure and ... when Jon had exhausted himself, kind of inspiring everybody to ... get this arrangement going, then he would sort of like leave the room or something and I'd carry on a little bit on another bit.
 So it was a kind of shared push, towards, keeping the story as opposed to getting halfway and turning back or anything. We didn't want to do that."

Steve Howe, Yes Music Podcast, 2025

Steve told me that they always went into rehearsals with a sketch of some kind. During the *Close to the Edge Tour*, when Anderson and Howe were developing the musical ideas for *Tales*, Steve recorded their demo versions on a Revox tape machine with a couple of microphones or sometimes, " ... just a cassette player with a built-in mic." He says they, "really sounded dreadful". However, it was essential to do this for *Tales* as there was so much music.

In his sleeve notes to the Steven Wilson remix of *Tales*, Sid Smith described how White, Wakeman and Squire would add detail into the broad outlines provided by Howe and Anderson. He quotes Alan White laughing about how Squire would never turn up at Manticore before midday. He said the process involved a lot of trial and error – "We had to find a way of joining the jigsaw puzzle together to make it work."

Jon Anderson playing a Gibson Firebird electric guitar at Manticore, note what appears to be the framework created by Michael Tait for the Roger Dean drum canopy behind him, photo by Martyn J Adelman

According to Chris Welch, Rick Wakeman believes the band were not properly prepared for the album due to a lack of material. This seems odd considering that the original plan was to create a single album containing 4 songs which was then expanded to a double album and even longer versions of the 4 movements did exist at one point in the process. Of course, Rick Wakeman famously believes that the album was heavily padded out with unnecessary material. Michael Tait explained it like this:

> "Jon was often way out ahead of people and possibly couldn't always guide them ... easily enough."

Michael Tait, Yes Music Podcast, 2024

Quoted in the Gottlieb Bros.' tour book for *The Classic Tales of Yes Tour*, 2023, Steve Howe explains his view of the material and how it was assembled for *Tales*:

"The fact that everyone would get writing credits is not irrelevant, because everyone did help with some of the arranging. Chris came up with some lines, and other people put their ideas in more freely, because they were going to get some respectful credit. Arranging is really the key to Yes. I mean, a lot of those ideas came from Jon and me about the arrangements, but they didn't all come from us. Chris would jump on it, guys would put things on. So there was a sense of driven collaboration in the rehearsal room, and then forming it in the studio, where really, a lot of it was created. We had gathered material, and there was a lot of material. Even by today's standards, we had a lot of material to gather."

Jon Anderson with newspaper in hand, pictured at Manticore Studios, photo by Martyn J Adelman

After what must have been an intense period of collaboration, the band moved on, as prepared as they could be, to Morgan Studios.

The site of Manticore Studios today, photo author's collection

4
RECORDING AT MORGAN STUDIOS

Jon Anderson contemplates the progress of the *Tales* recording, photo credit: Laurens Van Houten / Frank White Photo Agency

"It's an enthralling experience. We're working as five people all hurtling down the same road."

> Jon Anderson speaking to Chris Welch for *Melody Maker*, 4th August 1973, courtesy of Doug Curran

" ... we had life-size cardboard cows and real bales of straw in the studio."

> Steve Howe, *All My Yesterdays*, 2020

There was disagreement about where *Tales* should be recorded. Jon Anderson and Steve Howe wanted to record in the country, with Anderson even suggesting they use a tent in a forest in the middle of the night, complete with electrical generators built into the ground to avoid noise. Howe also felt at home in the countryside. After successful rehearsals for *The Yes Album* at Langley Farm in Devon, he bought the property and has been based there ever since. Chris Squire, on the other hand, preferred the urban setting of London. Alan White, typically, didn't mind either way. Eddie Offord, who had long experience of how fractious relationships in Yes could become, supported the countryside idea in order to try to make everyone calmer but, in the end, London was chosen. However, there was to be a break from the band's traditional Advision home in favour of Morgan Studios whose technical advantage came in the form of the first 24-track tape machine in England which was the 3M M79, installed in Studio 3. The increased number of tracks available is one of the factors identified by Miguel Falcão (see chapter 8) which led to a significantly different sound on this album. Steve told me:

> "Well, each time there was a new piece of technology just like today, you know, me and Yes and most musicians want to know what's going on and how it can help them go forward. So yeah, the development from, you know, Joe Meek [with whom Howe worked when he was in The Syndicats] with a couple of tracks and then early Yes albums on eight and then 16. Having 24 would seem like the absolute bees' knees."

Left – the 3M M79 tape machine between Jon Anderson and Eddie Offord, detail from photo by Laurens Van Houten / Frank White Photo Agency, right – 3M M79 from the instruction manual

"I don't think it let us down. I think Yes' manager at the time, Brian Lane, had gotten a super, super-duper deal, so it was cheaper to go there! But Morgan was fine. It was okay. Advision was like home. I grew up there, but Morgan was not bad. It wasn't a challenge. It's just another studio. It was no big deal."

Eddie Offord, quoted in the Gottlieb Bros. tour book
for The Classic Tales of Yes Tour, 2003

Squire took a little persuading to agree to the Willesden studio, according to Yes author Chris Welch, because he had grown up in that area of London and disliked it. However, the bassist was attracted by the availability of the latest technical equipment (see page 46).

Morgan Studios had been set up in 1967 by four musicians who owned a jazz record label. The studios were named after one of the quartet, Barry Morgan, and premises at 1 Maybury Gardens, Willesden, London were secured, initially as office space (see page 47). In another intriguing twist of fate in the small world of the London music scene, an assistant engineer at Morgan was the late Roy Thomas Baker (RTB), now famous for his work with Queen and The Cars. RTB was to preside over the abortive Yes Paris sessions of 1979 and the difficult recording process for Yes' 2014 album, *Heaven and Earth*. Also, Karen Jackman's first job was as an engineer at Morgan in 1971 (she was then known as Gregg). She is the younger sister of the late Andrew Pryce Jackman. Karen, Andrew, their other brother Jeremy and Chris Squire were all members of St Andrew's Church choir in Kingsbury, London. Andrew went on to play with Chris in The Selfs and then The Syn, alongside Yes' original guitarist, Peter Banks. Both Karen and Andrew worked alongside Squire and Yes, with Andrew creating the orchestrations for *Fish Out of Water*, 'Onward' from *Tormato* and other pieces. Karen recalls the first 24-track machine in Studio 3 at Morgan, which she describes as her 'stomping ground'. This new technology wasn't without its problems, however. In his autobiography, Steve Howe says that the 3M machine had a surprisingly long tape path, more like a cinema film camera than a studio tape machine and was, " ... quite troublesome."

Morgan's pedigree was already established when Yes chose it as the recording location for *Tales*. Paul McCartney recorded overdubs for his first solo album there and, amongst many others, records by Free, Mott the Hoople, Bloodwyn Pig (before original Yes guitarist Peter Banks joined them briefly), Jethro Tull, Supertramp, Rod Stewart, The Kinks, Pink Floyd and Elton John had all been created there, as had part of Led Zeppellin II had all been created there. Perhaps most significantly, Rick Wakeman recorded a lot of his *Six Wives of Henry VIII* there the year before the *Tales* recording sessions.

Tales from Topographic Oceans - Yes album Listening Guide

ADVISION STUDIOS

Address: 23 Gosfield Street, London W1P 7HB.
Telephone: 01-580 5707.
Studio Director: Roger Cameron.
Engineers: Roger Cameron, Gary Martin, Martin Rushent, Mike Dunne, Geoff Young.
Bookings: June Kallenburg, Susan Ott.
Studio capacity: Studio 1 – 60 musicians. Studio 2 – for small line-ups and over-dubbing. Dubbing theatre for film work.
Instruments available on hire: Practically any when notice is given.
Extra facilities: Music to picture in Studio 1. Moog synthesiser if notice is given, and Dolby 361 system.
Rates per hour:
Studio 1, 16 track recording £38.50
All other recording and overdubbing – mono, stereo, quad or eight track £33.00
Recording to picture £38.50
Studio 2, 16 track recording £30.80
8 track, quad, stereo or mono recording £27.50
Dubbing theatre £24.20
Overtime rates: All overtime, outside 0900 and 1800 hours, Monday to Fridays– £5 for first engineer, £2 for second.
Cancellation arrangements: If less than 48 hours notice is given – excluding Saturdays and Public Holidays – 50 per cent of full rate booked will be charged. If less than 24 hours notice is given full rate is charged.

MORGAN RECORDING STUDIOS

Address: 165–171 High Road, Willesden, London NW10.
Telephone: 01-459 7244.
Studio Manager: Roger Quested.
Engineers: Mike Bobak, Robin Black, Roger Quested, Mike Butcher, Greg Jackman, Martin Levan.
Maintenance Engineers: Pete Smith, John Romer.
Bookings: Pat Church.
Studio capacity: 35 (Studio 1), 12 (Studio 2), 35 (Studio 3).
Instruments free of charge: Hammond organs, Leslie speaker units, Steinway grand pianos.
Instruments on hire: Fender electric piano, percussion instruments, and complete range of guitars and amplifiers. Other instruments are available on notice.
Rates: Apart from 24-track reduction at £35.20 all studios (including all facilities) are at £30.80 per hour.
Tape charges per reel:
(Scotch 206 low noise)
2" £30.80
1" ,, ,, £17.60
$\frac{1}{2}$" ,, ,, £11.00
$\frac{1}{4}$" ,, ,, £6.60
Spools:
2" NAB £8.80
1" ,, £5.50
$\frac{1}{2}$" ,, £3.85
$\frac{1}{4}$" ,, £1.37
5" spool £0.27
7" spool £0.38
Special facilities: Fully licensed bar and restaurant.
Overtime rates: £5 per hour after 1800 hours weekdays, and on weekends and public holidays.
Cancellation arrangements: 50 per cent of booking charged if less than four days' notice given. Total booking charges if less than 48 hours' notice given.

A comparison of what was on offer in 1973 from Advision and Morgan Studios, advertised in *Beats International Magazine*, author's collection

4 – RECORDING AT MORGAN STUDIOS

Morgan Studios in the mid-1970s, photo by Tony Harris

Rick Wakeman, probably at Morgan Studios during the recording of *The Six Wives of Henry VIII* in 1972, photo credit: Laurens Van Houten / Frank White Photo Agency

In his book, *The Great British Recording Studios*, Howard Massey explains that the original Morgan premises comprised 2 studios and were augmented in 1972 by the purchase of space on the ground floor of a building over the road. This is where the much larger Studio 3 was established. Yes arrived there in July 1973, after completing their rehearsals at Manticore. In 1974, another, even larger studio was established in a newly-purchased building nearby at 14 to 16 Chaplin Road. Nicknamed 'The Laundry' in reference to its previous use, Studio 4 confirmed Morgan as a major recording complex in London.

Pictured a few years ago, the site of Morgan Studio 4 in Chaplin Road, Willesden, nicknamed 'The Laundry', as identified and photographed by recording engineer Tony Harris

Morgan Studios continued throughout the 1970s but a downturn in fortunes led to Studios 3 and 4 being sold to Zomba Records in 1980 and Studios 1 and 2 to producer Robin Millar in 1984. Millar's Power Plant Studios lasted for 6 years. Despite many changes of ownership and name, 'The Laundry' is still in operation, now owned by Mercury prize shortlisted producer/engineer/mixer, Andy Savours. Unfortunately, from a rock history perspective, the building which housed Studio 3, where *Tales* was recorded, is now The Lewinson Centre, home to a collection of community groups.

According to different accounts, in order to compensate for the urban setting of Studio 3 at Morgan, some combination of Rick Wakeman, Jon Anderson and manager Brian Lane brought in hay bales, flowers, pots of greenery, a 2D cardboard model of a cow with 'electronic udders' and a white picket fence to surround Rick Wakeman's keyboards. As quoted by Chris Welch, Wakeman said,

The site of Morgan Studios today with Studio 3 on the left, over the road from the main location, photo author's collection

"I was the only keyboard player who ever had to send his keyboard back for repair because it had lice."

In his book, *All My Yesterdays*, Steve Howe also mentions the later addition of palm trees – not very traditional in the English countryside. Unfortunately, the cow was soon covered in graffiti and the plants died, according to Eddie Offord.

> " ... what we did was we created a sort of farm, farm yard likeness about what the studio was like inside. You know, we had some fake sheep or something, and we had some bales of hay. I mean, that was really quite preposterous, but ... it amused us at the time. And that was a good thing to keep spirits high ... we weren't taking ourselves seriously ... I think ... the world thought we were very serious. And in fact, you know, that's not strictly true."
>
> Steve Howe, Yes Music Podcast, July 2024

In an even more bizarre move, Jon Anderson asked Yes' lighting designer Michael Tait to build a bathroom in the middle of the studio. This was because Anderson liked the sound of his voice in his own bathroom at home and wanted to replicate it at Morgan. So a 3-sided, tiled booth was created despite Tait's reservations, and recording takes were punctuated with tiles falling off the plywood construction.

> "Now, let me tell you, Jon's no engineer. And he said, "Yeah, well, you get some plywood, then you glue some tiles to it, and you just stand

it up around there." I said, "Jon, I don't believe that's going to give you the sound that you're looking for ... you need some mass." And he said, "It doesn't matter. Just do it." So I did it. And, you know, it is what it is. I don't think it did anything. ... But I just did it because, you know, Jon would get his way."

Michael Tait, Yes Music Podcast, 2024

While Yes were working on *Tales* in Studio 3, the Birmingham-based heavy rockers Black Sabbath arrived to record *Sabbath Bloody Sabbath* in Studio 4. Lead singer Ozzy Osbourne recalls that Rick Wakeman seemed to spend more time in Studio 4 than with his Yes colleagues and ended up providing keyboards for their song 'Sabbra Cadabra', for which he refused payment, except in beer. A lot of time was spent by the pre-teetotal Wakeman in the studio bar, drinking and playing darts. According to Chris Welch, when the band were due to start recording at noon, Rick Wakeman would turn up at 9am and make his way to Morgan Studio's bar across the road from Studio 3.

Jon Anderson and Rick Wakeman during the recording process, photo credit: Laurens Van Houten / Frank White Photo Agency

"Well, to be honest, Rick was kind of an outsider in the band at that time," says producer Eddy Offord. "The rest of us loved to smoke hash and spend hours in the studio. Rick was happier going to the pub and having a few pints. He didn't really do that kind of stuff. I love Rick. He was fantastic, and he did wonderful things with the band, but he was definitely kind of an outsider, a little bit."

Eddie Offord, quoted by the Gottlieb Bros. in the tour book for *The Classic Tales of Yes Tour*, 2023

4 – RECORDING AT MORGAN STUDIOS

Despite Wakeman's unhappiness, the band managed to record the backing tracks to all four sides of *Tales*, one a week, and then started to work on overdubs.

> "I woke up in the night scratching my face to a complicated part of an arrangement," said Jon. "I thought I was still in the studio. It can affect you in the strangest ways. I was waiting in my sleep for an accent that we had kept missing in the studio. We've been there four weeks and we've got six weeks to go. We've been at Morgan which has really helped us as there are plenty of good vibrations around. We played some of the music back last night, and admittedly we were well stoned, but it sounded good."
>
> Jon Anderson speaking to Chris Welch for Melody Maker,
4th August 1973, courtesy of Doug Curran

Steve Howe describes working closely with Jon Anderson to try and steer the band through the recording of the album, taking on the lead role each time Anderson had done all he could to cajole and support White, Wakeman and Squire. The bass maestro reportedly spent 16 hours a day, 7 days a week working on the music, which must have meant sessions lasting well into the night, as his tendency to arrive late every day continued. One of the main reasons Bill Bruford had found recording sessions with Yes so difficult was the time keeping of some of his colleagues and their insistence on analysing every note. In the case of *Tales*, it was Rick Wakeman who found the process practically unbearable, exacerbated by his oft-repeated assertion that he didn't understand the music.

Howe also remembers the pattern of recording a part of the music and then adjourning to the control room (only accessible from the studio itself, in an odd idiosyncrasy of Morgan's design) for each band member to critique his own playing and to rate the recording in terms of the direction and shape of the record overall. According to Howe, he had private meetings with Anderson to review progress and plan how to approach the other musicians to finish off the album in the best way possible.

> "I can't help but love the warmth of all those things. Some of the edits are a little crazy. But yeah, I mean, all I know is that that's as close as we could get at the time.
>
> It is fascinating how easy it is to do it and make it really good now. I mean, you can more or less edit ... anything together and make it work if you wanted to. But I think the edits were important if we were structurally building a big track, then we would only get like ... five or 10 minutes recorded each day and then we would stick it together.
>
> But the other aspects of the desk and the number of tracks, I

mean, you're being limited to 16 tracks. [That] would be unthinkable today. I mean, it's what I use here in my own studio, but that's adequate for what I need because I'm generally hooked into hard drive to Protools. So ... basically in those days, you couldn't record at home. ... So I mean, technology is just fast and ... I've welcomed it. ... I think it's all very well, you know, bigging up remastering and all that. And we should do that occasionally.

But you know, what the band did together, particularly with Eddie Offord ... in that period, in a way, there isn't a better version. ... I think the same with the Beatles. Although you might say, 'oh, could we have a bit more guitar?' 'Do you want this on the left?' You know, we can do all that. But in some way ... the original imprint, if you like, of Yes, is definitely there. It's ... not possible to make it better. There's nothing about it that needs making better, but there again, it's made in its time."

Steve Howe interview, Yes Music Podcast, 2024

Eddie Offord (far right) operates the desk at Morgan Studio 3 while Alan White and Rick Wakeman look on from the left, Jon Anderson sits on Eddie's right and Steve Howe rests on a sofa at the back between his future wife Janet and Alex Scott (a member of Brian Lane's management team), photo credit: Laurens Van Houten / Frank White Photo Agency

In April 2024 I had a remarkable conversation with someone whose name you may recognise in connection with Yes but his contribution to *Tales from Topographic Oceans* has been hidden for more than 50 years. He was nicknamed 'Generator' by Wendy (Eddie Offord's girlfriend at the time) and the name stuck. It was apparently easier for the band and crew to pronounce. I wonder if anyone remembered that fact in 1987 when Yes moved into the *Big Generator* era.

4 – RECORDING AT MORGAN STUDIOS

If you have a copy of *Relayer*, take a look at the credits. It will say something like 'Produced by Yes and Eddie Offord, tapes by Gennaro Rippo'. Gennaro, is 'Generator':

You may also have seen Gennaro's photo in the line-up of Yes crew in the 1975 US *Relayer* Tour programme (shown above right with alternative spelling). His picture is there alongside Adam Wildi, Ian Peacock, Ray Palmer, Jean Ristori, Nigel Luby, John Martin, NuNu Whiting and Claude Johnson-Taylor. The way he came to be involved with Yes is another of those remarkable tales that seems to have been almost commonplace in the world of 1970s rock.

For the origins of the story, we can read Richard North's review of Yes' 2 performances at the Whisky A Go Go in Los Angeles at the end of June 1971. Richard posted this to the Forgotten Yesterdays website:

> "I was a huge fan of Yes at the time of this show and followed closely club and concert announcements. There was absolutely no mention of these two shows at the whiskey [sic] in the local papers. I got a call from my brother the afternoon of the show saying that he had happened to drive by the whiskey [sic] as Yes were unloading their equipment and had met the band and was calling from Jon Anderson's room at the Hyatt on sunset blvd. [sic] I was completely blown away. My brother is Christopher North the founding keyboard player of the best American prog band Ambrosia. I raced up to Hollywood and saw the show both nights. It was great to finally see and hear Yes live. They did two complete sets each night. Most of the songs were from *The Yes Album*. I also was able to meet the band and the road crew which was the beginning of a friendship that would lead to going to some of the

recording sessions for *Close To The Edge* and *Tales Of* [sic] *Topographic Oceans*, but most importantly it led to one of my best friends, Gennaro Rippo, getting a job with Yes and becoming Eddie Offord's personal assistant."

Gennaro told me the reason he became involved with Yes at the Whisky A Go Go was because their equipment was late – he found himself helping to unload the kit when it eventually arrived and Yes' roadies, led by Phil Hepple, were most grateful. They told Gennaro to come and see them if he was ever over in London. It's the kind of throw-away comment often heard in these situations, but this time the recipient of the offer actually took it up the following year.

Incredibly, Gennaro found himself (perhaps with Richard North) alongside Eddie Offord in the control room at Advision Studios in 1972 while Yes recorded *Close to the Edge*. Gennaro tried to secure a role with the band at this point but none were on offer. Despite this initial setback, he did manage to see the band perform at Crystal Palace on 2nd September 1972, the world premiere of the whole of *Close to the Edge*.

After returning to London in 1973, Gennaro again took up position next to Eddie Offord and this time he stayed throughout every *Tales from Topographic Oceans* recording and mixing session at Morgan Studios, including through each night, Rick Wakeman's preferred time to work.

Jon Anderson and Rick Wakeman at the mixing desk in Morgan Studio 3, photo credit: Laurens Van Houten / Frank White Photo Agency

"I spent more time on that album and was there longer than Rick

4 – RECORDING AT MORGAN STUDIOS

Wakeman was."

Gennaro Rippo, Yes Music Podcast, 2024

RABBIT HOLE TALES – VEGETARIAN MANNA

A task the band asked Gennaro and Alex Scott (a member of Brian Lane's management team) to undertake was to provide sustenance while they worked on *Tales*. The two friends would go to the health food restaurant 'Manna' in Hampstead to pick up the band's preferred vegetarian cuisine. As Gennaro points out, Rick Wakeman wasn't included in these meals, being the only carnivore in the band.

Surprisingly, Manna is still in operation today (now a well-respected vegan restaurant) and its manager tells me that Steve Howe ate there fairly recently.

Left – 1970s advert for Manna Restaurant, right – Manna today, photos courtesy of Rob at Manna

Manna was only a short distance from Steve Howe and Alan White's health food shop, Brownies' (see chapter 1).

It is possible that Laurens Van Houten captured Alan White tucking into food from Manna when he visited Morgan Studios in 1973 and Martyn J Adelman might have spotted Chris Squire and Steve Howe doing the same:

Photo credit: Laurens Van Houten / Frank White Photo Agency

Photo by Martyn J Adelman

4 – RECORDING AT MORGAN STUDIOS

Gennaro describes his *Tales* experiences as a really good introduction to Yes world and remembers another 'Eddie' working at Morgan Studios at the time Yes were there recording *Tales*. It was Eddie Harris, the American Jazz saxophonist. The album he was working on was called *E.H. in the U.K.* and featured all sorts of familiar names such as Ian Paice (Deep Purple), Alan White and Chris Squire (perhaps on breaks from *Tales*?), Steve Winwood (Traffic), Tony Kaye (Badger, post-Yes), Jeff Beck, Boz Burrell (Bad Company) and others. In fact, 2 songs on the album feature the Kaye–Squire–White lineup that was to form the backbone of the post- and pre-Yes band Cinema, a decade later! It's amazing to think that musicians such as these were also working in Morgan Studios while Yes recorded their most ambitious project to date.

By chance, another Yes legend started working for Yes on the same day as Gennaro – Nigel Luby. While Gennaro worked alongside Eddie Offord, Nigel got a job with Chris Squire and his name does appear in connection with the recording of *Tales* (if you look carefully enough). Despite being there for the whole recording and mixing process, Gennaro's name does not appear anywhere because he didn't have a British work permit and so was never 'officially there'. Subsequently, he took a trip to Denmark in order to be out of the way while Eddie's manager Dennis Muirhead secured a work permit for him. This meant his name could be included in the Relayer credits and I'm very much looking forward to talking to Gennaro about those sessions at a later date. Both Gennaro and Nigel are named in the US 1974 *Tales Tour* programme.

> Sound Production & Engineering by
> Eddie Offord assisted by Genarro Rippo
> Sound Equipment by Clair Bros Audio
> with thanks to Roy Clair & Mike Roth
> Production Manager Mike Tait
> Lighting by Mike Tait assisted by Andrew
> Barker
> Slides by Alistair Robinson
> Stage Design by Roger/Martyn Dean
> made by Clive Richardson &
> Felicity Youette A & B Welding
> Stage set managed by David Goldberg &
> Adam Wildi
> General Tour Manager Phil Hepple
> Roadcrew:
> Phil Hepple Stage Monitoring
> John Cleary Keyboards assisted by
> Fred Stones
> 'Tasty' Guitar
> NuNu Drums assisted by Ian Peacock
> Nigel Luby Bass
> Personal Manager Alex Scott
> Secretary Krissy
> Photos Martyn Dean

Detail from US *Tales Tour* programme, uploaded to Forgotten Yesterdays by Steven Sullivan

As for tales of recording at Morgan Studios, Gennaro confirmed he was involved in the strange construction work that went on:

" ... Jon liked the sound in his bathroom. So we got plywood and ... we stuck tiles to it. We made a vocal booth."

Imagine for a moment Jon Anderson standing in the middle of Studio 3 at Morgan inside that hastily created, fake bathroom. All the accounts I have read say that it didn't work. Maybe that was no surprise.

"And then one time ... we got these cutouts of farm animals and put them in the studio."

Gennaro says this was all just a bit of fun but it was based on the fact that Jon Anderson was desperate to record away from the metropolis. Even if he thought it was a good idea, it's difficult to imagine Eddie being keen on trying to create a studio sound in a forest, so perhaps the bales of hay and other accoutrements brought into Morgan ended up being a better idea.

The famous cutout cow in the studio with Chris Squire, photo credit: Laurens Van Houten / Frank White Photo Agency

"The clock was ticking for Yes. A UK tour was already advertised for November and December. Factory time for the pressing of the finished album was already booked in. Every hour that swept by on the studio clock not only broke down into minutes and seconds but pounds and pence as well. 'God bless Eddy Offord,' laughs Anderson, referring to the period when the pair were literally camping out at Morgan Studios as they worked around the clock, even sleeping there in order to cross the finishing line as mastering and manufacturing dates loomed."

From a Prog Magazine online article by Sid Smith

"I was Eddie's bodyguard, student, studio manager, equipment man. It was all just me and Eddie," says Gennaro Rippo. I asked him what Eddie was like to work with and he stressed how clever he was. There is plenty of evidence for this but, to prove the point, Gennaro mentioned another character who was close to the band, Phil Carson. Phil was the London-based Senior Vice President of Atlantic Records (Yes' label) from 1968 to 1985 and a champion of both Led Zeppelin and Yes. Incidentally, both of these Atlantic stablemates used ELP's Manticore rehearsal facilities around this time (see chapter 3). According to Gennaro, there was an early link between Eddie Offord and Phil Carson whose background was in grocery stores. Eddie used to produce the kind of albums that were commonly found at budget prices in supermarkets. As Gennaro says, " ... they would do the whole album in one night from start to finish." I also remember an interview with Chris Squire where he recounted playing as a session musician on this kind of record and that he couldn't resist embellishing the bass lines rather than playing them straight – perhaps Eddie met Chris and Phil through this route.

Jon Anderson (left) and Eddie Offord (right) working out the mix for Tales, photo credit: Laurens Van Houten / Frank White Photo Agency

Eddie's contribution to progressive rock stretched much further than Yes, of course. Originally a tape op at Advision Studios, where he first worked with Yes when the band recorded *Time and a Word* in 1970, he graduated to engineering and then producing. Gennaro points out that Eddie engineered and arguably co-produced ELP's self-titled album, *Tarkus* and *Trilogy* at Advision. When they were ready to record *Brain Salad Surgery* in 1973, Eddie had to make a choice between continuing his ELP association or going with Yes to Morgan Studios. He chose Yes and maybe it had something to do with the way the three-piece ELP behaved in recording sessions. Gennaro said:

"Believe me, I went to a couple Emerson Lake and Palmer sessions with Eddie at Advision ... it was like the Marx Brothers, those three guys in the studio. And then Eddie was like, see, he kept saying, see, see, this is how crazy these guys are ... [with] Yes, it was different."

Gennaro agrees that Eddie's ability to edit takes together to produce seamless songs was remarkable. However, he thinks that some of the stories have been exaggerated, including tales of scratching about on the floor looking for lost takes. Here's how Gennaro explains one of the incidents he did witness at Morgan Studios:

"... well, basically, we took a bit of *Topographic Oceans* and it was ... an edit to send to, I think, Radio Luxembourg but [the engineer,] ... needed a blank reel, a metal reel, quarter inch ... [Eddie said,] 'Here's one with a little bit of tape on it. So let me cut all this tape off this reel and we can use this reel'. And then they realised, 'wait a minute, that's the mix we just did. Why did you cut that?' And so then he kind of put that [back] together."

The rather more extreme story often retold is included in the Gottlieb Bros.' epic tour book for *The Classic Tales of Yes Tour*, 2023:

"A funny thing, but only funny with the benefit of looking back on it now, happened on the way to delivering the master tapes. Jon Anderson and Eddy Offord had been encamped in the studio around the clock and under immense pressure to deliver the album to meet factory, and tour date commitments. 'I mean, cutting those tapes together was not easy,' says Eddy. 'It was like, "We'll use this take here, and then we'll try this take there. Oh, it doesn't quite fit. Then I'll put that on the floor over there. This bit is one I had tried, let's cut this one here and then cut that piece there. Where does that go?" So you wind up with a whole bunch of piles of tape around the studio and end trying to kind of fit it all together. But it all worked out. It was okay. It worked out in the end,' thanks in no small part to Eddy's preternatural skill with a razor and tape, along with an uncanny knack for keeping track of little bits of tape.

But when he and Jon Anderson jumped in a car, bleary eyed, having rested the precious masters on the roof of the vehicle and sped away, it was almost curtains for Tales. Jon Anderson recounts hopping out to scoop them up off the pavement just in the nick of time to save them from going under the wheels of an oncoming red double decker London bus. It is the stuff of legends, and gives Eddy Offord a chuckle over the fact that he can't quite deny, or tellingly, fully recall the episode. 'It sounds possible. I can't say I totally remember that. But I wouldn't be surprised,' he laughs. What is it they say about those heady

'60s and '70s days? If you can remember them, you probably weren't there!"

Eddie was not only a brilliant engineer, he also provided some, perhaps very necessary, structure for the traditionally long-winded Yes composition and recording process. The Gottlieb Bros. quoted Eddie reflecting on this part of his role:

> "I felt that my job was in not just being an engineer and a producer, but I also a bit of a psychiatrist. So if Chris wants to do this, and Jon wants to do that, how do we resolve it? So yes, what we'd do was, instead of talking about it, and arguing about it for hours, I'd say 'We're going to try it with Plan A, and then we're going to try Plan B, and then we're going to vote on which one we like.' So it was a matter of just kind of moving things along and trying to help them resolve their differences."

I asked Gennaro about his experiences of the Yes musicians as they recorded Tales. Of course, he spent all his time in the control room and Morgan studios were known for their unusual setup. In order to get to the control room, you had to go through the studio, so presumably Gennaro, Eddie and others didn't spend a great deal of time traipsing through the 'live' area. Despite this, Gennaro remembers the contrast between Rick Wakeman at the *Close to the Edge* sessions and the *Tales* ones.

> "I could tell that he wasn't happy with the record."

Gennaro had and still does have great respect for Rick Wakeman and many commentators agree that what he contributed to *Tales* includes some of his best keyboard work for Yes. It may not always be at the top of the mix but even when it is more subtle, it complements the other instruments and voices beautifully. Wakeman's intuitive understanding of the construction of musical structures adds a great deal to the success of the album. His choice of instruments, tones and textures is excellent throughout and I certainly don't agree with Yes author Bill Martin when he says that Wakeman could have been replaced with a 'competent sideman'.

Typical of Gennaro's experience of the master keyboardist was the following story concerning a trip to Rick's house alongside Nu Nu Whiting, Alan White's drum tech:

> "We brought some equipment out to Rick's house and then, on the way there, the windshield broke on us. And there was glass everywhere. When we got there, he was very nice to us. Very concerned to ... see how we were."

As already mentioned above, Black Sabbath were in another Morgan studio at the time Yes were recording *Tales*. In an interview from 1974, Black Sabbath lead singer Ozzy Osbourne showered Wakeman with praise:

> "Rick Wakeman is, he's incredible, man. I love that guy ... I hope the band [Black Sabbath] never splits. But if the band ever did split ... And I chose another guy to work with. I think I'd choose Rick ... He can blow anyone off the f***ing stage. I think he'd wipe the floor with Keith Emerson as far as I think." [sic][8]

Gennaro remembers meeting Osbourne on his regular visits to the Morgan Studios canteen.

> "He was a very happy Englishman ... drinking and telling jokes at the Morgan canteen ... luckily I got to eat there on Yes's tab every day. That's what I was paid."

Clearly, as an unofficial member of the Yes setup, Gennaro's remuneration was 'in kind' only.

From Gennaro's point of view, the whole band contributed a great deal to the creation of *Tales*, despite the music being Jon Anderson and Steve Howe's original creation:

> "Jon was in his space, he read that book, you know, about the yogi ... very spiritual ... Jon was being Jon."

The work was clearly not over when all the parts had been completed. Gennaro said:

> "The Yes ... mixing sessions at Morgan, they started around midnight ... I would get there at four and came home at five in the morning. I was there the whole time."

Although it is impossible to read the majority of the labels, we can see that Steve Howe literally has his hand on 2 of the 4 faders marked 'GUIT' in one mixing photo (see page 64).

Also visible in this photo is the track list for 'The Revealing Science of God'. This is confirmed by the file sent to Steven Wilson (see chapter 17):

After the mixing process, reel-to-reel tapes were made of the music and given to band and crew for review. London-based Yes collector Clive Ayer showed me the ones he has (see page 65).

According to Gennaro, Eddie Offord was becoming tired from the continual producing, engineering and live sound work he had been doing for several years by the time the *Tales* sessions happened. However, he recognised

---

[8] https://tormatobook.com/farout

4 – RECORDING AT MORGAN STUDIOS

Left to right - Chris Squire, Rick Wakeman (reclining at the rear), Alan White, Eddie Offord, Steve Howe, Jon Anderson, photo by Martyn J Adelman

The whole team involved with mixing *Tales* - front row left to right Rick Wakeman, Chris Squire, Alan White, Eddie Offord, Steve Howe, Jon Anderson - back row left to right Nu Nu Whiting (drum tech), Krissy (Yes office staff), Guy Bidmead (tapes), Michael Tait - identified by Gennaro Rippo, photo by Martyn J Adelman

Tales from Topographic Oceans - Yes album Listening Guide

Detail from a photo by Martyn J Adelman

Detail from a photo by Martyn J Adelman, plus Rhino image of the original track list for 'The Revealing Science of God', courtesy of Rhino

4 – RECORDING AT MORGAN STUDIOS

Quarter-inch reel-to-reel tape boxes, courtesy of
The Clive Ayer Collection, photo by Clive Ayer

Jon Anderson (left) and Chris Squire (right) listen as Alex Scott (centre) perhaps gives some
drumming tips to Chris, photo credit: Laurens Van Houten / Frank White Photo Agency

Gennaro's dedication and hard work and hatched a plan to include him for the next stage of work with Yes – going out on tour (see page 65).

PART 3 – THE INSTRUMENTS AND TECHNICALITIES

5
RICK WAKEMAN'S KEYBOARDS

Rick Wakeman amongst the tools of his trade for Tales, photo credit: Laurens Van Houten / Frank White Photo Agency

To find out about Rick Wakeman's keyboards on *Tales*, we turned to the remarkable Chris Dale. Chris is a keyboard expert and is responsible for rescuing two of the most important Yes keyboards – the fabled Birotron and Rick's unique Double Mellotron. The Birotron was invented after *Tales* was recorded and the fascinating story of 'the world's rarest musical instrument' is told in detail in *Yes – The Tormato Story*.

Chris has managed to identify the following keyboards on *Tales*:

Hammond B-3 Organ

RMI Rock-Si-Chord electra-piano 668

Minimoogs

Double Mellotron

Mander single manual portable (or 'portative') pipe organ

Piano

A 'harpsicord' (sic.) is mentioned on the track list for side 3 – 'The Ancient' (see chapter 14), but it isn't clear whether this is an acoustic instrument, a synthesised version or a harpsichord voice on the Mellotron.

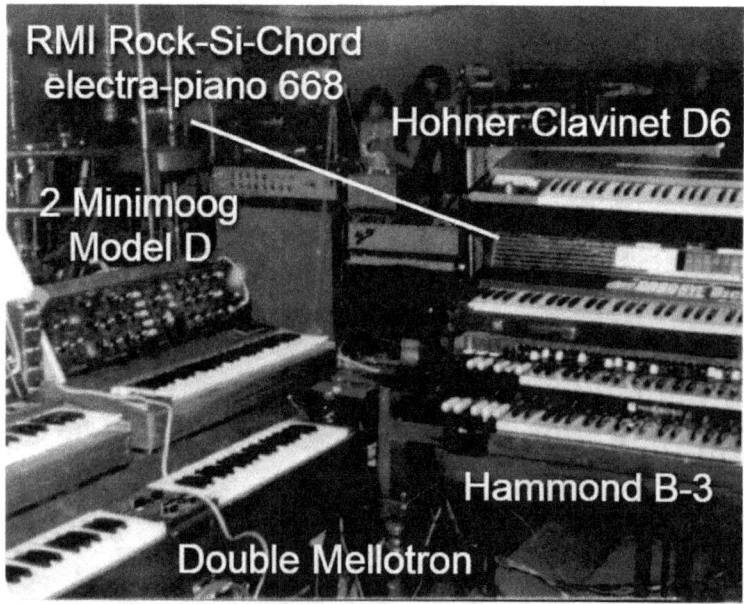

Rick Wakeman's Tales Tour keyboard setup, photo courtesy of Chris Dale

5 – RICK WAKEMAN'S KEYBOARDS

When we spoke to Chris about Tormato, he covered some of these keyboards so I've included edited extracts from *Yes – The Tormato Story*[9].

Hammond Organ

The Hammond organ was invented by Laurence Hammond in 1929 and uses internal tone wheels, combined with the later draw bars that can be moved in and out by the player to alter the sound. The original idea was that the Hammond organ would be marketed as a home instrument, or for churches, to replicate a pipe organ. However, a lot of people were sceptical because of the lack of pipes, so the draw bars were developed to provide a similar experience to pulling stops on a pipe organ.

The Hammond was renowned for its robustness. It was incredibly heavy to transport but it would withstand all kinds of rough treatment, which made it ideal for use in a rock band. This was in stark contrast to a lot of the newer instruments which were comparatively fragile and prone to damage when being carried around in tour trucks. In fact, Chris suggests that part of the reason Mellotrons and other keyboards were often damaged by roadies was that they were used to dealing with Hammonds which would soak up extreme mistreatment (as proved by the deliberate actions of Keith Emerson!).

An essential part of the Hammond sound for rock music comes from its pairing with the Leslie speaker. Hammond had their own speakers, but Don Leslie also developed separate speakers after the Hammond was released. Laurence Hammond was upset because he thought Leslie speakers ruined the sound of the Hammond, but owners, especially in the rock world, appreciated the Leslie's ability to make the sound appear to come from all directions simultaneously. This was partly due to its unique, rotating action.

Chris told us that the most common Hammond setting is achieved by pulling the first three draw bars out. This produces the characteristic rock sound used by many players, especially when combined with chorus or vibrato.

Yes – The Tormato Story, 2023

Speaking about the use of the Hammond Organ specifically on *Tales*, Chris said that Wakeman employs unusual sound settings to create a variety of sounds, including a 'chiming' effect, almost like Christmas chimes.

RMI Rock-Si-Chord electra-piano 668

Rocky Mountain Instruments, to give them their full name, were an innovative US company who also produced the RMI Music Computer played by Rick

9 https://tormatobook.com/

Wakeman on *Tormato* and elsewhere. The earlier RMI Electric Piano was used to wonderful effect on Wakeman's solo spot on the iconic live album, *Yessongs*. He plays 'Catherine of Aragon' and then incorporates other music. This electric piano had advanced features such as the ability to set a simulation of attack and decay, which means that Rick could use the same instrument to imitate a pipe organ and then later in the solo it could be more like a harpsichord. The same instrument can be heard in the background of 'The Revealing Science of God', side one of *Tales*. An example is around 8 mins 35 secs of the full piece, the version with the introduction. It sounds more like an organ vamp than a piano. It's interesting to compare this passage to the sound at the beginning of Elton John's 'Crocodile Rock', also played on an RMI Electric Piano.

Minimoog

"I actually got my first Minimoog off Jack Wild – the former child star who played the Artful Dodger the 1968 film, Oliver! He bought it and thought something was wrong with it because it only played one note at a time. I explained that it was monophonic, but he said, 'Ah, keep it'. I think I gave him 30 quid. Even if it hadn't worked, I'd have bought it and had it on stage with me. Just because it looked so fantastic."

Rick Wakeman interview on Music Radar[10], 2020

2 Minimoogs on top of the unique Double Mellotron, photo courtesy of David Kohn

---

10 https://tormatobook.com/rick5

Chris Dale believes that Rick Wakeman plays two Mimimoogs at once in various places on *Tales*. For me, the Minimoog solo on 'The Revealing Science of God' possibly defines the standard to which all other synth players aspire. Along with Keith Emerson, Wakeman practically invented the prog rock synth solo and here we have the pinnacle of the art. Chris agrees and says that part of Wakeman's ability to startle with the Minimoog is down to the way he sculpts the sound. The Minimoog has no memory capacity like modern digital synths – whatever the switches are set to at the time is what comes out of the speakers. Rick combined 'sawtooth' and 'square' waveforms, set via the complex-looking Minimoog controls:

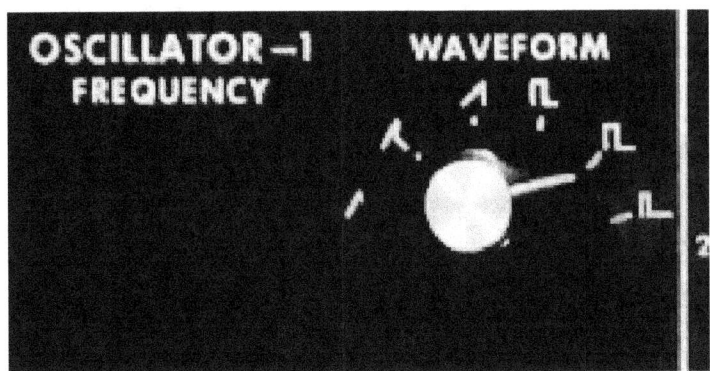

Detail from Minimoog control panel
This file is licensed under the Creative Commons Attribution 2.0 Generic license. Minimoog_(Buffalo_Museum_of_Science).jpg: Alex Harden from Harrisburg, PA, USA

Only one of the controls can be seen here – in fact a Minimoog has 3 separate oscillators, each one of which can be set to a different waveform pattern. It's Wakeman's proficiency with blending sounds as he plays that makes him remarkable. He also developed a technique using 2 Minimoogs together, set to the same sound, to create the illusion of one instrument with a huge, rich sound and polyphony (playing more than one note at a time).

Dave Watkinson:
" ... that Moog solo on side one has to be right up there as the perfect example of everything coming together at once to create greatness."

Steven Sullivan:
"Though that solo, as heard on the original mix, is an edit. An example of Eddy Offord's genius."

Comments on Yes Music Podcast, 2024

In addition to his comment above, Steven Sullivan also pointed out that keyboard pioneer Larry Fast worked with Rick Wakeman on his Moog setup for

Tales. Larry spoke to music journalist Anil Prasad about that time[11]. Larry was renowned in the 70s and 80s as an electronics wizard and he built custom synthesizer sound modules for himself. He met Wakeman when the Yes man first toured the US with the band and spoke to him shortly after he joined in late 1971 or early 1972. Rick was impressed with Larry's work and commissioned him to produce similar modules for himself. He used the resulting equipment on *Yessongs*. After this success, Wakeman suggested that Larry join him at Morgan Studios for the *Tales* recording sessions.

"I worked on hardware for Rick. I was doing electronic music before recording professionally and I wasn't very set financially. The Moog equipment was phenomenally expensive back then, even in today's dollars. I had a good background in electronics, so I was designing custom modules for myself. I first encountered Rick through my early work in US college radio when Yes was first starting out (1971). They were still traveling around in a station wagon and doing tiny, little concerts. I spoke to Rick literally a couple of months after he joined the band and we naturally touched on electronics and when I described some of the things I built for myself, he said "I'd like to have those for myself. Would you build some of those for me?" And in fact, he had the road manager give me the deposit that night. About six or seven months later, I delivered a finished, custom sound synthesizer module to him which he ended up using on the Yessongs live album. The first time I heard myself on the radio in a sense was hearing him use those modules on that album.

He suggested I come to the studio when the band was recording *Tales from Topographic Oceans* to see how the device was working and offer some tips and techniques, as well as do a little upgrading. So, I went to England for that, among other things. It was a very good opportunity. I was able to spend a lot of time in the control room watching Eddie Offord work. I learned a lot about the techniques that were important to the way British albums of the time were engineered. It was quite different from the way American recording was done in the studios in the New York area. I brought a lot of those techniques back with me and they have stayed with me. So, whether I was working with Peter Gabriel, Nektar, Kate Bush or acts in America that had British roots like Foreigner or Bonnie Tyler, I always had a cross-Atlantic thing to offer."

Interview with Anil Prasad[12]

Long-time Yes Music Podcast listener, Patron and supporter Doug Curran met Larry a few times with various artists and bands.

---

11 https://tormatobook.com/anil
12 https://tormatobook.com/anil

Doug Curran with Larry Fast, photo courtesy of Doug Curran

After working with Yes on *Tales*, Larry secured a recording contract with Passport Records, and started work on the first Synergy album, a project that was to establish his reputation as a pioneering keyboard figure.

Doug writes:

"He is best known for his 1975–1987 series of synthesizer music albums as Synergy, and for his keyboard playing and production work with Peter Gabriel, Foreigner, Nektar, Bonnie Tyler, Kate Bush, Hall & Oates, Meat Loaf, Jim Steinman, Dr. Buzzard's Original Savannah Band (morphed into Kid Creole and the Coconuts), Kool & the Gang, Annie Haslam, Randy Newman, FM, and the Tony Levin Band. He also composed music for the "Cosmos" tv series, and other shows and movies, including "Streets of Fire."

Larry served as a consultant to Moog Music in the development of the Polymoog (1976) and Memorymoog (1982) synthesizers, including voicing many of the original Memorymoog factory presets. On associated projects from 1975 until 1982 at AT&T Bell Laboratories, where the transistor was invented, Larry worked with groundbreaking digital recording, sampling and resynthesis, computer control of synthesizers, computer generated FM synthesis and other techniques years before they entered the mainstream."

Mander single-manual portable pipe organ

After recording the organ parts for *Close to the Edge* at the Church of St. Giles' Cripplegate, London, Rick Wakeman opted to use a portable pipe organ for his next recording with Yes. Coincidentally, the organ at St. Giles' was built by Mander Organs in 1970 using parts of another organ, only a short time before the *Close to the Edge* recording. The company also produced single and double-manual portable pipe organs.

When I was researching the Mander Portable Pipe Organ used by Rick Wakeman on *Tales*, one of the very few photographs I could find of a single manual version was from an auction site where one was for sale. It was owned by Dee (formerly known as David) Palmer who had played it live with Jethro Tull while an official member of the band from 1977–79. Dee was involved with the band from its earliest days as an arranger and was responsible for the orchestral arrangements on Jethro Tull's concept album *A Passion Play*, released, like *Tales*, in 1973.

Further searches took me to Dee's website where the photos reproduced below show her playing the Mander pipe organ. Looking closely at the left-hand image, you can just see the 2 XLR cables hanging down inside the glass case which is closed on stage to avoid the sound of the organ bleeding into other microphones. In concert or for recording, these cables would be connected to an amplifier. Coincidentally, the photographer is Elayne Barre, daughter of Dee's former Jethro Tull colleague, the legendary guitarist Martin Barre.

The organ was withdrawn from the auction which pre-dated the 2018 UK ban on selling ivory (the Mander keyboards were made with ivory). However, it has long been illegal to import items containing ivory into the US so that may have been a factor.

Dee Palmer playing her Mander portable, single-manual pipe organ, photos by Elayne Barre

Perhaps unsurprisingly, given the cross-pollination of rock and prog personnel throughout the decades, Dee also has a strong Yes connection. She wrote the orchestral arrangements and conducted the London Philharmonic Orchestra on *The Symphonic Music of Yes*. The album featured Jon Anderson, Bill Bruford and Steve Howe on selected tracks.

Dee commissioned both a single and a double portable pipe organ from Mander Organs so it seems reasonable to assume they were very similar to the ones used by Rick Wakeman on *Tales* – the single manual on the recording and the double manual live on tour.

RABBIT HOLE TALES – PORTABLE PIPES

The concept of portable (also referred to as 'portative') pipe organs has a surprisingly long history. Fortunately, Yes fan and Yes Music Podcast listener Chris Berry is also an organist and enthusiast of the history of the instrument. He kindly provided the following explanation of the fascinating topic of the portative organ.

Early history of the portable organ

Early drawings of organs dating back to the 800s, and indeed to Roman times, show them already to be large contraptions, and not portable in any clear sense, often with several burly chaps pulling levers or treading on bellows to create enough wind to make loud noises outdoors. Large organs eventually found their way into churches, in a more refined form. However from 12th to 15th Centuries in Europe there are also many representations in church windows and paintings of small organs carried or held in the hands of monks, angels or saints, perhaps with the help of a neck strap. Think mediaeval keytar. Necessarily (due to size and weight) the pipes were quite short and therefore the pitch in the alto or soprano voice range. They were generally played from a small keyboard by one hand while a bellows was pumped by the other.

Detail of an angel with a portative organ from 'Maria with child' by Marcellus Coffermans (fl. circa 1549–1575), uploaded to Flickr by sharethewisdom, image Creative Commons Attribution 2.0 Generic license[13]

---

13 https://tormatobook.com/CC

Slightly larger organs are also seen in illustrations placed on a table, a stand or sitting on the floor. These are often referred to as positifs. In positif organs the pipes could be of larger size, therefore with a deeper tone perhaps even suitable for accompanying male voices, and the pipes were supported with more elaborate decorative supporting pillars and rails. We see the pipe lengths decrease from left to right, each adjacent to the key from which they were played with a simple mechanical mechanism to open the valves. In the famous Unicorn tapestries at the Cluny museum, such an organ stands on a table played by a noble lady, while a maid lifts and closes two bellows behind it. Some of the larger floor-mounted positif organs were likely to have had more than one pipe per note, and to be only moveable with poles, sedan-chair style.

Detail from tapestry at Musée de Cluny, uploaded to Flickr by ho visto nina volare, image Creative Commons Attribution 2.0 Generic license[14]

Developments in larger organs included transmitting the key action sideways so that pipes with bigger diameters could be spread out on larger windchests in more dramatic cases, adding further rows of pipes at different pitches of the harmonic series, adding vibrating reeds with resonators instead of flue pipes, being able to turn off (stop) each row of pipes with stop knobs or sliders, combining more than one organ into an instrument with multiple keyboards, and adding pipes playable from foot pedals. Some of these advances were added to portable positifs.

Dee Palmer's 'Portative' pipe organ

Dee Palmer's instrument was made in 1970s by Mander. It consists of a 44 note keyboard with two ranks of pipes, and two sliding stop knobs that allow each rank to be either switched on or off. As the pipe ranks do not sit side by side the key action must be electrical rather than directly mechanical. Be-

---

[14] https://tormatobook.com/CC

hind the keyboard, in a glass enclosure, the front rank of pipes comprises 44 metal open principal pipes arranged chromatically, with the bass on the left and the mouths facing into the organ. Behind that are c. 33 metal tapered flute pipes which are longer than the corresponding principal pipes, spaced slightly further apart. To the left of the metal pipes are two rows of 5 or 6 wooden stopped pipes, at right angles to the keyboard, which make up the bass of the flute rank. Being stopped, they sound an octave lower than their length would suggest, so some appear shorter than the longest metal pipes.

A small metal tab is soldered to the upper part of each metal pipe foot, and this is screwed directly into the top of the rack board. This unusual feature means that the pipes are secured firmly onto the instrument, rather than just held by gravity. This appears to be a deviation from normal practice to allow for use as a touring instrument.

Assuming that the keyboard has a regular spacing (c.165 mm per octave) then the speaking length of the 8th note (the lowest C on the keyboard) of the principal rank is 1 foot (i.e. one octave above middle C in pitch). The speaking length of the flute rank of the same note is 2 feet (i.e. middle C, an octave below the principal).

Therefore the organ can be considered to have a short compass, starting at tenor f (i.e. F below middle C), playing at traditional piano pitch (i.e. the equivalent of an 8 foot pitch flute stop) and a keener principal stop sounding an octave higher. As it was not carried but sat on a stand, it is effectively a positif rather than portative. (In *Tales*, this is more or less what you hear on 'The Remembering' – often just the flute (for example in the opening bars – the sweet, ornamented melody, various countermelodies) or with the principal added the crunchier chords. No bass notes are obvious?).

Rick's two manual touring organ

In the 1950s, Noel Mander, a then Suffolk-based organ builder, advertised a new range of pipe organs, 'designed to meet the needs of those churches where both space and funds are limited'. In the Denham model, the pipework was mounted above the console in an elegant case. In the Hoxne model the pipes were arranged in the open on a platform built behind the organ. Both organs had a single keyboard and no pedalboard. At their most simple, they contained a flute and a principal rank of pipes. However, because electrical transmission was used between the keys and the pipes, it was possible using relays to sound notes one or two octaves higher than played, and these were activated using the 4 and 2 foot draw stops. This saves considerable space and expense, rather than in the traditional organ where at least one unique pipe is provided for each note for every stop. To accommodate this, extra octaves of small pipes were added at the top ends of the windchests. In addition, the flute could be made to sound at an octave and a fifth above piano pitch. Unlike in Dee Palmer's portable organ, the keyboards extended down to two octaves below middle C, and so the deepest sounding pipes in the instrument were 4 foot long stopped flutes sounding at 8 foot pitch (piano pitch), meaning that much more room was needed.

The Denham model organs in particular, of which a few still exist, are well regarded today because of the quality of the pipework and woodwork, clear refined speech, and the elegance of the case and console. The electrical components are not so durable apparently, and now require renewal or refurbishment if not already attended to.

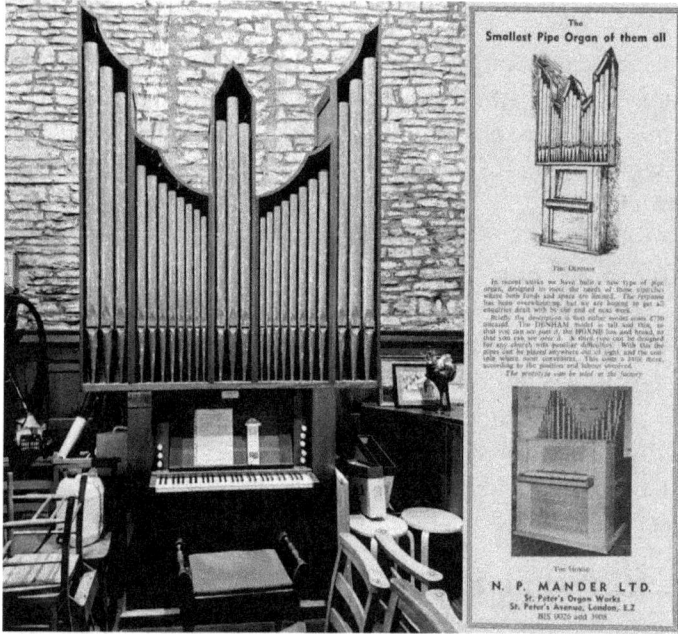

Left – Denham organ, Old Cogan Penarth, photo courtesy of Chris Berry, right – Mander's advert for the Hoxne and Denham range

A later, more versatile version of the Hoxne organ was produced from around 1959. One was recorded by Barry Rose (Guild GRM 304) in 1968. This had a traditional 2 manual console with draw stops, and the pipework was placed on a small platform with the 19 or 20 longest pipes of the principal rank (4 feet long) mounted symmetrically above a triangular toe board at the front, to hide the rest of the otherwise open pipework behind. In addition to the flute (c. 80 pipes starting at bottom C) and principal (56 pipes starting at tenor C) ranks, another partial rank was introduced to supply the pitches at a fifth as these pipes need to be tuned exactly to be effective. Two manuals did not mean more pipes, but different stop combinations could be drawn on each allowing rapid transition between timbres, or soloing out a melody

– important in a live rather than recording environment. It is undoubtedly this type of instrument which was adapted to the needs of Rick's touring organ. Rick was already familiar with the work of Noel Mander, now based in London, because of his recordings of Six Wives and Close to the Edge on the impressive, almost brand new 1970 3 manual 39 stop organ in St Giles Cripplegate (where by chance I had lessons in the late 1980s).

ABOVE: Left – two manual Hoxne organ console, right – Hoxne organ platform, with bellows visible under, and principal pipes of the façade, photos courtesy of Prof David Shuker

LEFT: Inside a Hoxne organ, photo courtesy of Prof David Shuker – Here we see from left to right: 19 bass pipes of the principal in the façade; 32 pipes of the quint rank, sounding one octave and a fifth above the note played, from middle C to the top of the keyboard; 38 treble pipes of the principal rank; 80 pipes of the flute rank, including open flutes (extreme treble), 13 stopped flutes with turned wooden stoppers, 11 chimney flutes, 38 flutes stopped with metal cannisters, and 12 wooden stopped flutes at the side and back of the case (which forms the bass octave of both flute and principal ranks).

> Photographs of Rick's touring organ, such as the famous photos from the Rainbow Theatre late in 1973 (see chapter 20), show it to have a traditional two manual console, but with sliding stop levers rather than draw stops to the left of the keyboard, much like in a Hammond organ. This console unit is little bigger than the two keyboards and stop levers alone, and so much more compact and portable than the traditional Hoxne console pictured above.
>
> The pipework is enclosed in a wooden case. Unlike the Hoxne organ, the 19 visible principal bass pipes of the façade are mounted with the deepest speaking pipe in the centre, and likely the tops of the longest pipes are folded into the wooden cabinet to reduce the overall height. The shorter pipework would have been mounted on top of the bellows (reservoir) inside, the bellows being neatly hidden by paneling. It is joined to the console via a multicore cable, so the pipework was not necessarily onstage.
>
> It was later also used in studio albums with Yes, as well as solo albums such as *White Rock*.

Rick Wakeman confirmed to me that he believes he used a Mander portable pipe organ on *Tales*:

> "If I recall correctly, I used a Mander pipe organ on a few little bits but not my double manual Mander as that was ordered during the recording."

The newly-acquired double manual instrument was used on the *Tales Tour* and Gennaro Rippo remembers setting it up. I wondered if Rick still has the double manual organ somewhere. He said:

> "I do and it is in need of restoration. John Mander at Mander's was going to do the restoration for me but then Covid struck and destroyed so much including the demise of Mander's. I'd love to have it restored and record an album on it."

Chris Dale explains that the organ sounds on *Tales* are definitely made using a real pipe organ because, " ... the Moog, Mellotron and RMI Electra Piano don't do this exact pristine sound at all ... " He can hear the Mander organ on 'Ritual' as 'little pipe organ chords' and he can hear that it's definitely using a single manual setting. Chris is impressed with the way Wakeman employs the pipe organ on side 4 of *Tales*. He finds it tasteful and says Rick uses the high range of the instrument where it 'sings' best.

From his work restoring Rick's fabled Birotron (see *Yes – The Tormato Story*),

Chris has also discovered that the single manual Mander organ is likely to have been used to create the 'Pipe Organ Sound' on the second set of Biroton master tapes. Peter Robinson (Birotronics CEO) agrees that the Birotron tape sounds almost identical to the pipe organ on *Tales* and Wakeman's 1977 solo album, *Criminal Record*, which is one of the very few records to feature the Birotron. Telltale aspects of the real pipe organ that are audible include the clarity of the sound and what Chris calls the 'slight out-of-tune-ness' that would not be present if this was a synthesised instrument.

Other listeners have identified the Mander Pipe organ on 'The Remembering'. Yes fan and organist Chris Berry has timed more than 7 minutes of pipe organ on the movement and Joey Wise commented:

> "I've come to understand from listening to an isolated keyboard mix[15] that it's used all over ['The Remembering']! Anything that sounds like it could be pipe organ is likely the Mander and not the Hammond. The entire last section from " ... we don't even need to try we are one ... " to the end of the track has it to some degree. It seems to be used to fill out a lot of the sonic space and accent the Mellotron. I'm certain it's the only keyboard being played while Jon and Chris sing, ' ... rainbows, soft light, alternate tune, sun light, tell me, ... ' etc. until the ending where the Mellotron overtakes it."
>
> Yes fan, Joey Wise

Once the double manual version of the instrument arrived, Wakeman employed it live on the *Tales Tour*, at least on the UK leg. It cannot be seen in photos of the North American leg of the tour so, presumably, Rick used another instrument to recreate the pipe organ sound. Comparing bootlegs of shows from the UK and North America, it is possible to hear a very different organ tone, for example at the beginning of 'The Remembering'. The tone of the organ in UK performances is more mellow and sounds more like real pipes while in the US the tone is more 'reedy' with lots of high frequencies like one would expect to hear from a synthesised, general-purpose church organ sound.

Reportedly, Rick's Mander instrument was similar to the one here (see p.84), although it's not clear whether this is the actual instrument Wakeman used:

The portable size of this instrument made it a relatively easy way to add an authentic pipe organ sound to live performances. As can be seen above, the keyboards were housed in a separate unit to the pipes. Originally, a huge bundle of cables carried the signal from the console to the pipes which were set up off stage. When we spoke to Derek Dearden on the Yes Music Podcast, he

---

15 https://tormatobook.com/isolatedkey

Mander double manual Portable Pipe Organ, image source unknown, published in *The Musical Instruments of Progressive Rock* by Gerard Bassols

The Mander double-manual pipe organ console in use on what looks like a bespoke stand at The Rainbow Theatre, as shown in the 1974 *Tales North American Tour* book, detail from a photo on Forgotten Yesterdays

explained that he was asked to try and do something about the heavy and cumbersome 'snake' of wires that connected the 2 elements. He ended up designing a system that used just a single coaxial cable instead. This was years before the Midi musical instrument control system was invented and is another example of Yes collaborating with some of the brightest minds in musical technology.

Chris Dale adds that the Mander organ was the only way at that time to achieve a 'real-sounding' pipe organ in concerts. In fact, the splitting of the Mander organ into 2 parts probably inspired a similar innovation in the design of Hammond organs a little later and also predicts the look of the Korg BX-3 keyboard.

Chris agrees that Rick Wakeman's single manual Mander organ was indeed similar to Dee Palmer's (see the Rabbit Hole Tale above). Chris was actually offered that Rick Wakeman Mander by a late collector but, sadly, he never saw the instrument, which was in a state of disrepair. The organ is now reportedly restored, possibly in either a Canadian or a Philadelphia museum.

Double Mellotron

> "I burnt three of them in a field in Switzerland. They had great sound but they were a total nightmare in every other way."
>
> Rick Wakeman (possibly an apocryphal story), 2009 interview about Mellotrons, quoted on Planet Mellotron[16]

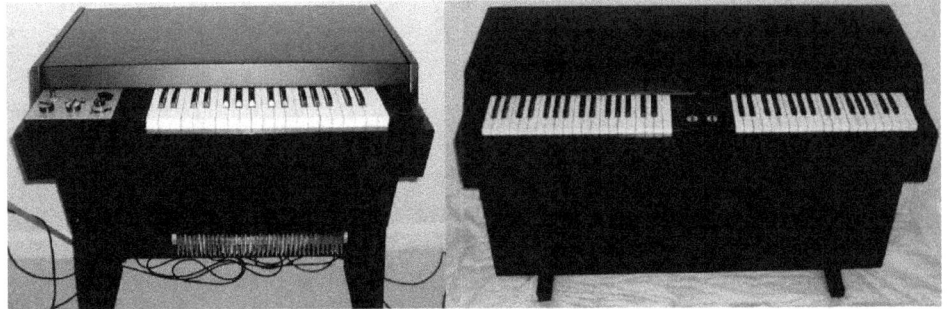

Left – single Mellotron once owned by Rick Wakeman, right – fully restored Double Mellotron, photos courtesy of Chris Dale

On *Tales*, Wakeman used his own, personalised version of the Mellotron. In order to try and fix some of the disadvantages of the tape-based machine, Rick had two of his own Mellotrons built into a unique, double configuration. The resulting instrument had a different build to standard Mellotrons as well as a different set of tapes.

---

16 https://tormatobook.com/rickmellotron

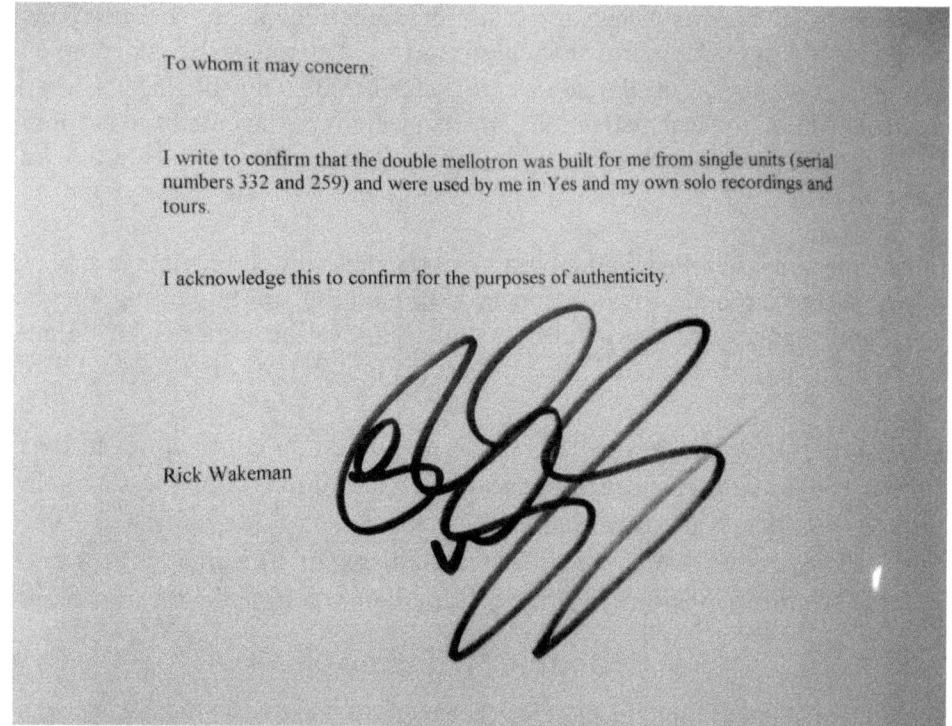

Note of authenticity from Rick Wakeman, photo courtesy of Chris Dale

Previously, for example on the *Fragile Tour* in 1971–2, Wakeman had 2 Mellotrons and chose to use whichever one was most in-tune on the night of each concert. Certain electronic components in the Mellotron were unreliable, being sensitive to humidity and temperature fluctuations. Also, the more notes played concurrently on the keyboard, the more likely the sound was to 'sag' – to dip lower in pitch – because the speed of the motors controlling the tapes could be affected by the demand on the system as well as electrical and climactic conditions. Unfortunately, due to the periodically dramatic contrasts in Yes music, the Mellotron could be left exposed. A good example of this is in 'Heart of the Sunrise'. If the sound began to sag in a concert, Rick Wakeman literally had nowhere to hide. Clearly, there was a need to try and stop these musical disasters.

This is one of the main reasons for the development of the Double Mellotron. Yes' own legendary lighting and hardware genius, Michael Tait, and the staff of the Mellotronics company collaborated on the project.

> "Well, it was my idea, I believe, because the problem with the Mellotron is you can only get, you know, one, you could have different cassettes for different sounds. But that was it. And it wasn't enough sounds for him. So the idea was to double it up. So we just bought another

5 – RICK WAKEMAN'S KEYBOARDS

Inside the Double Mellotron, photo courtesy of Chris Dale

Mellotron and I made a device to hook them together. ... Yeah, I mean, the only trick was keeping the spindles travelling at the same speed."

Typical understatement from Michael Tait, Yes Music Podcast, 2024

Chris explained to us that the inner workings of two Mellotrons (previously used by Wakeman live and for recording *Close to the Edge*) were extracted from their cases and put together in a new, single box. The original frames were replaced with a stronger, bigger, aluminium frame used to try to avoid warping. A host of other changes were also made including preamp card configuration, sound processing output electronics and balanced line transformer. The motors were stabilised and re-positioned to make the drive belt tighter.

Chris has detailed knowledge of the provenance of the two instruments used for the Double Mellotron. The instrument on the right hand side is the slightly older one. It has a lower serial number and a brass capstan (the metal roller bar that takes the tape forward). This was the type used on all early models before the company adopted the less expensive, nickel-plated variety. The original brass capstan was prone to tarnishing but this actually helped to grip the tape better as it moved, making tape spillage less likely. This was Mellotron #259 and was finished/released on 30th June 1972 at the same time Yes were recording *Close to the Edge* at Advision Studios. This brand new Mellotron would most likely have been used for overdubs in the very last hours of recording the Yes classic as well as being used live on the *Close to the Edge Tour* that started in July. It is also featured on the *Yessongs Tour* and album, of course.

The left hand Mellotron is numbered #332 and was finished or released earlier than the other one, although the date is unknown. It arrived back at the Mellotronics workshop to be integrated into the Double Mellotron on 21st May, 1973. There is a reference to this machine being 'BLACK YES MACHINE No 3' on the document. The timing of the creation of the Double Mellotron makes it undeniably the machine used for recording *Tales*, beginning in July 1973. This seems to be confirmed by Eddie Offord in a Melody Maker album preview towards the end of September 1973 (see chapter 19). He mentioned Rick Wakeman's Mellotron now featured new tapes and the ability to play both violins and cellos at the same time.

Production certificates for both Mellotrons used to create the Double Mellotron, photos courtesy of Chris Dale

The Double Mellotron is also pictured on the inside gatefold sleeve of Wakeman's *The Six Wives of Henry VIII* album. It is one of the keyboards identified in a large photo of Wakeman along with Minimoogs, RMI and others. It has a bright, reflective, red-pink thumbscrew unlike the usual, slightly darker red paint used on most other Mellotrons but identical to the Double Mellotron's right hand thumbscrew. The control panel on this side of the Double Mellotron is marked 'Brass Strings Flutes', just like this single Mellotron was.

Mellotron tapes were created by recording real instruments and then making a continuous loop of magnetic tape for each note of the keyboard. Occasionally, a Mellotron note included a mistake, captured in the recording process, that remained on the tape, rather than being edited out. For example, the highest note of the cello sound ends with the cellist accidentally banging his bow on the body of the instrument. Somehow, this was retained on the take used for the Mellotron tape! An example of this can of vagary can be heard at the beginning of 'Trio' from King Crimson's *Starless and Bible Black*. The flute sound is a Mellotron and, if you listen carefully, one of the notes is a lot brighter than the others and sticks out.

Understandably, Rick found these sorts of errors annoying and so he asked Mellotronics for alternative takes of the notes he didn't like. They delivered what he wanted and, if you were to play the same flute notes as King Crimson used on Rick's Double Mellotron, all the notes would sound similar, unlike on all other Mellotrons. With the addition of the different tapes, the Double Mellotron was not only unique in terms of its physical construction, it also sounded different to all other Mellotrons. This was one of the reasons Wakeman's keyboards on *Close to the Edge* and *Tales from Topographic Oceans* sound different – as Chris points out, the Mellotrons are even at different pitches on those two records.

The ability to play polyphonic combinations of sounds (more than one note at a time) with each keyboard of the Double Mellotron at the same time was a significant advantage and led to some interesting effects. Even the fact that the two keyboards could be slightly out-of-tune with each other added unique possibilities. To control this, each integrated Mellotron had its own 10-turn pitch knob. This feature was later copied from the Double Mellotron to the forthcoming Birotron (see *Yes – The Tormato Story*).

Another unique facet of the Double Mellotron was explained by Chris after Yes Music Podcast listener Mark Jones asked Rick Wakeman (via his website) what instrument is heard at the beginning of 'The Ancient'. Mark imagined that the fast part was played by Alan White on a marimba but Rick said it was actually him playing that part on the Melllotron. Chris said he found this particular sound while he was restoring the Double Mellotron. It is actually a vibraphone sound but without any vibrato. The other surprising aspect is that Rick is able to play it so quickly. It isn't possible to play ordinary Mellotrons at this speed but Rick had the double Mellotron's keyboards specially adjusted when it was created and this made the technique possible. Chris isn't sure if it was a deliberate attempt to enable different playing styles or if it was simply a bi-product of the adjustments.

Rick used this remarkable instrument live and in the studio extensively up until about 1977. It can be seen in his keyboard setup with two Minimoogs on top of it on the front cover of his 1974 live album, *Journey to the Centre of the Earth*. He also used it on albums such as *No Earthly Connection* and *The Myths and Legends of King Arthur and the Knights of the Round Table*. It even, possibly, appears on an album by the prog band Wally whose album Wakeman produced alongside 'Whispering' Bob Harris, presenter of the BBC's *Old Grey Whistle Test*.

Rick Wakeman playing the Double Mellotron on the Tales Tour, 1973, with additional single Mellotron also visible, photo courtesy of Chris Dale

The Double Mellotron idea inspired Mellotronics to create the Mellotron MK V in 1975, basically a production version of Wakeman's instrument. It was purchased and used by some notable players including Jimmy Page, Klaus Schulze, Mike Pinder, Neil Diamond, Joni Mitchell, Paul McCartney, Tangerine Dream and, most importantly for us, Patrick Moraz, who used it in the recording of *Relayer* and with The Moody Blues. Despite this stellar lineup of musicians, only between 25 and 35 MK Vs were made.

Chris Dale's own story with the Double Mellotron is equally fascinating. He acquired it decades after its creation. It had reportedly been stolen (at least once!) from Rick Wakeman's storage facility in High Wickham, known as Complex 7. It was here that the Birotron was being developed, an eventually unsuccessful endeavour that became a huge drain on Wakeman's finances (see *Yes – The Tormato Story*). Rick believes that his financial woes, compounded by a divorce, encouraged his own crew to steal items of value from him before they could be sold off to pay his debts. Unfortunately, the storage used at Complex 7 was not temperature-controlled so the condition of everything there was at risk. This probably contributed to the wrecked state of the Double Mellotron when Chris found it.

Advertisement for Rick Wakeman's Complex 7 facility from International Musician and Recording World Magazine, October 1975, author's collection

Like he did with the Birotron, Chris spent years renovating and restoring the Double Mellotron. By the time it reached Chris, the black paint on the cabinet was flaking off to reveal white paint beneath and mould had invaded the wood. Chris decided to save some flecks of the original black paint and mix them into the new paint to preserve a little authenticity. However, it took a year of mould removal and the addition of new wood where the damage was most severe before painting could even begin!

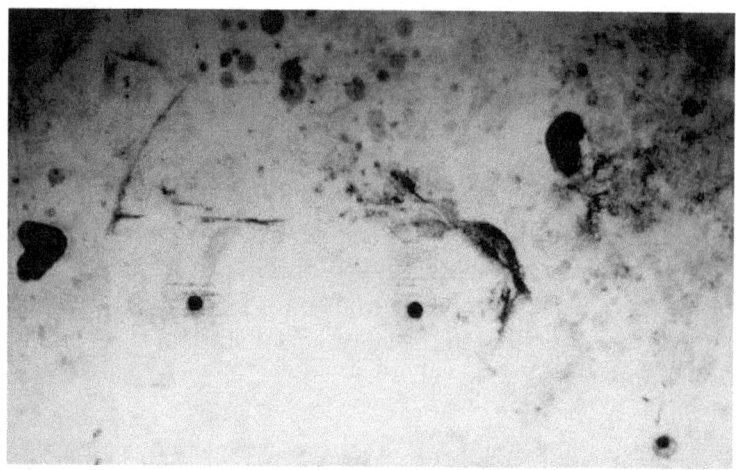

An example of the mould affecting the case of the Double Mellotron, photo courtesy of Chris Dale

The Double Mellotron after mould removal, the addition of strengthening wood and sanding down, photo courtesy of Chris Dale

The next step was to return the electronics to a working state. Initially, Chris contacted Frank Levi, who was credited as a technician on *Yessongs*, but he was unable to help. Another ignominy was then to be visited upon this remarkable instrument when Chris took it to a Mellotron convention to look for help. In a bizarre twist, it was 'mistreated' by some Yes-loathing King Crimson fans while unattended! Chris was dismayed to find that beer bottles had been left on the machine and there were even 'dings' in the cabinetry of the newly-refinished case. One attendee advised him to cut the machine in half and return it to two individual instruments. It seemed that a certain section of Mellotron enthusiasts were jealous of Chris owning this iconic instrument and this extended to a conspiracy to encourage him to sell it cheaply to them (including denigrating it as 'junk' to his face) so it could be resold at a profit. Chris eventually found out who was behind the plot and managed to cut off the whole group of what he calls 'toxic' people. Fortunately, Chris was then to contact people who were rather more interested in helping him to return the Double Mellotron to a working state.

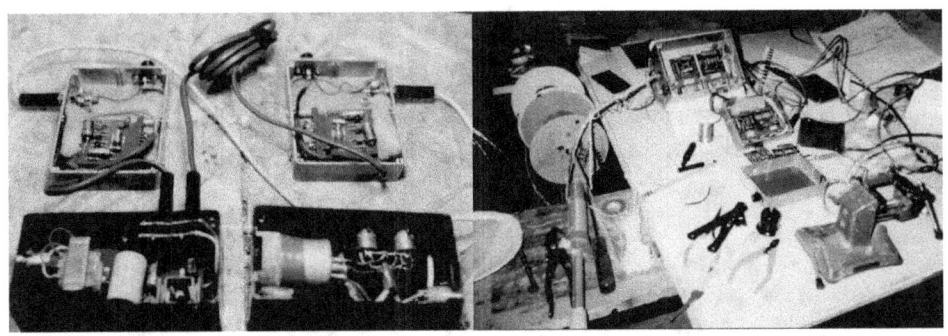

Double Mellotron electronics, photos courtesy of Chris Dale

One of the issues which led to the electronics containing an unusual preamp and crazy wiring was that the machine had to work reliably in all the different countries in which Yes and Rick Wakeman toured. It was shipped around the world at least 9 times from 1973 to 1977. This complexity led to many unsatisfactory attempts to fix the electronics. As Chris puts it this resulted in:

> " ... years and years of people mal-adjusting the mechanical bits, screwing around with the wiring, and trying to get it working ... being defeated by not having any specs or schematics ... "

This time it had to be done properly and so Chris enlisted the help of 'Mellotron fix-it professor' Jerry Korb, one of the most knowledgeable specialists on the planet. Jerry and Chris worked on the electronics for a week together and were able to devise schematics to help. Finally, the Double Mellotron was completed and in a playable state (see page 94).

Chris is planning to create a piece of music combining the Double Mellotron and the Birotron. This would be highly appropriate because Dave Biro, who was responsible for the invention of the Birotron, was heavily influenced by the Double Mellotron. He listened to *Tales from Topographic Oceans* repeatedly on 8-track cassette while he worked on his very first prototype in 1974.

Tales from Topographic Oceans - Yes album Listening Guide

The completed Double Mellotron, signed by all the members of the Tales lineup of the band, photo courtesy of Chris Dale

6
ALAN WHITE'S DRUMS AND PERCUSSION

Alan White arrives at Morgan Studios (the white building behind him) for the *Tales* recordings, possibly with Steve Howe's future wife, Janet, walking behind him, photo credit: Laurens Van Houten / Frank White Photo Agency

Tales from Topographic Oceans - Yes album Listening Guide

For the majority of his career, Alan White used Ludwig drums and *Tales* was no exception. In addition, there is a huge variety of percussion on the album. Below is an inevitably incomplete list of what Alan and the other members of the band played at some point on the album, based on my own observations and other sources.

Ludwig Drum Kit	Orchestral Cymbals
Hi-Hats	Ride Cymbals
Crash Cymbals	China Cymbals
Finger Bells	Hand Claps
Triangles	Tambourine
Orchestral Bass Drum	Metal Tent Pole(?)
Tam-Tams	Gongs
Metal Thunder Sheet	Whistle
Castanets	Steel Drums
Congas	Log Drum
Vibraphone	Bells
Crotales	Tubular Bells

As a dedicated Yes concert-goer from childhood, friend of Alan White and the drummer for the Total Mass Retain Yes tribute band, Joe Cass was an ideal Yes Music Podcast guest to ask about the percussion on *Tales*. Our first question was around how Alan coped with his first Yes studio recording experience at Morgan Studios. It must have been a daunting task to take on an epic, double studio album as your introduction to making records with the already legendary band. However, as Joe points out, Alan had just been 'thrown in at the deep end' on the *Close to the Edge* tour. He had to learn the whole set and develop musical relationships with the rest of the band in only a few days. This must have been a huge advantage when it came to Alan's mindset as he entered the rehearsals at Manticore and then the recording sessions themselves.

Although Alan has the well-deserved reputation of being a generous, self-effacing personality, this didn't mean he was tentative about making contributions to *Tales*. In addition to remarkable drumming and percussion, Alan also composed and played piano on the album and even provided some backing vocals. He was clearly intent on being a lot more than simply 'the new drummer'. Joe believes that Alan would have been the most receptive member of the band when Jon Anderson and Steve Howe presented the ideas for *Tales* to their fellow musicians.

There are precedents for White's all-round musical contributions. When he played drums for John Lennon on the iconic album *Imagine*, for example, he also added vibraphone to the songs 'Jealous Guy' and 'I Don't Want to Be a Soldier'. Joe recalls how proud Alan was of his writing on all sorts of Yes records such as 'Turn of the Century' from *Going for the One* and 'In The Presence Of' from *Magnification* and his ability to fit into many different musical settings was well-known. This also supports the belief, held by many Yes fans who understand Alan's artistry more fully, that he was not simply the 'powerhouse' drummer, compared to his predecessor Bill Bruford's jazz sensibilities and lighter touch. Joe points out the many examples of Alan's rhythmical creativity – "... from the period of *Tales* through *Drama*, and there's even a lot of it on things like *90125*, ... the switching of where the beat lies below the rest of the band creates a dynamic." The easy stereotype cannot be upheld when players try to replicate Alan's playing on the albums from *Tales* to *Drama*.

One clear example of Alan's remarkable, complex percussion writing and playing is the battle sequence in 'The Gates of Delirium' from *Relayer*. However, there are moments in his first album with the band that are just as remarkable. From the beginning of side 3, 'The Ancient – Giants under the Sun', Alan chooses sounds to help create the mood. When Joe Cass asked Alan exactly how he created the metallic sounds here, he simply replied, with a twinkle in his eye, "Well, that's a trade secret."

Just like the famous scene in the *Going for the One* behind-the-scenes video, Joe is convinced that Alan and the other band members frequently joined forces to create the percussion parts for *Tales*, especially in 'The Ancient' and 'Ritual'. Clearly, there was also overdubbing but, for example, at 36 secs onwards, there are tom parts and at least two more metallic-sounding parts. Joe imagines that Jon Anderson might be playing the tom parts with Alan providing the intricate parts above. This is how sections like this and 'Ritual' were reproduced live, with Jon Anderson and Chris Squire playing alongside Alan to create the essential percussive soundscape.

From side 2, 'The Remembering', onwards, Alan adds more unusual, exotic-sounding instruments, highly appropriate for the stated themes of the album. Little touches of tiny bells occur near the beginning of side 2 and, at around 1 min 39 secs, what I think are crotales add a beautiful, high-pitched background colour to the soft section. Also, not all the percussion sounds are instruments. For example, at 7 mins 22 secs in 'The Remembering' some off-beat hand claps appear. In a foreshadowing of 'Ritual', at 13 mins 50 secs, there is not only some intricate kit drumming but also some kind of instrument with bells like on a tambourine. It sounds heavier than a tambourine though, so maybe it's something like a large, stout stick being hit on the ground.

The exotic sounds take centre stage at the beginning of and throughout 'The Ancient'. The piece starts with a gong – or the instrument more correctly termed a Tam-Tam because it is unpitched. In the 1970s these huge, circular items adorned many a drum set-up in concert. Roger Taylor of Queen had one that was only used once per gig, for the final note of 'Bohemian Rhapsody' and iconic drummers like Neil Peart of Rush, Terry Bozzio of the Frank Zappa band and Carl Palmer of ELP all liked the visual and musical impact of Tam-Tams. Also common in symphony orchestras, the glowing, mighty sound of the Tam-Tam is augmented by White with another symphonic form of metallic percussion – a set of 2 crash cymbals played by hand by a standing percussionist who hits them together in front of his/her body. This produces a sound quite dissimilar to a standard, stand-mounted crash cymbal. Tinkling bell sounds – or perhaps crotales also take part in this mix but the most remarkable sound, for me, begins at 4 mins 33 secs. White plays what sounds like a pitched gong (to use the correct expression) to hold the beat of the passage. There is other, lighter, untuned percussion as well but listen out for the way Alan subtly changes the note of the gong at times to produce a quasi-melodic structure. Alan's use of a pitched gong here reminds me of the orchestras of tuned and untuned percussion in Balinese and Javanese gamelan music. This type of traditional Indonesian music was starting to appear in the west in the 1970s alongside Indian musical traditions. The result is a hypnotic, repeated pattern, ideal for invoking a meditative state.

Alan White working on his first Yes album at Morgan Studios, photo credit: Laurens Van Houten / Frank White Photo Agency

" ... the cymbal on the beginning of 'Ritual' was 20" inverted China, made by Zildjian. Played along with it was a wafer-thin metal plate, which gave the cymbal another texture and a unique sound."

Modern Drummer Magazine, March 2001

6 – ALAN WHITE'S DRUMS AND PERCUSSION

The opening of side 4, 'Ritual *Nous Sommes Du Soleil*', is an iconic moment in Yes music. Not only does it feature a bass solo from Chris Squire and a soaring electric guitar solo from Steve Howe, but also some remarkable drumming and percussion from Alan White. At first, he ties this section back to side 3 with some exotic gong sounds, or perhaps cymbals but then, from about 20 secs in, he combines with Squire to create a rhythm which exemplifies Alan's ability to invent parts that fit – and augment – the mood of the music perfectly. The rhythm at this point could have been in a fairly 4-square, ordinary-sounding pattern but White accents the first 2 quavers (eighth notes) of the bar, set up via a preceding grace note, and then lets the second crotchet (quarter note) beat hang in the air:

Simplified Alan White drum pattern, showing the main stresses of the rhythm

Joe describes this effect as 'letting the music breathe' and is only one example of the many instances of synergy between White and Squire across the record. Perhaps my favourite is at 13 mins 12 secs in the middle of the bass solo section that is mainly accompanied by tuned and untuned percussion. There is a hiatus in the motion of the music and Squire plays a high, tuneful line. White joins in with this on the snare drum and, somehow, he seems able to replicate not only Squire's rhythm but also the shape of the melody being played on the bass.

After this section, Howe adds his own boisterous, almost madcap line and then at 14 mins 20 secs comes what you could describe as Alan's 'moment' on the album. It's a drum kit solo and percussion section with lots of additional sound effects thrown in. After the dramatic bed of tinkling, clanging metallic percussion with Alan's toms and cymbals above has been established, timpani enter at about 14 mins 58 secs. This is the section in which Chris Squire and Jon Anderson take part in live performances of the song. As pointed out by Joe, however, it would be impossible to play the piece exactly as it was created in the studio due to the sheer number of overdubs and different types of percussion required. In fact, 'Ritual' is the most different of the 4 sides of *Tales* when played live, according to Joe who is one of the few people who has played it (on the Cruise to the Edge). This section captures a strong sense of the fourth Shastra, 'Tantras', and its fight between sources of evil and pure love. Presumably, this drum and percussion break is meant to evoke the chaos and threat of evil so that when the resolution of 'Nous Sommes du Soleil' appears from 16 mins 58 secs the feeling of pure love triumphing over evil is reinforced as the previous section fades away.

The second 'Nous Sommes du Soleil' section of 'Ritual' contains one of the most subtle and, arguably, important contributions Alan White made to *Tales*. This is where his piano composing and playing is heard. At 17 mins 33 secs, his gentle and perfectly-judged piano comes in for the first time. At 18 mins 10 secs, he plays a beautiful counter-melodic line that extends beyond the 'flying home, going home' vocal line and emerges again a little later as well. It's a wide-ranging, unusual line which climbs and falls with a lovely lilt.

Apart from the percussion and piano parts, Joe also believes that Alan took part in the 'Yes choir'. The usual voices at this time would have been Jon, Steve and Chris but Alan is credited with backing vocals and Joe thinks it's him in the lowest part of the choir that begins at 2 mins 28 secs of 'The Revealing Science of God'. This lowest part is particularly noticeable at 2 mins 59 secs – 3 mins 30 secs. It could be Rick Wakeman or even Eddie Offord helping out but perhaps the most likely answer is Alan. It certainly doesn't sound like Steve (who usually sings the bottom part) or Chris.

> "... I think that Alan White is the glue of 'Tales' ... and for a person's first album with such a band, I would go as far as to say that Alan White is a genius on Tales from Topographic Oceans."
>
> Joe Cass, Yes Music Podcast, 2023

7
STEVE HOWE'S GUITARS

Steve Howe in a contemplative mood during the recording sessions for *Tales from Topographic Oceans* at Morgan Studios, photo credit: Laurens Van Houten / Frank White Photo Agency

"... no one guitar has everything although the [Gibson] ES-175 and I are pretty inseparable. It *is* a luxury being able to choose, but I enjoy choosing, because it broadens certain aspects of my performance for me. If I had to cut it down to one – which would be ridiculous – it would have to be the 175, because I can actually play acoustic pieces on it as well. But since there isn't that sort of crisis, and I own about a hundred guitars, I don't really think about it. The importance of them is justified by the fact that I use them. I'm not overemphasising my importance to myself, but I'm the only one who can make that decision. I'd love to have the ease of a tour with just one guitar, but it's just not possible. Slide and acoustic guitar, for example, are different instruments and they help make up a varied show of guitar sounds. It's the same in the studio."

Steve Howe, interviewed in *Guitar Player* magazine, May 1978

Guitars on *Tales from Topographic Oceans*:

Gibson Les Paul Junior

Gibson 345TD

Gibson L5CESN*

Danelectro Dane/Hawk A2N12

Kohno N0. 10**

'Portuguese' 12-string

Danelectro Coral Sitar

Gibson BR9 (Steel Guitar)**

The Yes Music Podcast benefits from a resident guitar expert, co-host Mark Anthony K. He describes Steve Howe's approach on *Tales* as 'experimental'. Steve decided to expand his palette compared with previous Yes albums, such as *Close to the Edge*. He uses a wider variety of guitars on *Tales* in order to achieve different sounds, tones, colours and textures.

However, as Mark points out, the guitar work on *Tales* is still clearly in Howe's recognisable style, even if the choice of guitars is different.

"You can give him Eddie Van Halen's guitar and it's going to sound like Steve Howe still, because it's the way he plays. It's in his technique – it's the way he picks."

Mark Anthony K, Yes Music Podcast, 2023

Gibson Les Paul Junior

Howe identifies the Les Paul Junior as the 'main' guitar on *Tales*. Compared with other Gibson Les Paul models such as The Les Paul and the Les Paul Special that Steve uses on other albums, a lot of commentators describe the Les Paul Junior as a 'cheap' or entry-level model. However, as pointed out by Mark, everything is relative and, if you wanted to buy a new Junior today, it would cost at least £1,500 GBP or $1,599 USD. (Steve told me Les Paul Junior models from the 1950s sell today for around £10,000!)

It is true that the Les Paul Junior was first introduced as an electric guitar for students and that it is a much simpler design than other models in the range. It consists of a slab of mahogany with a neck attached and a single, 'dog ear' P90 pickup (so-called because of the shape of its mounting flanges). The tail bridge for connecting the strings is also of the simplest possible design. The string goes through a hole, wraps around and is connected to the tone tuning peg.

The single pickup makes the range of sounds available from the Les Paul Junior significantly restricted in comparison to other models but there are many guitarists who say that the single volume and tone controls are all you need to create a wide range of sounds from this guitar. Mark says this is partly due to the fact that the single pickup is 'hot', meaning that distorted sounds are easy to make from lower gain levels on an amplifier. This means that there's no need to add a distortion or other effect pedal to the setup to achieve that rock sound.

Howe playing the Les Paul junior on 'Ritual' in 2001, image from the *Symphonic Live* DVD

Bearing in mind the varied character of the music on *Tales* and the kind of tone that Steve Howe likes to play with, it may be a bit of a surprise that the main guitar he chose is known to be restricted in tonal range. Steve does say that he was partly aiming to provide a level of consistency in the sound of the whole album, but he also admits that the Les Paul Junior did cause him difficulties.

> "Of course, it was hard for the guitar to cope with some of the things I wanted to play. I don't think all of it sounded sweet. Looking back, I probably would have chosen different guitars more often, but at the time I stuck with it for continuity and simplicity."
>
> Steve Howe, *The Steve Howe Guitar Collection*

Listen out for the Les Paul Junior on sides two and three, and especially side four. As Mark says, if you want to hear what the Junior sounds like with Yes, just listen to Ritual. It has a lot more 'crunch' to its sound than most of Steve Howe's other guitar work for Yes.

Gibson 345TD

As pointed out in the quote which begins this chapter, the guitar most commonly associated with Steve Howe is the Gibson ES175D, but he uses a different variety of Gibson hollow-bodied guitar on both *Close to the Edge* and side one of *Tales*. Whether it was intentional or not, this provides a tonal connection between the end of the previous album and the opening of *Tales*. If you have seen Yes in concert with Howe, you will almost certainly have seen the Gibson ES345 used on *Tales*. Contrasting with his ES175, the 345 has a dark brown finish.

> "The 345 came off the back at 'Close to the Edge.' That's the guitar feature on 'Close to the Edge' and starting 'The Revealing' with that guitar just felt right, because at the time, I'd perfected a two amp and two volume pedals technique. If you put headphones on, there's a whole lot of volume pedalling going on, and kind of tremoloing going on with two pickups, one on each side of you. So it was a fascinating guitar approach. But what happens as the song goes on is, I use a few other tricks. One of them is a little amp called a Pignose."
>
> Steve Howe quoted in the Gottlieb Bros.' tour book for *The Classic Tales of Yes Tour*, 2023

In his *Guitar Collection* book, Steve tells the story of how he acquired the Gibson ES345TD. He was given it in return for appearing in a print advertisement endorsing Gibson guitars. It is interesting to note, therefore, that he didn't go out to buy himself this instrument that ended up providing the major tonal character for the genre-defining *Close to the Edge* and the beginning of *Tales*. He must have been very pleased with his 'payment in kind'.

Mark says the reasons for Howe's preference for the 345 on *Tales* may lie in its name. 'ES' stands for Electric Spanish, while 'T' means 'thin line' and 'D' means 'double pickup'. The ES175 has a much deeper body than the 345 which means that the 345 is easier to handle. Both models have two pickups, indicated by the letter 'D' but the 345 has an additional 'varitone' rotary switch known as a 'bird nose'. This enables five different tones to be selected quickly, although Howe says he only ever uses two of these settings. He mentioned to me that he believes only position 1 and 2 are full-sounding and the others are much less effective.

Another key difference between the two types of Gibson guitars is the length and playability of the fretboard. The ES175 has 20 frets while the ES345 has 22. So the 345 offers more scope in terms of playing parts high on the fretboard.

Perhaps the biggest difference between the two series, however, is the ES345's stereo wiring. As Steve mentions in the quote above, this means he can send two signals from the guitar – one to each of his two amplifiers. One signal could be 'clean' with maybe some digital delay, while the other could be slightly 'dirtier' with perhaps a touch of distortion. This helps him to create a dramatic, stereo sound, in a similar way to Chris Squire's Rickenbacker 4001 which he converted into a stereo instrument himself.

In the studio, the two outputs from the guitar would be sent to the two amplifiers and then either microphones would pick up the sound separately but at the same time or Steve would play the same guitar line twice, with the sound picked up from one of the two amplifiers at a time.

Gibson L5CESN*

Steve took this guitar (also known as a 'Super 400' or 'L5') to the rehearsals at Manticore (see chapter 3) but ended up not using it on the album at all. Despite being a very expensive and beautiful looking guitar, hand-made with ebony and abalone inlays, Mark is in no doubt about why Steve rejected it. 'CES' stands for Cutaway Electric Spanish and the guitar is semi-hollow. It has just 20 frets of which only about 17 are are fully accessible because of the shape of the body. Like the ES175, this guitar's body is deep, making it more difficult to play, as discovered by Mark in his local music store. In addition, Steve says that the guitar was, "... prone to feedback at the levels I was playing at, which wasn't incredibly loud."

Steve told me:

> "And I remember one thing quite distinctly is that when I started *Tales*, I brought this beautiful blonde Gibson L5 jazz guitar. I mean, this is really a jazz guitar [from the] 50s too, with these other, earlier pickups,

not humbuckers. So I'm in Manticore, standing on the stage with my amp and everything ... I'm playing this guitar and it keeps feeding back and I'm thinking, well, you know, I want to play this guitar. This might be the *Tales* guitar ... so I wrestled with that."

Danelectro Dane/Hawk A2N12

This 12-string guitar (known as both a 'Dane' and a 'Hawk') is very obvious in 'The Remembering – High the memory', side 2 of the album. Steve didn't have the highly-regarded Rickenbacker 12-string at the time he recorded *Tales* but he was keen on his rather cheaper Danelectro alternative. He pointed out to me that Danelectro guitars were famous at the time for their tone. This was the second 'entry-level' guitar to take a major role in *Tales*, after the Les Paul Junior. Apparently, its pickup covers were made from recycled lipstick tubes and the whole range of guitars, made by New Yorker Nathan I Daniel, was known for its use of cheap materials. Despite this, the sound they produced was surprisingly good.

Steve Howe playing the Danelectro Dane/Hawk A2N12, screenshot from 8mm film of the *Tales Tour* concert in Atlanta on 11th February 1974, courtesy of Ron Gerber Films and the Classic Rock Media Archive

It is perhaps a surprise that Howe chose this guitar for a major role on *Tales* because of its 12-string configuration. Mark points out that once you get used to the different feel of the 12-string, it can be as natural as a 6-string. However, it is far more usual for guitarists to play strummed, chordal parts on a 12-string than intricate, fast-moving, finger-picking solos. Listen again to 'The Remembering' and you will notice the comparatively slow-moving electric guitar parts, particularly around the opening of the song. There are more typical sections, for example around 13 mins 8 secs onwards but this sounds more like the Les Paul Junior again.

Kohno N0. 10**

A Kohno N0. 10 Spanish guitar was bought by Steve Howe on the first Yes tour to Japan in 1973. He describes it as his first choice Spanish guitar for all recording work since then, but this was after recording *Tales*, so another guitar was needed. Spanish guitar features heavily on 'The Ancient' from 12 mins 31 secs. This beautiful section leads into the lovely 'Leaves of Green' duet with Jon Anderson, accompanied by harmony singing and a high-pitched synth solo. It is one of the most touching passages in all Yes music.

For the *Tales* recording, Steve told engineer/producer Eddie Offord he wanted to sound like the iconic classical guitarist Julian Bream for this sequence. He believes the guitar he ended up using was hired specifically for the *Tales* recording and may well have been a Kohno but he can't be sure.

> " … we actually listened to Julian Bream in the studio when we did 'Leaves'. I put it on and I said, 'Well, that's what a Spanish guitar is really supposed to sound like.' … Eddie and I used that as a reference point because, … his approach is one of the most impressive classical guitar approaches that I've seen. I was very familiar with his work, so that was a bit of emulation there."
>
> Steve Howe, Yes Music Podcast, 2025

In a recent interview with the Gottlieb Brothers for *The Classic Tales of Yes Tour* book, Steve says, "I was actually playing a guitar from 1810 at that point. It had such a lovely lute-like sound." Perhaps he has now worked out which guitar he used.

'Portuguese' 12-string

Another iconic Yes acoustic guitar is Steve's Portuguese 12-string, wrongly called a 'vachalia' in the sleeve notes to *The Yes Album*. The instrument was brought back from a Spanish holiday by Howe's sister and given to him when he was about 15.

Perhaps the most obvious use of this guitar is on the 1977 song 'Wonderous Stories', which is based around its sound and strumming style but it also appears notably on 'And You And I' from *Close to the Edge* and 'I've Seen All Good People' from *The Yes Album* (its first appearance on a Yes record). In his *Guitar Collection* book, Howe says that it is used on *Tales* to provide colour on side one – 'The Revealing Science of God – Dance of the Dawn'. Its jangly tones

(Howe's expression) should be audible but I find it difficult to hear it at all. As Mark says, it is probably mixed in with the 12-string Danelectro to add a slightly different flavour to the tone.

It turns out this guitar is actually a Spanish laúd and its strings use an unusual tuning which possibly contributes to its unusual sound as well as making the chord fingering a little easier.

Danelectro Coral Sitar

> "On *Tales*, the Danelectro Coral Sitar guitar is featured on Side 4 through the "Life seems like a fight" song, verse and choruses."
>
> Steve Howe, 2025, via email

Before the development of electronic instruments, Howe sought out interesting and unusual sounds by collecting instruments from around the world. For example, he has used a Japanese koto in solo work as well as on recent Yes albums and there is a South Asian sitar pictured in his *Guitar Collection* book. The sitar became a popular instrument in Europe and the US in the 1960s and 70s, partly due to The Beatles' George Harrison using it on songs such as 'Norwegian Wood' from *Rubber Soul* and 'Within You Without You' from *Sgt. Pepper's Lonely Hearts Club Band*. Howe said he first heard the instrument in the 60s on records such as 'Green Tambourine' by The Lemon Pipers.

After initial experiments with the instrument, George Harrison became a pupil of Indian sitar legend Ravi Shankar and at one point even considered learning the instrument full-time. Steve Howe loved The Beatles' music and incorporating some of the sound of the Southern Asian musical tradition he had heard on their records must have been an obvious choice for *Tales*, considering its thematic basis in the Shastric scriptures.

Although it looks fairly similar, the sitar is a very different instrument to the guitar and requires a radically different technique. It is much longer than a guitar and requires the player to sit on the ground. Its trademark 'buzzy' sound comes from its combination of 2 types of strings. There are 6 or 7 strings running over moveable frets and more than twice as many sympathetic strings, beneath the frets. These additional strings are not played with the fingers but instead reverberate in sympathy with the played strings. The large distance between the frets means that it is not possible to play chords like a guitarist and sitarists generally only use their middle and index fingers to create notes.

The many guitarists who wanted to incorporate this sound into their songs in the 1960s and 70s must have been daunted by the time it would take to learn the techniques needed so guitar manufacturers saw an opportunity. Howe bought one of the resulting Coral Sitars on a Yes tour of the US, probably in 1972 and used it for 'Siberian Khatru' on *Close to the Edge*. He describes its special 'flat' bridge which helps to create the sitar-like sound in combination with 13 extra strings, arranged next to the main strings that act just like the sympathetic strings on a sitar. However, the Coral Sitar has 6 main strings, arranged in the same way as a traditional 6-string guitar. So this instrument can be played just like a 6-string guitar but produces a sound closer to that of a sitar.

Steve Howe playing the Gibson 345TD with the Coral Sitar on a stand in front, photo by Barry Plummer

Although Howe doesn't mention the Coral Sitar being used on *Tales* in his *Guitar Collection* book, its characteristic sound can be heard clearly, for example at 15 mins 30 secs on side 1. When I asked him about this guitar on *Tales*, he told me:

"Well, they were very cheap guitars. It wasn't like buying a Gibson, this was like buying a Hofner ... so they were very crude guitars. All Danelectros are quite crude. But the genius of them was that those little lipstick pickups they had were really good. Jimmy Page used his Danelectro a lot and I used the six string bass on my solo album *Beginnings* quite a bit, which was adventurous ... the way that [the Coral Sitar Guitar] made that sound was incredibly crude. It was just kind of rattling on this surface that they'd found that the string could vibrate across."

Howe also mentioned that the sympathetic strings could be switched off which was essential at times to achieve a 'tighter' sound. He even used those additional strings on their own to create unusual sounds for his solo albums at times.

Gibson BR9 (Steel guitar)***

The steel guitar's origins lie in Hawaiian music. Its use in 1950s jazz/country by such legendary artists as Speedy West in his collaborations with Jimmy Bryant, might make it an unlikely choice for progressive rock. Yet Steve Howe wasn't the only prog guitarist to wield a variety of steel guitars. For example, the music of Pink Floyd would be rather different without David Gilmour's steel. Howe used the sliding characteristics of the instrument to create unusual solos but didn't transfer some of the more typically Hawaiian or country music strumming, chordal-shifting and vibrato techniques.

Along with the Gibson ES175, Steve Howe has long been associated with the Fender Dual 6 Professional or 'Stringmaster' steel guitar (identifiable by the two pickups on each neck). Invented in the 19th Century, 'steel' refers to the small metal bar used in the left hand on the fretboard. Many variations of terminology exist, for example slide guitar, lap steel (played on one's lap) and pedal steel (with the addition of extra foot controls) but the important factor is the sound that can be created with these instruments.

If you have ever seen Yes live in person or on film, you will probably have seen the cream-coloured, double-necked Fender Dual guitar in use on songs such as 'And You And I', 'Going for the One' and many others. Since the *Drama Tour* of 1980, it has been mounted on what Steve describes as a 'clever rail system'. This enables him to slide it from the side of the stage in front of him and then back out of the way when he is finished with it. It's an unforgettable sight, in my experience.

The Fender has been Steve's preferred steel guitar since the early 1970s but when I asked him about *Tales*, he was understandably a little unsure about the exact chronology of the acquisition of certain instruments. In his *Guitar Collection* book he states that he bought the Fender in October 1973 in the US but Yes weren't in the US at that time. Perhaps he meant October 1972 when the band were on tour in North America to support *Close to the Edge*. So, more than fifty years after the recording of *Tales*, Steve isn't 100% sure if the Gibson BR9 or the Fender Dual 6 Professional was used at Morgan Studios, although he most recently told me, "I think [the Fender] is the featured steel on Side 3 [of *Tales*]."

He is sure that the steel guitar on *Close to the Edge* is the Gibson and the Fender was definitely used in 1974 for *Relayer*.

Steve's BR9 was made in around 1953, and it's a strange combination of a cream wooden body, brown wooden fretboard and brown plastic (perhaps Bakelite) hardware. To the untrained eye, it looks a little like a child's toy. Despite this, the instrument that was picked up in New York on a Yes tour in the early 70s has worked rather well. The evidence is clear on both 'And You And I' and 'Siberian Khatru'. He also played the BR9 in many live concerts, placing it on a simple table to which he had to move in order to access it. As we will learn, once the Fender steel appeared in concert, other, rather more elaborate arrangements, were made.

Steve told me that he modified the BR9 in order to extend its range:

> "And I did things like I put ... a bit of string or something ... where I could get more notes. Sometimes the frets ran out a bit and I needed some more frets because the adventurism about the steel is just how high it can go ... I was always into being somewhere up there in the gods ..."

Although, again, not mentioned in his *Guitar Collection* book, I think the BR9 appears in several places on *Tales* including at 12 mins 54 secs in 'The Remembering – High the Memory'. At this point, there is a sliding electric guitar solo and, although some of the notes are picked and it turns into what is clearly a Les Paul Junior solo, I think Howe is using the BR9 at the start.

The beginning of 'The Ancient – Giants Under the Sun' is much clearer. This is definitely the BR9 in an extended passage from 45 secs to after 5 mins. Considering the comparative simplicity of this instrument, it sounds great here, providing a wonderful contrast to the fast and frenetic percussion beneath. Howe describes the sound of the BR9 as, "... a sort of sliding, bending, slippery sound" and this passage in 'The Ancient' certainly does have the character he calls, "... a kind of haunting atmosphere in the background."

8

CHRIS SQUIRE'S BASSES

"So, as the songs are different, so the bass playing is different, so the instruments were different."

Miguel Falcão, Yes Music Podcast, 2023

Chris Squire playing his Rickenbacker 4001S bass at the Rainbow Theatre on the *Tales Tour*, detail from photo by Barry Plummer

Basses used on Tales from Topographic Oceans

Rickenbacker 4001S bass

Rickenbacker 4008 8 string bass

Fender Jazz bass

Guild Jetstar II short scale fretless bass

Ernie Ball Earthwood acoustic bass

Miguel Falcão has recorded many bass covers of Yes songs and related Chris Squire songs on his website, miguelbass.com. Two of these are of particular interest to us – 'The Remembering – High the Memory' and 'The Ancient – Giants under the Sun'. He takes a forensic approach to reconstructing bass lines which extends to the instruments Chris used both in the studio and live. Miguel kindly wrote a section of 'Yes – The Tormato Story' to explain the origin and importance of the first instrument in the list above:

Rickenbacker 4001S bass

"The Rickenbacker International Corporation (RIC) was founded in 1931 by Adolph Rickenbacker and George D. Beauchamp and developed from a company named Electro String Instrument Corporation, that created and manufactured electric musical instruments and amplifiers. One of their inventions was the development in 1930 of the 'magnetic horseshoe' pickup to translate string vibration into an electric, amplifiable signal. This was the first ever electric guitar, also known as the 'frying pan'. Hawaiian guitars were the main products to take advantage of the 'frying pan' electrification system, which was then extended through the decades to several kinds of string instruments including guitars, mandolins, violins, cellos, violas and even harps. Right up to the present day, Rickenbacker is regarded as one of the most high-quality and distinctive instrument manufacturers in popular music. The Rickenbacker 4001 bass guitar was the first bass manufactured by RIC with two pickups and came out in 1961 as the follow-up to the single pickup model 4000. The 4001 was the model that cemented Rickenbacker basses' success in a market dominated by Fender and was soon to be the instrument of choice for Paul McCartney, John Entwistle, Pete Quaife and Roger Waters.

Just like its six- and twelve-stringed siblings, the 4001 and later the 4003 basses are often said to have a distinctive sound, sometimes described as a 'twang' (Definition from Oxford Languages: a strong ringing sound such as that made by the plucked string of a musical instrument or a released bowstring). Of course, other factors can significantly change the timbre of a stringed instrument such as the type of strings or amplifiers, but the tone of a Rickenbacker bass is immediately recognisable. Owing to the specificity of the 4001's sonority, it is not considered an all-purpose bass for standard applications where, once again, Fender and sound-alike brands continue to be pervasive and dominant.

Influenced by Paul McCartney and especially John Entwistle, Chris Squire acquired the third Rickenbacker 4001S model to be imported into the UK in 1965 (John Entwistle and Pete Quaife had the other two). Chris' bass was manufactured in 1964 and the model's name was RM1999, the designation for the importer Rose Morris, where Chris was working and thus able to get a good discount. The RM1999/4001S differed from the standard 4001 model, sporting a more simplified look (regarding binding and neck inlays) and no stereo output. However, Chris Squire ended up routing the bass to stereo some years later.

Chris never stated specifically why he kept the Rickenbacker as his main instrument. As we know, he was able to add his own sonic fingerprint to whichever bass he was playing at the time, but he became one of the world's most acclaimed bass players and arguably the one with the most distinctive sound in rock with that very same instrument. Perhaps one sign of how irreplaceable the 4001S was for him, was that for some periods he toured it with serious issues such as neck cracks, one of which was fixed by luthier Mike Tobias. Also, when the limited-edition Chris Squire signature bass was made (a 1000 unit signature series), Chris declared on several occasions that it didn't sound anything like his own bass."

Miguel Falcão, 2022

Miguel points out that the use of the 4001 provides a link back to Squire's previous work on *Close to the Edge*. Side one of *Tales* contains bass playing which was typical of Squire's career up until that point. Chris was certainly looking around for new sounds at this time and, as we shall see, *Tales* includes some significantly different bass instruments. However, throughout his career, Squire always came back to his 4001 because, as he said in interviews, there are so many possibilities with this bass. He said he could create virtually infinite combinations of sounds with the single bass and the different approaches he took to amplification.

There are examples of great Squire bass writing on side one. In the, "all fighters past" section (around 15 mins 45 secs), there is plenty of space for his part to come through. In other sections where the keyboards or guitars are flying around, he is more content to let those other parts shine. Chris is also singing backing vocals a great deal on side one, providing counterpoint to the other parts. Unusually, here Chris often sings a lower part than Steve, who more generally takes the lowest. This is audible at 7 mins 58 secs onwards.

Differences in bass writing from previous albums can be seen on *Tales*, particularly from side 2 onwards. Miguel says this was due to a number of factors. Firstly, Squire was now working with a new drummer, Alan White. It was a kind of re-start and Squire had to adapt to White's completely different style after working with Bill Bruford on five albums. Miguel describes Bruford's style as opening up a lot of empty space which could be filled by Squire's lines 'breathing'. Alan's kit was physically bigger than Bill's and White liked to ride the cymbals, whereas Bill's style was more closed. Secondly, the bass playing on the previous album, *Close to the Edge*, is consistent throughout the three songs whereas on *Tales* the bass on each side is different in style, in approach and in instruments used.

An aspect Miguel can hear in the sound of the bass on parts of side two and particularly side four of *Tales* is a Jack Bruce influence. Chris mentioned his liking for the Cream bass player's more mid-frequency, rounded bass timbre and he tried to add some of that on *Tales*. Previously, Squire's bass tone had been more thunderous, metallic and edgy. Perhaps the best place to listen out for the Jack Bruce approach is on Squire's classic solo album of 1975, *Fish out of Water*.

Chris Squire playing his Rickenbacker 4001S bass, screenshot from 8mm film of the *Tales Tour* concert in Atlanta on 11th February 1974, courtesy of Ron Gerber Films and the Classic Rock Media Archive

Production also changed for this album. Miguel says that from *Tales* onwards the tendency on Yes albums was to place the bass further back in the mix, making it harder to distinguish. In particular, he notices this on *Relayer* and *Going for the One*. He describes the mix on these albums as, "... a little bit messy and a little bit saturated on the high end." *Tales* was the first time the band had recorded in 24 track as opposed to their previous 16 track recording process. Unfortunately for Squire, a band with access to 8 additional tracks are unlikely to hand them all over to the bass player. More guitars, more stacked keyboards and more layered vocal harmonies (a lot of them doubled) meant less visibility for the bass, according to Miguel. There is also much more use of atmospheric textures on *Tales* with reverb and special effects.

This isn't to say that Squire was dissatisfied with his contributions to this album. Miguel recounts the times Chris said that he liked his bass line on 'The Remembering', for example. This is significant because it's not one of Squire's signature towering, epic performances. It's comparatively discreet and perhaps that is partly due to the way the production was handled. However, as mentioned by author Will Romano in his book *Mountains Come Out of the Sky: The Illustrated History of Prog Rock*, "Squire worked in the studio for as long as sixteen-hour days, seven days a week," so he put plenty of effort into his bass lines.

Rickenbacker 4008 8 string bass

Chris Squire acquired the Rickenbacker 8 string bass shortly before the recording of *Tales*. Miguel believes it is used for overdubbing on side one and for soloing on side four. For example, Miguel believes the first bass lick of 'Ritual' is the 8 string instrument because only its expanded range could reach this note – it's just too high for the 4001. Squire changed this bass line when the piece was performed live because he played the 4001 in concert as he needed it for the rest of the song. Instead of an ascending, major third, he opts for a descending minor sixth so plays the second note in a lower octave than on the record.

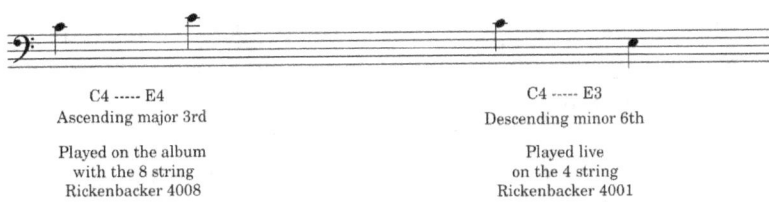

C4 ----- E4
Ascending major 3rd

Played on the album
with the 8 string
Rickenbacker 4008

C4 ----- E3
Descending minor 6th

Played live
on the 4 string
Rickenbacker 4001

Not to pitch – for illustration only

I asked my e-newsletter subscribers for their opinions on what Squire does on the record and on various live recordings and here is how Joost Doesburg responded:

> I for one certainly don't agree that on the QPR version Chris is sliding up (like on the album), I can clearly hear him sliding down from the high D to the low F#, though he does it quickly.
>
> To me, in that Zurich recording (1974), the QPR one (1975) and Yesshows (Detroit 1976) he's playing the same line sliding down.
>
> Remember that this is an effect with distortion, delay and an octaver adding a lower octave to the bass, therefore mimicking the 8 string effect.

Excellent points from Joost.

At the beginning of side four of *Tales*, there seem to be two separate bass lines – the 'theme' and also accents underneath. One of these, according to Miguel, is the 8 string Rickenbacker. Squire sets up a kind of dialogue between the two parts, with a soloing bass and a background or rhythm part. There may also be some bass pedals in the mix, in order to accent the bass 'hits' but, as Chris never played the bass pedals live on this song, it's not easy to tell.

Guild Jetstar II short scale fretless bass

There aren't many examples of Chris Squire playing fretless bass. Notable exceptions include 'Total Mass Retain' from the song 'Close to the Edge' but there he used a very distorted tone.

Not only was the bass used on side two of *Tales* fretless, it was also 'short scale'. This means the fretboard is significantly shorter than a standard bass. Electric guitars have a 'scale length' (the distance between a guitar's nut and its bridge) of around 24 inches, short scale bass scale length is usually around 30 inches and standard basses usually around 34 inches. The effects of the shorter scale length include different tone and lower string tension, which makes bending the notes up or down easier than on a longer, tighter string.

Chris' fretless bass technique was very different to some of the most well-known players such as Jaco Pastorius (Weather Report, Pat Metheny etc.) or the Yes-influenced Pino Palladino (Paul Young, The Who, Jeff Beck etc.) who played with finger-style rather than Squire's preferred pick. Incidentally, Bill Wyman (Rolling Stones) mentioned in his diary that he purchased a Guild Jetstar II short scale fretless bass in 1973 but this is probably a co-incidence (see p.119).

On side two, we can hear what Miguel refers to as Squire's short scale fretless

8 – CHRIS SQUIRE'S BASSES

Chris Squire playing the Guild Jetstar II short scale fretless bass, screenshot from 8mm film of the *Tales Tour* concert in Atlanta on 11th February 1974, courtesy of Ron Gerber Films and the Classic Rock Media Archive

bass coming in as if wearing 'woollen shoes', producing a woody effect. There is some lovely bass playing, creating a discreet counter-melodic line with the Mellotron. After about a minute, you can clearly hear the slightly sliding fretless bass which then continues under Rick Wakeman playing a church organ sound at about 2 mins. At the end of some phrases, Squire incorporates a slight downwards glissando (slide), a highly effective fretless bass effect.

When the "Don the cap" section arrives, the Jetstar II comes into its own, according to Miguel, as it integrates perfectly with the Spanish laúd acoustic guitar sounds provided by Steve Howe (9 mins 10 secs onwards). This part is a little like a mini acoustic set in the middle of the song.

Around 10 mins 30 secs, Chris returns to the Rickenbacker for the rockier section. If you listen to the studio run-through version of 'The Remembering', available on the Steve Wilson Remix collection, you'll hear that there is a completely different bass line from this point, still played on the Guild fretless bass. Chris clearly changed his mind and employed the Rickenbacker for the final version on the record. When he played side two of *Tales* live, the Guild fretless bass can be seen in photos to be on a stand so that he could change back to the Rickenbacker (see p.120).

Fender Jazz bass

Squire used his Fender Jazz bass on 'The Ancient' with a wah-wah pedal throughout. Originally designed to appeal to upright bass players (hence the name), this bass has a brighter tone in the mid-range and treble than the other Fender bass used by many rock musicians, the Fender Precision Bass. It was

Chris Squire playing the Rickenbacker 4001S at The Rainbow Theatre with the Guild Jetstar II short scale fretless bass on a stand to his left, detail from photo by Barry Plummer

introduced in 1960 as the Deluxe Model bass.

Miguel calls the bass line of side three 'mad' and it's easy to hear why. As soon as it appears, under the fast Double Mellotron pattern (see chapter 5), we can hear a syncopated, repeated approach that complements the Mellotron and the percussion parts perfectly. Around 1 min 28 secs, it is possible to hear the pattern more easily in its fragmented, wah-infused brilliance. Miguel likens the bass part here to Squire's line in the introduction to 'Close to the Edge', but he was always trying to come up with something new for each song – hence the choice of the Fender Jazz bass and the Crybaby Wah pedal, that he regarded as the best one available.

In response to the widely-held view that 'The Ancient' is random, formless, meandering and appears to be improvised by the band, Miguel points out that it is possible to analyse what is happening and discover patterns and structure, including in the bass lines. However, the depth of study required is more than the casual or even the dedicated listener is likely to be willing to undertake. Also, 'cracking the code' of the music would probably remove a lot of the enjoyment that the apparent chaos creates.

Ernie Ball Earthwood acoustic bass

At 15 mins 36 secs of 'The Ancient', these words appear: " ... Where does reason stop and killing just take over? ... " This is the second verse of what has become known as 'Leaves of Green', an acoustic passage in the piece. In this verse, an additional instrumental line is added by Chris Squire on an acoustic bass. This serves to move the music forward by elaborating the accompaniment beneath Anderson's beautiful lead vocals. Later on in the chorus section, the acoustic bass is heard more clearly.

The instrument used by Squire here was the Ernie Ball Earthwood acoustic bass. This is the same Ernie Ball whose company is still famous for producing guitar strings.

Chris Squire playing the Ernie Ball Earthwood acoustic bass in concert, photo from a video entitled 'Yes – Live Tales from Topographic Oceans Tour 1974 8mm Footage'[17], compiled by Duke Albert

At first glance, this instrument looks like a huge, 6 string acoustic guitar and was based on the fretless Mexican guitarrón, most familiar from traditional Mariachi bands. When it is played by Chris Squire, of course, the instrument doesn't look particularly over-sized!

Ernie Ball had experimented with the concept of an acoustic bass by installing frets on a guitarrón. He tried to persuade various guitar manufacturers to produce his acoustic bass idea, but none were interested. Instead, he launched one himself, working with legendary ex-Fender guitar maker, George Fullerton.

---
17 https://tormatobook.com/8mm

The instrument appeared in 1972 and was renowned for using wood where it would have been more usual to see metal or plastic. In some versions, even components such as truss rod covers, headstock binding, fret markers and sound hole trim were all made from wood.

Ernie Ball only produced instruments for a little over a decade but players like Squire and The Who's John Entwistle appreciated the Earthwood bass' loud and resonant sound.

Listening carefully to the second verse of 'Leaves of Green' from 'The Ancient', it's clear that the bass line starts very high (as many Squire bass lines do) but then goes much lower than a standard acoustic guitar. Chris' style is also discernible in the shape of the line as it progresses. Miguel describes it as, " ... almost like a classical bass player ... It's like Chris trying to be in Steve's domain because [the song is] so much driven by Steve's guitar." Squire interprets the feel of Steve's classical guitar here and displays his tendency to invert harmonies and play rhythms his own way.

Chris' Earthwood bass is now in the care of Yes collector Clive Ayer in London (see p.123). Clive told me that the bass had to be repaired (perhaps by luthier Sam Li) because Chris dropped a bottle of champagne onto it. The expert mend is still visible today. I was surprised to see that the bass has an internal pickup and an accompanying jack output in the side. I had assumed it was entirely acoustic and would need to have a strategically-placed microphone to be heard in concert.

Bass pedals

Despite my assumption that some of the strongest and lowest bass parts I can hear on the album were created by bass pedals, Miguel believes all the bass sounds on *Tales* were created by bass guitars, sometimes with effects applied, or maybe synthesizers. Of course, bass pedals are themselves synthesizers which is one of the reasons it's so difficult to decide how the lowest notes are created on audio-only albums. Chris doesn't include bass pedals in album credits until 1978's *Tormato* and before this he doesn't use them in the studio. Even in songs like 'Awaken' from *Going for the One* in 1977, Miguel says the lowest bass notes are probably played on the pipe organ. Squire often used techniques such as doubling bass parts, for example in 'And You And I' from *Close to the Edge*, or a fuzz pedal in the vocal introduction to 'Yours Is No Disgrace' on *The Yes Album*. However, Chris' extensive use of bass pedals in live concerts tends to lead us to assume that he also used them in the studio. Of course, Miguel can't be 100% sure but after many hours' research, this is his belief.

Chris Squire's Earthwood acoustic bass, courtesy of The Clive Ayer Collection, photo by Clive Ayer

One example of the difficulty in identifying bass sources, according to Miguel, is in the long bass solo of 'Ritual' before the drums come in, (equivalent to the beginning of 'Ritual' part 2 in *Yesshows*). Some low bass notes can be heard at the same time as the bass solo. Those could be played by any synth – it could be the Dewtron Mister Bassman pedals famously used by Anderson with his hands in concerts or another instrument – once again, there is no indication in the credits. In the video of the 1975 QPR Yes show, we can see that Chris definitely doesn't play the lowest bass notes on bass pedals, so those notes are being played by Patrick Moraz on one of his many synthesizers. However, at a different part of the 'Ritual' solo on 1980's *Yesshows*, Chris decided to use the bass pedals to produce a more conventional drone note. This can be heard at around 15 mins 15 secs. However this is completely different from the album version, as Joe Cass pointed out (see chapter 6), 'Ritual' live and in the studio are (almost) completely different arrangements.

Chris Squire tries out Alan White's drums at Morgan Studio 3 during the recording of *Tales* (or has he actually just finished eating?), photo credit: Laurens Van Houten / Frank White Photo Agency

PART 4 – THE MOVEMENTS

9

MY MOVEMENT REVIEWS

Legendary journalist and friend of the band Chris Welch's 1973 review (see chapter 19) of *Tales from Topographic Oceans* contains some harsh views. He called it:

" ... [a] fragmented masterwork ..."
" ... brilliant in patches ..."
" ... curiously lacking in warmth or personal expression ..."

I established the Yes Music Podcast in 2011. The first task I took on was to review every Yes studio album. I reached *Tales* on 28th October 2011 and what follows here is a recently fact-checked and slightly edited version of what I said back then. In those early days, I simply listened to the music and gave my honest reactions to it, rather than doing the kind of in-depth research I have done for this book. I include this review as a historical document from a time when the current Yes album was *Fly from Here*, Alan White and Chris Squire were still with us, Benoit David was the lead singer of the band and my knowledge was 14 years less developed than it is today.

Tales from Topographic Oceans – My review from 2011

This is probably Roger Dean's most well-known album cover, and probably prog rock's most well-known album cover as well. The artwork perfectly complements the concept of this album, with its South American looking temple in the distance and some fish which appear to be swimming through the air on the back cover.

The album itself is remarkable for the sheer audacity of producing a double album with a consistent concept over the four sides. It's interesting to compare it with TV programmes which are given the opportunity to develop into feature films. Can the successful formula from the TV programme be transferred into a longer format without losing the aspects which made the original so successful? With Yes albums, the songs have been moving to longer and longer forms, as we have seen ending up with *Close to the Edge* taking up a whole side on the album of the same name.

The subject matter of this album captures the early 1970s obsession with mystical eastern philosophy. Anderson's lengthy sleeve notes describe how the album concept came about. It's very biographical. The four sides are based on four parts of the Shastric scriptures, four interlocking pieces of music, says Anderson. We will see how this is translated into the music.

The personnel on this album obviously sees another huge change with the departure of original drummer, Bill Bruford, and the arrival of Alan White. A different drummer with a very different style, as we will see.

Side one of the album is 'The Revealing Science of God – Dance of the Dawn', and here's what Anderson says in the sleeve note description of this side.

> "First movement, Srutis. The Revealing Science of God can be seen as an ever-opening flower in which simple truths emerge examining the complexities and magic of the past and how we should not forget the song that has been left to us to hear. The knowledge of God is a search, constant and clear."

It's interesting to note that the move towards a classical music structure even includes referring to the parts of tales as movements, just like a symphony.

The opening of the piece is very unusual, with Anderson chanting with only a small variation in pitch. I think this is meant to evoke meditative practices of this kind of spirituality. Anderson gets through a lot of text in this opening, and is having to solve the same problem as others before him. In classical opera there's often the need to tell the story in lengthy passages of text. Rather than stop the music and have the actors speak the lines, composers developed a technique called recitative. This was very much like what Anderson is doing here – a quiet, simple accompaniment with lyrics principally on one or two notes with shifts in pitch towards the ends of phrases. There's also an interesting parallel in Church choral traditions, particularly of the Roman Catholic Church, and in a different way the Greek Orthodox Church, where a lot of the text of services are intoned by the priest. The technique used is quite similar to this passage on *Tales*, and there are set rules on how to end phrases, depending on the pattern of syllables.

Gradually more vocal parts come in, as well as instrumental parts, and the whole thing crescendos and moves towards another classic Yes moment when Squire and Wakeman introduce the startling and deeply moving theme, which seems like an incredible release of tension after the previous build up. Alan White's heavier style comes through here, giving a different, driving, solid backbone to the theme. Bruford would have done something rather different here, perhaps. It's a memorable hook, again like the ones on *Close to the Edge*, with Howe and Wakeman in between, trading elaborate, improvised-sounding passages. Between the beautiful vocal harmonies of 'talk to the sunlight caller' and then the verses come in, listen to the instrumentation. It's one of the most powerfully immersive passages of all Yes music for me. All the instruments are interweaving beautifully, underneath the strong, yet subtle vocal line.

The drum parts are undeniably simpler than those which Bruford might have contributed, but they are entirely consistent with the feel of the music, and there's no sense in which Alan White misinterprets that feel, it's just accomplished in his style rather than trying to copy Bruford's.

The texture and mood changes at 'starlight movement' and we have a reappearance of the short vocal phrases Anderson employs on previous records. This is a short section of more agitated-sounding music before the band moves seamlessly into a quiet passage of repeated melodic lines before the main theme reappears. It is calmer this time with Howe playing a bluesy solo above washes of keyboard.

Yet another section enters with 'they move fast' and another hook makes an appearance, 'getting over overhanging trees'. It's a combination of catchy tunes in loose verse-chorus structure. We're then back to the more disconcerting mood for a short time, followed by a Howe solo passage of initially heroic sounding guitar work, but this is followed soon after by one of the passages which I think *Tales* detractors probably point out as less successful. The guitar moves into a strange tonality for an extended section, with many changes in mood. I think this is where some lose interest in this first side. There are so many ideas surfacing without being fully developed that it doesn't seem to be a coherent passage in the same way as the rest. Don't get me wrong, I love the melody and feel when Anderson comes in with 'and through the rhythm of moving slowly'. It's a great passage for me and a great effect when the previous theme comes back as echoes. But again, there are a couple of passages which don't quite flow as they might. Chris Squire said in later years that he didn't think anyone should be asked to listen to the whole of *Tales*. There are fantastic moments, particularly with Wakeman racing around the keyboard in one of his most dramatic solo passages, but maybe it's all just too complex. Perhaps some more development of fewer ideas would have been more effective. As I said, don't misunderstand what I'm saying, I love the song, I'm just trying to be objective.

It has some of the most fantastic Yes moments of all time. When Anderson sings 'what happened to this song, we once knew so well' it's spine-tingling prog rock genius. Maybe it's even more effective after the preceding complexity. There is a semi-chanting section again making a really effective ending to side one out of four. It's remarkable to think this is only a quarter of the album. I'm emotionally drained already.

Side two is called 'The Remembering – High the Memory'. Here's what Anderson says about it in the sleeve notes:

> 2nd movement. Suritus. The Remembering. All our thoughts, impressions, knowledge, fears have been developed for millions of years. What we can relate to is our own past, our own life, our own history. Here it is especially Rick's keyboards which bring alive the ebb and flow and depth of our mind's eye. The topographic ocean. Hopefully we should appreciate that given points in time are not so significant as the nature of what is impressed on the mind, and how it is retained and used.

So this piece I think has many fewer ideas than side one. It's a fairly consistently medium-paced song for more than eight minutes. There are different sections but much more of a feeling of a simple structure. Repeating vocal lines create another mystical chant-like meditative feel, with passages of high-pitched melody making a good contrast. There is suspension of the pulse and quite a number of cymbal washes for example, but the main chant-like ideas and themes reappear several times. In the context of the whole album, it's a worthwhile section but maybe there are too few ideas this time, which have been stretched out too far.

Once again it's great music for Yes fans, but I wonder how new listeners feel about it. There's less to capture their attention. It needs more work to appreciate it, maybe. In the passages where a recognisable hook appears, it disappears just as quickly.

There's a lovely Wakeman theme around the 8 minutes mark, if you're still listening by then. The tempo picks up as Howe brings in acoustic guitar beneath Anderson singing 'Don the cap and close your eyes'. It's a passage that provides a great contrast to what precedes it – a jaunty little song with a great arrangement. 'Distant suns – will we reach' – here we have short phrases again in typical Anderson style.

A lovely Howe solo brings us to an up-tempo passage, with some great ensemble playing supporting a strong melody as Anderson sings about 'Relayer'. Of course, that's the name of the next Yes album, so it's interesting to see the word used here. A bit too soon for me, the slow mood returns, but only temporarily. I would ask if it's really necessary to split it up like this, it feels a bit like padding. Anyway, the recap of the 'Relayer' section is great, and leads to a recap of previous material now at breakneck speed with Squire's bass pushing the band on and on. There are echoes of the earlier 'America' cover bass line here. It's another great ensemble section with strong vocal line again, before yet another slower moving passage. Again, it feels a bit broken up despite some amazingly creative Wakeman keyboard effects, and inventive Howe moments.

Through those washes of sound, eventually there come new strong and triumphant song-like sections interspersed with instrumental sections, which build with Squire's ascending bass line to reveal one of the original themes recapped and fading out to finish.

As I said, I think this side rewards repeated listening. I'm sure it's quite difficult for someone listening to this for the first time to come to terms with the multitude of different sections and the complexity of the piece. Maybe the scale is just too grand for some. We're only halfway through the album and it takes a lot of dedication to get a real understanding of the whole work, which is possibly why this album is not as universally liked as *Fragile* or *Close to the Edge*. Perhaps it's a bit like a book by Tolstoy or an opera by Wagner – you need to take the time to understand, fully to appreciate the rewards it brings, and I think there are many rewards to be found in *Tales*. Maybe it doesn't fit in with the current mindset of music listeners of the streaming generation, where the short, single track is the currency, rather than the grand work of art which is the province of albums like *Tales from Topographic Oceans*.

Side 3, often viewed as the most difficult side of the whole album, is introduced by Jon Anderson on the sleeve notes like this:

"Third movement, Puranus. The ancient probes still further into the past beyond the point of remembering. Here, Steve's guitar is pivotal in sharpening reflection on the beauties and treasures of lost civilizations. Indian, Chinese, Central American, Atlantean, these and other peoples left in an immense treasure of knowledge."

The opening of side 3 features a vast array of different percussion instruments. There are very fast passages of ostinato patterns beneath Steve's improvised-sounding, mostly high-pitched soloing. The percussion includes pitched and unpitched instruments. Is that Rick Wakeman on the keyboard, or is there an actual glockenspiel part? (See chapter 5.) There's an ancient feel to the music as if it could have been written by some long-lost society. It also puts me in mind of the minimalist classical music movement which was in full flow during the time that this album was created. Composers such as Steve Reich and John Adams created music from short note fragments repeated again and again. These composers influenced prog rock musicians like Mike Oldfield. Incidentally, Jon Anderson included music by minimalist composer John Adams in his 1994 solo album *Change We Must*.

The percussion bed shifts quickly between right and left in the stereo, creating an even more complex rhythmical texture, while Steve's guitar has much longer lines. This is the kind of juxtaposition seen several times before in previous albums. The pulse breaks and several different sections appear. I think there's little sign of Wakeman on this side, and I think this is one aspect that diminishes its effectiveness. As we will see, there is really none of that Howe-Wakeman sparring that we talked about before that was so noticeable in the previous albums. I wonder if this has a lot to do with who the co-creators of *Tales* were – Jon and Steve. Chris Squire also plays a supporting role on this side, I think. His trademark playing is there, but it seems oddly muted in comparison with his normal flamboyant style.

I do think it's an effective opening to side 3, however, and when the lyrics come in around 4 minutes 17 seconds, it's a great effect. There's a pulse set up in the percussion, which this time sounds like an Indonesian Gamelan (see chapter 6). Again, this gives an appropriate air of mysticism and fits the theme of the side. The pattern is interspersed with a Wakeman theme, which reappears several times on this side, as well as a choppy-sounding passage before we have yet another example of short words uttered in semi-chant-like style by Anderson. Strange harmonies mix with great off-beat, syncopated passages and sweeping themes, but once again, the undoubted energy that it has feels a bit forced somehow, and the very frequent changes in tempo and style make it difficult to get a grip on what's happening. It's certainly not easily-accessible music, and maybe, like sides 1 and 2, it rewards repeated listening. Perhaps the fact that I know it really well enables me just to enjoy it for what it is. Also, I'm wondering if the fact that I am a classically-trained musician, used to large format works like symphonies also helps me.

It's certainly true that Side 3 features Steve Howe's solo guitar, but also gives Alan White a huge amount of freedom to experiment with different instruments, timbres and techniques. White sounds like he is revelling in the freedom, whereas Squire and Wakeman seem to be less convinced. Howe produces a huge amount of heroic soloing here, and I'm reminded of Frank Zappa's more's self-indulgent moments, for which he became notorious. Howe's style here isn't like Zappa's, I'm referring to the similar amount of confidence and audacity. Perhaps these extended solos are one of the reasons why some people don't rate this side of the album very highly. There are various points at which I feel that the band are just about to turn a corner and develop a more memorable theme or hook but instead the rhythm just shifts slightly and Howe starts off again with more of the same histrionics. To be clear, I can – and do – shut my eyes and really enjoy the sound washing over me, but I do appreciate this side of the album leaves some people cold and I'm trying to analyse why that might be.

If you listen to the music around 11 minutes 10 seconds, there's a section which is quite reminiscent of King Crimson in their *Larks' Tongues in Aspic* phase, featuring the former Yes drummer Bill Bruford. This can be heard in the choice of percussion tonality but here we have the music building towards a really odd section where Wakeman is pushing the boundaries of what sound effects can be produced. There are quite a few 'Doctor Who'-type moments.

At last, at about 12 mins 30 secs, the mood changes, with Anderson singing and Howe playing just acoustic guitar beneath. This leads to a Howe guitar solo, the equal of any Steve Howe acoustic solo for Yes – a lovely tune. Listen out for the moment when Steve knocks the body of the guitar. I always remember finding that really exciting even though I know it's quite a common technique in Spanish guitar playing. This grows into one of the most beautiful passages not only in the Yes canon, but, I would argue, in all rock music. 'Do the leaves of green stay greener through the autumn?' sings Anderson. I absolutely defy you to listen to this, with headphones on, and the hairs on the back of your neck not stand up. It's amazing how this affects me every time I hear it. Maybe this would be my Desert Island Yes selection, my champagne moment. I feel really sorry for those Yes fans who skip side 3 of the album because they miss this, and I feel sorry for everyone who's never heard this. So please spread the word if you can. If you read the words of this section, this is practically a protest song, it's about peace, the collective power of people, and, as Anderson says in the sleeve notes, "The treasure of knowledge left to us by peoples of the past." All this is achieved in a few, short lines. Howe takes up the solo acoustic guitar again, and then a short recap of previous themes with full band takes us to the end of the movement, where the sound spirals up and away into nothing.

Side 3 is actually a work of genius. The massively-extended, complex first part, with very disturbing tonality and structure is counterbalanced by the sublime melody and guitar sweetness towards the end. The question remains though, can you make it through the first 12 and a half minutes to reap the benefits?

Finally, we arrive at the last side, 'Ritual – Nous Sommes du Soleil'. Here's what Jon Anderson's sleeve notes say:

> "Fourth movement – Tantras. The ritual. Seven notes of freedom to learn and to know the ritual of life. Life is a fight between sources of evil and pure love. Alan and Chris present and relay the struggle out of which comes a positive source, Nous Sommes du Soleil. We are of the sun, we can see."

Chris Squire's bass starts the side with stabs of percussive accompaniment, then Steve Howe introduces a soaring theme. It's one of those uplifting segments common in Yes music of the early 1970s. This time it's Howe's guitar which starts at a low pitch in the instrument's range and then climbs, repeating the material shifted up until he reaches high notes towards the top of the guitar's register. It's this upward movement that creates the uplifting feeling, I think. There's a Wakeman keyboard section and then Howe repeats the theme again with louder and more insistent accompaniment. There are, once again, the usual Wakeman hallmarks here but the keyboards sound like they have been sunk into the background of the mix a bit.

Another Yes trademark arrives with a wordless chorus from Anderson with a catchy bright theme. Keyboards reinforce the tune and the music seems to be pushing on, with quieter breaks common to so much of the music on this and other albums. It's a great tapestry of sections, very effective, with a compelling sense of forward motion. A particular favourite of mine is around 3 minutes 30 seconds, with Chris Squire soloing in typically dramatic fashion. Then there is a quiet, mystical passage where Steve Howe introduces fragments of the 'Nous Sommes du Soleil' theme above some intriguing percussion parts. This segues into the actual rendition, or exposition, of the 'Nous Sommes du Soleil' theme. To Yes fans, this is one of the most important sequences of the album. It's beautifully-constructed and when Anderson talks about 'harmonic convergence' in later years, I think this is what he's talking about. Listen to the bass line weaving in and out, the perfectly judged drum part and the keyboards providing the glue to hold everything together beneath the transcendent melody.

Interestingly, there are only two lines of lyrics in the first section of 'Nous Sommes du Soleil', repeated again and again. I think it's meant to be chant-like. Howe's guitar sounds quite sitar-like here (see chapter 7), and this helps the exotic character of the passage and the album. The verses grow towards the triumphant recap of a theme on keyboards and guitar at about 8 minutes 30 seconds and then the verses take us on a journey of almost ecstatic joy, surrounded by the soundscape. It's a long passage, but the movement pushes on, and the interest is sustained, maybe more effectively than in some of the preceding movements. At about 11 minutes, Squire's opening material reappears to usher-in a fast, ensemble instrumental development section, led by Squire's bass guitar.

The music gradually gets wilder until it stops and a very odd percussion section appears around 14 minutes 25 seconds, featuring a remarkable drum solo from Alan White, involving some timpani. Wakeman joins in with his strangest synthesiser noises and effects yet and everything grows until it sounds like the band will explode. However, at about 16 minutes 58 seconds, Steve Howe appears with a solo and the percussive section just fades out under him. I have to admit that I would have liked this previous section to segue more naturally into the next, rather than fading to leave Howe playing on his own, but it's a minor point. This is a kind of variation on the theme of Nous Sommes du Soleil, with dreamlike vocals supported by what I have now discovered is

Alan White's piano accompaniment of the theme, foreshadowing the acoustic segments of live shows of over 30 years in the future, culminating in the *Yes Acoustic Live* project of 2004. It adds to the feeling of peace and tranquility. We're not finished yet, though, as Howe takes up the mantle again and adds a louder, much more insistent repeat of previous material as the band all move as one to a mini climax. This dies away to complete the side and the album.

What is there left to be said about *Tales from Topographic Oceans*? Well, sometimes I feel that there should be a compilation of the best bits from the four sides, rather like classical composers rearranging suites from ballets. An example of this is *The Firebird Suite* by Stravinsky, the ending of which has been used countless times as an introduction to Yes concerts. The music Stravinsky collates for this work is distilled down from a longer ballet score. However, for the reasons I've tried to explain, I think this would diminish the album. It stands as a colossus in the world of progressive rock. Excessive, perhaps, difficult to access, maybe, but definitely well worth the effort for anyone serious about the history of the band, the genre, or indeed music itself. So if you've been putting off playing Side 3 of Tales, or if the whole album is gathering dust on a shelf or in the loft, go and find it, pour a drop of your favourite liquid and give it a try. I don't think you'll be disappointed.

10

THE LYRICS

"The doctor overrates me in my room
And with the regularity of doom
A geezer with a double-necked guitar
Comes and tells me Tales From Topographic Oceans"

'This Leaden Pall' by British indie band Half Man Half Biscuit

"I've always said about Jon Anderson, that he always had that bigger lyrical idea that was more improvised, if you like, or more kind of colourful and not so clear about what it was really about, which was a great ingredient to have ... "

Steve Howe, Yes Music Podcast, 2025

The topic of Yes lyrics has always provoked strong reactions, especially among those who like to criticise progressive rock music. If you find Yes lyrics impenetrable and annoying, that is of course your prerogative, but in this chapter I hope to present some more positive perspectives on the words in *Tales* [18].

Nick Kokoshis is the originator of the Facebook group, *Tales From Topographic Oceans: studio and live performance discussion group* [19]. His responses to unsubstantiated opinions on *Tales* are always entertaining and well-informed. Here, he corrects a common misconception about the lyrics on *Tales* and indeed many other Yes albums in which Jon Anderson was involved:

"The lyrics of all four sides of *Topographic Oceans* are written by Anderson AND Howe. The arrangements were written largely by Howe but credited to the band as a whole. Sometimes ... I'll see people quote Yes lyrics and then attribute them to Anderson, when I know the lyrics

---

[18] All songs published by Topographic Music, Inc., ASCAP administered by WB Music Corp.
[19] https://tormatobook.com/facebooktopo

cited were written by Howe. I would say that Howe is just as obtuse of a lyricist as Anderson. He can still pull that style off-- listen to 'Unknown Place' from their 2023 album *Mirror to the Sky* – a very strong arrangement and lyric, all written by Howe. And that was written at age 75!"

Perhaps one of the most effective passages of lyrics on 'Tales' was, indeed, written by Howe. As Kokoshis puts it:

"Steve Howe wrote the main song on 'The Revealing Science of God', it came from his demo that goes '...what happened to this song we once knew so well.'"

Steve Howe told me:

" ... one of the benefits of Jon and I working together is that my lyrics and my songs were really quite straight ahead, you know, 'What happened to this song we once knew so well'. I mean, it's simplistic, but Jon would add the complexity – 'Dawn of light lying between the silence ... ', you know, so there was that kind of thing like we did on *Close to the Edge* when I had some of *Close to the Edge* written a few years earlier. [That music] was looking for a home, so that's how Jon and I kind of came across *Close to the Edge* and the same thing happened to *Tales* ... [Jon] had this kind of cosmic lyrical approach and I had a very, as I said, more of a straightforward story.

Interestingly, Steve likens Jon Anderson's ability to come up with lyrics to Trevor Horn's. Horn took that Anderson role on for 1980's *Drama* and when we spoke to Jon Davison, the current Yes lead singer, he mentioned being surprised when writing and recording music for 2014's *Heaven and Earth* that the other band members looked to him for lyrical inspiration as well. Howe told me that Jon Anderson used to be able to come up with additional verses to songs Steve had started:

"I would write a verse and a chorus and Jon would go, 'I really like the chorus. The verse, yeah, that starts it off good.' But then we needed three other verses. And that's where at the time (it's not the same now), but at the time that's where my limitations stepped in. I thought, 'I don't know, I haven't got any other verses' ... So I had a kind of intro and I had a chorus and then Jon would elaborate in the most wonderful way. And then as he wrote lyrics, then he'd incorporate little bits of a tune or a sequence or something he had into it. And that's where the extensions to the song came along."

Once again, I am indebted to Simon Barrow for the following insightful and detailed essay, this time concerning the lyrics on *Tales*.

10 - THE LYRICS

TALES: A LYRICAL LONG DISTANCE RUNAROUND

by
Simon Barrow

The lyrics on *Tales From Topographic Oceans*, located between the Herman Hesse-influenced *Close to the Edge* album and *Relayer* (the latter supposedly inspired by Tolstoy's *War and Peace*, specifically on the 'The Gates of Delirium'), is perhaps the most intense example of Yes stretching out towards the esoteric and the mystical. More than anything else in the band's catalogue, the album also illustrates the inextricable interdependence of musical and lyrical form in the way Yes managed to synergise its members' differing talents and temperaments at the height of their artistic powers.

People responding to Yes lyrics, predominantly those written or shaped by Jon Anderson, tend to fall in or between four categories. There are those who dismiss them as gibberish; those who regard them as personally inscrutable; those who develop elaborate schemes of interpretation and philosophy around them, and those who see them primarily as 'sound sculpture' or 'sound paintings' rather than meaning-conveyors.

What the first three responses have in common (the fourth operates a little differently) is that they move towards either forsaking meaning altogether, or alternatively towards what literary scholars call *eisegesis*. That is, over-interpreting particular words and metaphors by imposing upon them certain larger ideas or categories which reinforce the reader's particular wishes, expectations or imaginations. Arguably, neither approach (abandoning sense-making or wishful over-elaboration) pays sufficient practical attention to the intriguing ways in which the album's lyrics shape – and are in turn shaped by – the intense, shifting musical environment in which they are embedded.

Taking that as our clue is the pathway, I would suggest, to more organic 'ways of reading' (that is, ways of perceiving) what is going on lyrically in *Tales*. In other words, ones which explore the different connections which can be made between its sonic, poetic and visual elements. For some that may lead to making a truce with the type of imagistic language which resists obvious resolution and which will not yield to any straightforward "this is what it means". For others it will involve discovering avenues of engaged appreciation which enable them to weave personal meaning out of what might otherwise seem obtusely abstract – but without trying to fix that reading as one others have to follow.

Such a flexible, creative approach is explicitly encouraged by the lyrical material itself: "The strength of you seeing lies with you" in the search for what is variously termed an "alternate tune", an "alternate view" or "alternate ways". Indeed, that word "alternate" occurs seven times across the album. To quote part of a line from another Yes track ('Parallels', on *Going for the One*), *Tales* is appropriately seen as "an ever-opening flower".

As with those methods of dream interpretation employing Jungian or other typologies, it is helpful to start modestly, acknowledging that while we may be able to discern certain 'archetypes' from different sources within the allusive words and ideas that abound on *Tales*, there is no single, unambiguous or universally agreeable message to be derived from them. That does not make these lyrics meaningless. On the contrary, it opens the door to a superabundance of meaning. That is often how poetic and painterly language works. It indicates that meaning is to be found as much (if not more, on occasions) in the reader as in the writer. This is what is known as the "reader-response" theory of literary interpretation. It suggests that the way a text is appropriated is as much part of its richness as the intention behind its creation, which will often remain inaccessible and may vary over time.

Thinking about how abstract impressionism or surrealism works in art provides a helpful analogy here. In both forms the impulse of the artist is to alter, displace, recast, expand or challenge the viewpoint of the viewer; to move consciously away from a standard definition of 'the real', from offering precise guidance as to what or how we should see, or from fixing the artist's own mind on one particular idea.

Another reason why the intertwined elements of musical and lyrical imagination are the place to start when examining *Tales* is that Jon Anderson and Steve Howe worked on both elements together. Realising that, we will soon notice, for example, that there are many instances of the rhythm of spoken words influencing various irregularities of melody, tone, tempo and texture in the accompanying music. One of the most obvious examples is to be found on side three, 'The Ancient' – "So the flowering creativity of life wove its web face to face with the shallow. And their gods sought out and conquered. Ah kin." Here the shape of the words evidently directs the speech-like form, pace and rhythm of the music.

By contrast, there are other moments on the album where strong melodic or harmonic ideas seem to require a certain pattern, modulation or inflection in the choice and use of words. Consider these stanzas from side two, 'The Remembering' – "Relayer, we advance, we retrace our story" (four sets of three syllables) and "Stand on hills of long forgotten yesterdays. Pass amongst your memories told returning ways" (sung as two sequences of eleven stressed and unstressed syllables). At the same time, and contrary to the 'it's just nonsense' accusations, both these poetic stanzas address – albeit in elusive ways – the variable relationship between memory, time and place in the way we look at the world. They do indeed 'make sense', I would argue. But evocative and allusive (rather than literal or representational) sense. They are about generating feelings through emotional or mental responses rather than imparting fixed propositions to which we are all expected to conform in some way or other. What we have here are resources for the exercise of exploration and imagination, as is often the case with lyrics – words specifically designed to work with and serve music – which gravitate towards the poetic more than the prosaic.

Then there are the larger themes mapped out across the album, where words and sounds are also required to operate together to achieve particular effects. Famously, *Tales* draws its fourfold pattern from a footnote in Paramahansa Yogananda's *Autobiography of a Yogi*. This spiritual memoir of an unconventional American-Indian Hindu mystic, written in 1949, became something of a 'hit' in the West in the 1960s and early 1970s, well after his death in 1952. George Harrison, Elvis Presley and Ravi Shankar were among Yogananda's celebrity advocates. The discipline of Kriya Yoga (seeking unification with the infinite through focussed body energy, actions and rites) took off in the West largely because of his influence.

This is reflected especially in 'Ritual', which pulls together – both lyrically and musically – the respective quests for knowledge, memory and (en)light(enment) on sides one to three, taking them to a new level in the unifying realms of personal illumination ("Nous sommes du soleil") and "pure love" (Anderson's term). Here it is the contrast and balance between the alternating tenderness and sheer physicality of the music – especially the percussion-led struggle between sources of life-giving and death-dealing – that presses towards a denouement which is both adventurous ("We hear a sound, and alter our returning") and gently consoling ("We love when we play"). The closing of the whole album is also exquisitely beautiful, resolving the gloriously jarring dissonances and Eastern-inflected, chromatic harmonies of the mainly instrumental side three (and the warlike sequence on 'Ritual' itself, moments earlier) into something truly sublime.

Characteristically, Jon Anderson always seems far more concerned with the grand themes that play on his mind than with smaller details. In the opening liner notes he gets both Yogananda's name wrong and misconstrues two of the four elements of the Hindu *shastras* ("treatises" in Sanskrit), *shruti* ("that which is heard") and *Smriti* ("that which is remembered"). That said, the introduction to the album's themes sets out a fairly clear schema – albeit one which Anderson and Howe seem to have developed without much specific attention to the scriptural texts they reference, or indeed to the wider content of *Autobiography of a Yogi*.

Then there is the superimposition (a late choice, it seems) of the overall title for the album, paradoxically eliding the solidity of physical topography with the fluidity of an ocean. This is also reflected in the lyrical content and in the encasing imagery supplied by artist Roger Dean. In some instances, the symbolism has a socially constructed impact: "School gates remind us of our class" is surely derived from Anderson's distinctly non-privileged upbringing in the north of England – it speaks of socioeconomic class, as well as visually referencing the experience of going to school. In other cases, the metaphors float freely across a river of feeling and impression in a stream-of-consciousness way: "sunshower seasons", "whispers of clay", or "we relive in seagull's pages", and so on.

But what of the broader lyrical architecture of the album? The wider themes of *Tales* are first, on side one, the search for God in both the unfolding of life and the psyche (note the opening creation myth). Next, on side two, the mind's eye exploring the ebb and flow of both historical memory and the essential nature of human beings as remembering subjects. Third, on 'The Ancient', what C. J. Jung would call our 'collective unconscious', mining symbols and archetypes from diverse civilisations (Roman, Persian, Hindi, Norse, Armenian and Himyarite words are all used, along with references to the mythological Atlantis, a Jon Anderson favourite). And finally, on side four, the primal energy of ritual as a means of discovering sources of "pure love" and enlightenment in place of a hoard of destruction. Again, all of this is best treated as "an ever-opening flower" rather than as some sort of historical or mythological treatise.

A variety of references to the physical elements are also evidently present – in turn, air, water, fire and earth – offering another lens of interpretation. These could also be linked to the themes of creation, exodus, suffering and eventual return which occur in the Hebrew scriptures ("We must have waited all our lives for this moment"). Given his Catholic background, it is also not surprising that, for Anderson, "Young Christians see it / From the beginning". Equally, in Buddhism, the Four Great Elements (five if you include space and consciousness) represent fundamental aspects of existence which are used in meditation practices to understand the nature of the self and the world. They evoke qualities and characteristics of both the inner and outer world, and the correspondence between the two.

Tales is saturated with inner/outer world correspondences if you search for them. There are also a number of parallelisms that occur throughout, starting with the foundational ones in the opening fourteen lines of the album, sung in chant-like form. Here the sources (and goals) of life are mapped out as "dawn of light", "dawn of thought", "dawn of our power" and "dawn of love". It would not be inappropriate to think of each of these phrases as summarising the four sequential sides of the album as a whole. Another example would be the layers emphases throughout the lyrics of *Tales* that we humans are narrated and narrating beings: "ours the story", "retrace our story", "work out the story", "walk around the story", "acting out the story".

Then there is that curiously tender, standout moment on 'The Ancient' when the cascading instrumental otherness of the track subsides, and Howe's classically-shaped acoustic guitar interlude (it is much more than a 'solo') leads into a tender, melancholic and almost sentimental song that poses existential questions which could almost have come from William Blake: "Where does reason stop and killing just take over? / Does a lamb cry out before we shoot it dead?"

Of course many other 'meta readings' of *Tales* are possible. In *Yes, But What Does It Mean?* (Wyndstar, 1994) Thomas Mosbo offers one example of an approach to its lyrics and themes derived from their more religiously or philosophically inflected elements. Bill Martin, in *Music of Yes: Structure and Vision in Progressive Rock* (Open Court, 1996), leans more towards a social reading rooted in Romanticism. Each has merits, but arguably presses too far in the search for overall coherence. For what Anderson (and Howe) offer is assuredly multivocal rather than univocal. The imagery employed on each of the four sides of the album is so varied and accommodating, its eclecticism so irreducible, that any attempt at 'final determination' will always be rendered unviable.

Any work of art, Ezra Pound averred, always demonstrates some kind of tension between freedom and order, the transcendental and the earthed. That was no doubt part of Jon Anderson's procedure, implicitly at least. He is an auto-didact, after all. And, yes, sometimes he does seem to choose words primarily or complementarily for the effect of their sounds. Sound structure is a requisite of poetry, and since lyrics have to serve the music first and foremost, Tales draws heavily (and I would say imaginatively) on the realm of what Dylan Thomas called "the colour of saying".

T. S. Eliot observed that for verse to succeed, there always has to be some kind of musicality at work in it. Indeed, language itself probably developed out of abstract sounds, tones and vocal registers which are themselves the building blocks of music. The most obvious and extended example of Anderson using words for their sounds can be found on 'Siberian Khatru' (*Close to the Edge*), but *Tales* is another occasional source for that, where flowing or halting words enable the sounds to emerge as an almost instrumental voice: the "Starlight, movement" sequence on side one, say, or "Ours entrance we surely carry on" (where you have to wonder if what was being striven for was "in trance").

One final observation. While *Tales* is itself a lengthy musical journey, it often points towards the way in which stories or concepts spanning great expenses of time itself can be condensed into intense, momentary experiences through the medium of language. As such, our fragile human reality is not so much dwarfed by the vastness of the universe as it is somehow poetically reflected and encompassed within it. That feels to me to be a way of perceiving much of what goes on in Yes music/lyrics, and certainly on this album. You, of course, may hear and see it quite differently. That is its immense intrigue and joy:

Stand on hills of long forgotten yesterdays
Pass amongst your memories told returning ways
As certain as we walk today
We walk around the story
Out in the city running free
Days pass as seconds turn they key
The strength of the moment lies with you...

11

TALES LISTENING GUIDES

A few years ago, Yes fan and podcaster Charlie Nieland created a 'personal map' of *Tales* as a handy aid for listeners. He has kindly given permission for this to be reproduced here.

Yes's *Tales From Topographic Oceans* can seem like an unending series of ideas coming at you, but what I've found with many listens is that there's a tapestry of melodic themes that gives it shape; they come and go in different ways throughout all four sides. I'm always hearing more after years of listening; this is the first time I've tried to write them down.

These themes bring focus to what can sound like a lot of noodling and the dreaded 'padding' that *Tales* is accused of. But for me, they yield incredible enjoyment. Yes is brilliant at call and response and they are doing it at a very deep level on *Tales*. It's a musical conversation that continues throughout the 80 minutes.

This may help you enjoy the music or it may not. I've read the arguments, even from fans, that the melodies are dumb and it's not interesting that they are woven everywhere. But I think it's what makes this a work of art. You can tell that much of it is pushed by Howe and Anderson. Those simple melodies give wonderful contrast and familiarity as they are incorporated into thematic movements via Anderson's voice and Howe's deft guitar phrasing. It gives the whole thing an emotional pull that all the members dig into, Squire, White and Wakeman included.

Anyway, I've given the themes nicknames that may be confusing but this is, by definition, a work in progress. For example, in *Revealing*:

Triumph: 01:36
Flutter 01:58
Steps: 05:00

Imperial guitar melody 12:34
etc.

I know there are even more resemblances and similarities than these. We'll keep listening...

Tales Musical Themes

'Revealing Science Of God – Dance Of The Dawn' (side 1)

Opening Chant – hypnotic mantra reprised at the end of the song

Volume pedal guitar notes underneath hint at coming main Triumph theme, which arrives, synth-fuelled, along with the full band at the climax of the **Chant**

Main guitar **Flutter** theme established, woven with **Moog ornamentation**, the jumping intervals of which are recalled later at the end of 'Ritual' (side 4)

Bass and drum punctuation theme established, followed immediately by the bass line from **They Move Fast** at the introduction of

Talk to the Sunlight Caller vocal melody, itself a preview of the **Out in the City** theme later introduced in 'The Remembering' (side 2) and developed into the **Nous Sommes** guitar theme from 'Ritual', followed by

1st introduction of **Steps** melody on guitar (stepwise major scale; short-short-long-long-long, etc.) leading into

What Happened To This Song — 1st verse/chorus song section – anthemic

The first descending notes of the chorus melody, 'What happened ... ', So-Fa-Mi, long-short-long, is a foundation that is further developed in the **Imperial guitar theme**, later in 'Revealing', and even more in the **High the Memory** and **Relayer** vocal melodies in 'The Remembering' (side 2).

Steps melody developed more thoroughly on guitar in the break after each chorus

Starlight section – dark, tribal, electronic transitional passage with intense guitar – the last break briefly alludes to upward melody in **'Ritual' guitar theme** (side 4), followed by **Steps** melody featured on gentle volume pedal guitar, followed by a quiet refrain of the **Triumph** theme and then **Steps** on big Mellotron chords leading to

They Move Fast – verse/chorus song – uplift tinged with melancholy – much of this section is in ¾

The second occurrence of the **They Move Fast** vocal melody is underpinned by the **'Ritual' guitar theme** (side 4) playing counterpoint underneath

Skyline Teacher passage (recap of **Starlight**) – piano lick quotes **'Heart Of The Sunrise'** (from Fragile)

Instrumental break – this energetic guitar-led section has its own themes based around a three-against-four rhythmic phrase heard in **Starlight** and **Skyline**, with modulating step-wise melodies building to a solo that climaxes with the **Imperial guitar theme**, a recurring, descending/ascending motif – (So-Fa-Mi-Re, long-short-short-long; this theme resembles the descending **High The Memory** vocal melody) It is answered with a briskly strummed **Steps** theme recalled as the section concludes — then **Steps** melody walks gently up to

All Fighters Past – verse/chorus song – quiet, contemplative – **Minor key sitar melody** intro (with **Major Moog melody** played on Mellotron underneath) then the **Major Moog melody** is established, leading into each verse

Steps melody on guitar answers lines in 2nd verse 'Young Christians see it'

Gentle **Triumph** theme on volume pedal guitar quote under final **'All Fighters Past'** vocal phrase leads to

Steps melody big time Mellotron break

Then modulated, more **Steps** building with vocals – answered with **Pentatonic Synth melody** from 'The Ancient' (side 3) and a fragment of **Flutter** guitar melody then

Big Keyboard solo starts with **Major Moog melody** from 'All Fighters Past' and ends with rhythmic themes from **Imperial guitar theme** break

Walk back through sections, building up: **They Move Fast** recap – with **'Ritual 'guitar theme**, then **Flutter** melody – climaxing with **What Happened** chorus vocal return – winding down with **Chant** return from intro (alongside **Steps** theme on volume pedal guitar)

'The Remembering – High The Memory' (side 2)

Intro – pipe organ arpeggios reminiscent of future song **'Awaken'** (from 1977 album *Going For the One*)

Silence Of Seasons song – pastoral – guitar and vocal theme are a derivation of **Steps** melody

High The Memory vocal melody – kind of a one-time-only chorus – joyful – a derivation of **Imperial guitar theme**, and **What Happened** vocal melody

These two sections, in a slow 7/8, are subtly recalled, much faster in the **Relayer** theme later in 'The Remembering'

Keyboard break – brief preview of **Out In The City** melody

Ours The Story elegiac song section — the descending melody is later incorporated as a bassline in the **Don the Cap** section followed by

Alternate Tune theme

– containing a return of side 1's **They Move Fast**, and its 3/4 feel; they cycle twice, gradually building to

Out In The City vocal theme – then answered by the **Stand On Hills** vocal theme

– act as a new triumphant song section

'Ritual' guitar theme (side 4) directly quoted, but gently baroque with guitar and pipe organ, in the transition to first dreamy keyboard cloud section

Silence Of Seasons and **Out In The City** vocal recap then

sweeping ethereal modulating ambient transition leading to

Remembering Keys dreamy theme, which alludes to **High The Memory** and the **Imperial guitar theme**. Hard cuts to

Don the Cap song — jangling Celtic reel – transitions out with **Imperial guitar melody**, leading to

Relayer song – This is a powerful re-interpolation of the **Silence Of Seasons** (listen for the 7/8) in a circular crunchy guitar riff that recalls the first phrase of the **Remembering Keys** theme, set against a driving rhythm section. The vocal melody for the **Relayer** hook is Mi-Fa-So and back down Fa-Mi-Re, creating the same melodic color as **High The Memory**. It goes around twice with **Don The Cap** (both sections getting respectively softer then louder) before the powerful keys/guitar solo that recaps the actual **Silence Of Seasons** melody over fantastic bass and drums.

Then climaxing with the **Relayer** vocal melody returning on keys as it crashes back into **Stand On Hills Extended Keyboard break** – ambient swirling modulations, layered with guitar and bass

After the extended keyboard sequence, the final big return of **Ours The Story** ('Ours entrance we surely carry on') into

Big time revisit of **They Move Fast** as **They Move Time/Rainbows/Alternate Tune**, with a brief recall of **Bass and Drum punctuation** and **Flutter** guitar themes from 'Revealing' (side 1) before final vocal climax with Rainbows/Alternate Tune and one more flash of Flutter guitar to start the final solo

Remembering Keys theme end

'The Ancient – Giants Under The Sun' (side 3)

Intro – Marching Cymbals play **Big punchy stops** rhythm

1st slide guitar – establishes **Ancient Triplet theme**

Electric Guitar break foreshadows **Angular** theme

Ancient Triplet theme 2 leads to first instance of

Big punchy stops

under expansive Mellotron chords

As One With The Knowledge vocal melody arrives over chords, echoing **Flutter** theme (side 1)

Pentatonic Synth theme established – Sweeping motif over processional march with bass and drum punctuation

Big punchy stops – guitar throws in descending lick from the **Flutter** theme and lick from **'Siberian Khatru'** (from *Close to the Edge*)

Pentatonic theme continues

Big punchy stops – guitar throws in **Angular theme**

Sun Theme section – urgent 6/4 time with guitar/Mellotron recalling 'I just can't believe they really mean to' vocal melody from **They Move Fast** (side 1), alternates with **Sun chant** vocal theme and **Ancient Pentatonic Synth/tron** theme

Angular theme, full band, appears briefly and only once

Sun Theme continues, ending with single punchy stop into transition featuring high repeated bass note, gong/bell and tense Mellotron strings

Out In The City and **Steps** melody quoted by guitar in the transition

Electric guitar solo – expansive 3 part cycle, getting weirder and more intense – featuring slide then conventional electric

The **'Ritual' guitar theme** (side 4) can be heard in the ascending phrases of the first part of the guitar solo; **Flowering Creativity** theme is gradually hinted at, and then fully stated at the climax of the solo, which finally comes to rest with punchy stops.

Flowering Creativity vocal theme introduced with acoustic guitar after the ending of the solo, sounding very medieval

Classical Guitar theme established – the opening melody has similar upward stepwise motion to the first phrase of **Ancient Triplet theme** and features a quick quote from *Close To The Edge* (Thanks to Joey Wise for pointing this one out in the Yes Facebook discussion group)

'Leaves Of Green' song theme arrives – acoustic melancholy hymn

Classical Guitar theme recapitulated

Slide guitar transition—joyful recap of **Triplet theme 2**

Big stops return for end, final upward guitar hints at upcoming **'Ritual' guitar theme**

'Ritual – Nous Sommes Du Soleil' (side 4)

Bass Intro based on **'Ritual' vocal chant** theme

Ritual guitar theme introduced (arpeggiated melody related to *Steps* theme)

Punctuation theme on bass and drums and **Steps** theme on keys from 'Revealing' (side 1) underneath

Answered with **Out in The City** theme on keys

'Ritual' vocal chant theme established — joyful wordless vocal melody –

Drum pattern reminiscent of the **Relayer** theme from 'The Remembering' (side 2) – now in a compound meter, 5/4, 5/4, 6/4, 7/4.

Finished off with brief fiery bass break.

Spacey transitional section – sequence of LOTS of themes on guitar – **Steps, Minor Old Fighter's Past, Close To The Edge, Pentatonic Ancient, 'Ritual' guitar theme, Flutter, Triumph, Imperial, Out In The City** themes morphing into

Nous Sommes guitar theme introduced, derived from **Out in the City** theme

Nous Sommes Du Soleil vocal theme established, building to

Life Seems like a Fight

verse/chorus song section – wistful sitar-drenched Beatlesque pop song

Triumph theme as a bridge before 2nd verse 'maybe we'll just stand a while'

Soul Constant/At All coda crescendo leads to

Bass theme return, then propulsive bass solo based on **Ritual vocal chant** – breaks it up with a quote of **Ancient Triplet** theme

Guitar enters with **Silence Of Seasons** melody and its own intense solo over tension-building chord changes leading to a hard stop climax. Hard cuts to

Drum War — two-part section, cycles twice, featuring constant 8th note metallic strikes with Indonesian gong punctuations. First section features a drum kit solo; second section is a driving tribal groove for tympani and kit. There's a purely rhythmic restatement of the **Flutter** theme in the first phrases of the drum-triggered synth in the second half of this section (Thanks to **Peter Smorodin** for pointing this one out in the Yes Facebook discussion group)

The big rhythm motif at the finish is derived from the **Ancient Triplet** theme

Gentle guitar solo transition out — descending **Flutter** theme, rising **Ritual guitar theme** (maybe a little **Ancient**?), arriving at **Nous Sommes guitar theme**

Nous Sommes vocal theme returns, now a gentle verse/chorus song with some extra development

Piano motif that answers 'and course our way back home' in the final **Nous Somme Du Soleil** vocal refrain recalls the **Pentatonic Synth theme** from 'The Ancient' (side 3)

High piano notes also recall the **Moog ornamentation** from the beginning of 'Revealing' (side 1)

Finale – guitar climax revisiting **'Ritual' guitar theme, Flutter** theme, **Steps** theme over angular modulations that recall the chord changes under the solo before the **Drum war**

Minor key ending with a final little volume pedal guitar hint of **Steps** melody

Footnote: What Happened To This Song, Imperial guitar theme, High The Memory, Remembering Keys theme, Nous Sommes Du Soleil vocal theme are all related via a phrase in common: downward stepwise melody, So-Fa-Mi-Re, with a long, shot, short, (long) note duration

Time Index:

Initial occurrences of themes

'The Revealing' (Original version – without newer extended intro):
Opening Chant: 00:00
Triumph: 01:36
Bass And drum punctuation theme: 01:55
Flutter: 01:58
Talk To The Sunlight Caller: 03:04
What Happened To This Song section: 03:35
Steps: 05:00
Starlight: 06:52
They Move Fast Song section: 09:45
Skyline Teacher: 11:07
Imperial guitar melody: 12:34
All Fighters Past Song section – minor key sitar melody: 13:04
Major Moog melody: 13:48
Moog solo: 16:40
They Move Fast recap: 17:39
Flutter return: 18:58
What Happened return: 19:05
Final Chant: 19:44

'The Remembering':
Intro Pipe Organ: 00:00

Silence Of Seasons Song; guitar and vocal theme: 00:14
High The Memory vocal melody: 01:34
Ours The Story vocal theme: 02:36
Alternate Tune theme ("they move fast"): 03:04
Stand On Hills vocal theme (I reach over...): 05:41
Out In The City Vocal theme: 06:09
Remembering Keys theme: 08:11
Don the Cap: 09:14
Relayer Theme: 10:42
Extended Ambient Keyboard: 15:48
Ours the Story/Alternate Tune Return: 17:40
Final Keys Theme: 19:53

'The Ancient':
Intro Cymbals: 00:00
Ancient Triplet theme: 00:47
Ancient Triplet theme 2: 03:00
Big punchy stops: 03:41
As One With the Knowledge: 04:17
Pentatonic Synth theme: 04:41
Sun Theme: 06:08
Angular theme: 07:04
Guitar Solo: 09:01
Flowering Creativity theme: 12:31
Classical Guitar theme: 12:53
Leaves Of Green song: 14:42
Classical Guitar theme recap: 17:04
Triplet Theme 2 Recap: 17:45

'Ritual':
Bass Intro: 00:00
'Ritual' guitar theme: 00:19
Ritual vocal chant Theme: 01:46
Spacey many themes guitar transition: 04:03
Nous Sommes guitar theme: 05:26
Nous Sommes vocal theme: 05:30
Life Seems like a Fight song: 06:50
Soul Constant/At All Coda: 09:45
Bass Solo: 11:11
Guitar Solo: 13:35
Drum War: 14:21
Nous Sommes return song section: 17:40
Finale: 19:57

In the following 4 chapters, each movement of *Tales* has been analysed by several contributors. Each entry is labelled as follows:

KM – The author
GB – Gottlieb Brothers (from their *Classic Tales of Yes Tour Book*)
JM – Joost Maglev
PC – Peter Corda
DW – David Watkinson
JL – Jérôme Laffon
SE – Steven English
KJ – Ken Jonach
RN – Robert Nasir
AN – Andy Nicholes
JF – James Fitzmaurice
GDR – Guy DeRome
RVR – Richard van Roomen
CD – Chris Dale
NK – Nick Kokoshis
RK – Robert Keeley
CB – Chris Berry

There are passages in *Tales from Topographic Oceans* that contain exquisite music. This is largely due to Rick Wakeman's keyboards, despite his later disapproval of the album (describing it as bloated and too long). In Parts 1 and 2, he uses analogue synthesisers to create a wash of sound that evokes the deep expanse of seas and oceans. In doing so he cements the ethereal voice of Jon Anderson and the pivotal guitars and percussion into a truly orchestral blend, which at times is haunting and spine-tingling. It's true that the whole is probably less than the sum of its parts, but they're well worth waiting for. Listen out for them. JF

N.B.
- '–' denotes that the reference has the same timestamp as the previous entry
- All the timings are taken from the 2003 remastered version of the album except 'The Revealing Science of God' – in this chapter (12), the first entry is labelled -1:58 – 0:00 to show it precedes the beginning of the first versions of the record available in 1973

YouTube versions used:
Side 1 – https://youtu.be/4eMe5SRs_iA?si=DtbD0MvAQC5C7V09
Side 2 – https://youtu.be/6ILzyVz72yo?si=DxCZsQwUWUIuigen
Side 3 – https://youtu.be/HDbfT3YI_L4?si=bmXHlhM8tJvrj08Q
Side 4 – https://youtu.be/I4EPABbDdCQ?si=ox7MtXkzQYlnB07K

12
MOVEMENT GUIDE 1 – THE REVEALING SCIENCE OF GOD – DANCE OF THE DAWN

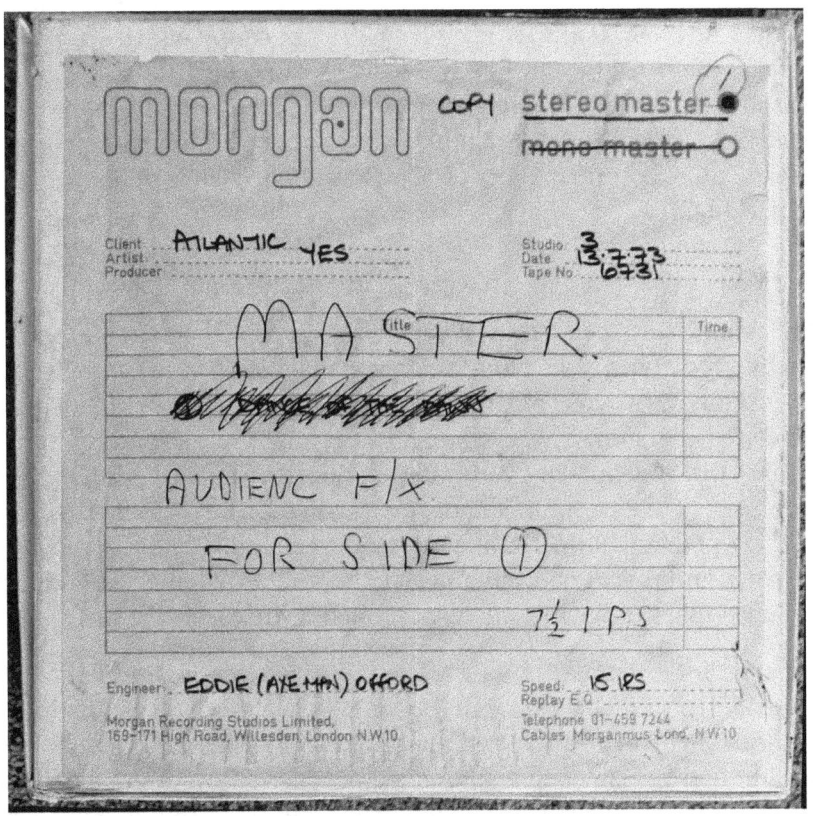

Review copy of 'The Revealing Science of God', courtesy of The Clive Ayer Collection, photo by Clive Ayer

> " ... side one was originally twenty eight minutes long. We had to lose something like eight minutes or so to fit on the LP. That sounds ridiculous. Maybe we did waffle on a bit, so we took out the waffle from *Tales* as much as we could."
>
> Steve Howe, quoted in the Gottlieb Bros.' tour book for
The Classic Tales of Yes Tour, 2023

When the *Fragile Definitive Edition* was released in 2015, one of the extras included was Steven Wilson's remix of a song called 'All Fighters Past' [20]. This was also included in 2024's *Fragile Outtakes* vinyl collection. As a fan of *Tales*, I'm sure you recognise the name of this song being mentioned in the lyrics of 'The Revealing Science of God'. Incidentally, the words appear on the inner sleeve of *Tales* as 'Move over glory to sons of old fighters past'. While this version makes sense (as much as any lyrics on *Tales* make sense), I think it's a mistake and it seems Steven Wilson agrees, hence his naming of the song, 'All Fighters Past'.

All artists recycle older ideas into new creations, of course (for example the 'Würm' section in 'Starship Trooper' from *The Yes Album* which Steve Howe recycled from the song 'Nether Street', by his earlier band, Bodast), but here we seem to have an almost complete song with Bill Bruford on drums, recorded at the same sessions as 1972's 'Fragile'. It was described online as 'incorporating ideas that would later form parts of 'The Revealing Science of God' and 'Siberian Khatru' on *Close to the Edge*.

I asked Steve Howe if he remembered recording 'All Fighters Past'. He said:

> "Well, not clearly ... You know, I've had things come back to me from Asia that I'm going, 'you mean we played that?' And so ... we revisited it and included it, as you said, into Tales ... if you have a musical idea and it doesn't work somewhere, who knows, it might work somewhere else better ... Other people are very radical with their music and they're going to say, OK, well, I said, I'm not re-visiting that, but it's whether it can be developed and quite often music's got a pliability where it can be one place and then it can actually be in another, particularly if it doesn't actually appear in the first instance, which is the case with that."

In the sleeve notes to the CD/Blu-ray Panegyric release, Sid Smith (see chapter 1) quotes Steven Wilson explaining how he came across the previously-unknown song. It had been worked on and recorded by the band at Advision Studios but had clearly been abandoned because Wilson found it on a *Fragile* master tape. It was revealed at the end of another track that had been recorded over the top of it, presumably to re-use the 'junk' tape. This is why the 'All

---

20 https://tormatobook.com/AllFighters

Fighters Past' recording starts in the middle of the song with the lyrics ' … rhythm work out the story … ". The lyrics in the corresponding passage of 'The Revealing Science of God' are:

> " … *And through the* rhythm of moving slowly,
> Sent through the rhythm work out the story,
> Move over glory to sons of all fighters past … "

It's only because the material recorded over the top of 'All Fighters Past' was shorter than the original recording that we have any of the previous song left to find. This serendipity allows us to glimpse part of the creation process of this part of Tales. It shows that re-purposing old material can result in very different musical outcomes. 'All Fighters Past' is an up-tempo romp, with a little bit of a 'Roundabout' feel. We are left with 2 mins 33 secs of the energetic song that benefits from both Bruford's charismatic drumming and Wakeman's fabulous Hammond organ playing – and soloing. When combined into 'The Revealing Science of God', the music is slowed to almost half the speed and there are no Wakeman Hammond fireworks. However, I am fond of both versions. The Steven Wilson remix of 'All Fighters Past' is a tantalising and expertly-mixed song that I think could have been a good addition to Fragile and the passage in 'The Revealing Science of God' works beautifully and seamlessly inside the rest of the movement.

Incidentally, if you are wondering what the 'Siberian Khatru' element is, Rick Wakeman plays one of the themes from that song in the accompaniment to 'All Fighters Past'. That also works surprisingly well.

1	2	3	4	5	6	7	8
Kick	Snare	Hi tom	Lo tom	OH	OH	Bass	Ocean FX, Mellotron & Moog Speaker, El Piano Dly, Bass, Group Vox
9	**10**	**11**	**12**	**13**	**14**	**15**	**16**
Ocean FX, El Piano, Ac Piano, Mellotron (Strings, Flute and Choir), B3	Mellotron (Strings, Flute & Choir), El Piano, Ac Piano	Moog, El Piano, Ac Piano,	Moog Toms, El Guitar, Room Organ, Group Vox	Perc, Piano, Hi Hat, Timp, Cymbals, Toms, Kit, Gong	Perc, El Gtr, Hi Hat, Toms, Timp, Cymbals, Kit, Gong	El Gtr, Sitar	El Gtr, Sitar
17	**18**	**19**	**20**	**21**	**22**	**23**	**24**
Sound FX, Drum FX, El Gtr, Sitar	Bass, Drum FX, El Gtr, Sitar	Jon Vox, Steve Vox, Moog, Piano, Mello Strings, El Gtr, Rev Cymbal	Ac Gtr, Steve Vox, Piano, El Gtr, Mello Strings, Jon Vox	Chris Vox, Jon Vox, Sitar, Piano, Mello Strings	Jon Vox, Chris Vox, Piano, Mello Strings	Jon Vox, B3	Jon Vox, B3

Track listing from the analogue to digital transfer, author's version (see chapter 17)

Tales from Topographic Oceans - Yes album Listening Guide

Timestamp Type Contributed by	Description
–1:58 – 0:00 Intro KM	The restored introduction that does not appear on the original version. It was reinstated in the 2003 remastered CD edition. It consists of what sound like waves, thunder or some other kind of soft percussion. I assume this is what is meant by 'Ocean FX' on the track list above. Howe's guitar plays individual notes and is joined by Rick Wakeman's synth. I like this quiet introduction which sets the scene for what follows.
0:00 Guitar JL	Steve Howe plays a slowed down version of the theme appearing from 1:36 to 1:42.
0:00 – 2:00 Vocals DW & KM	Slightly abrupt in the original version. The chanting vocal by Jon Anderson – a little reminiscent of the classical techniques of 'recitative' and Church intoning. Anderson's vocals are doubled initially.
– Vocals RVR	The chant that opens the album immediately signals that we are about to embark on a remarkable journey. No other rock album travels through such an ancient and mystical soundscape: this can truly only be *Tales*. For me, the decision to (re-)instate the keyboard intro in the 2003 remaster was a mistake: for me it reduces the opening to a sort of prog-by-numbers. It could be the start of any of a dozen or more pieces by Yes, or Pink Floyd, or a number of other bands. The original opening chant is pure pagan magic.
0:35 Vocals KM	Backing singing perhaps by Alan White?
1:04 Keyboards KM	Dramatic, wailing, high-pitched synth sounds help to ramp up the tension, descending in a fabulous sequence.
1:36 Bass SE/KM	The sustained bass/bass pedal is a startling and wonderful addition.
1:42 Keyboards KM	A towering theme on synth blasts out in the first of many spine-tingling moments, combining with rasping bass playing an answering phrase.
3:38 Drums KM	Drums immediately provide atmosphere behind the chanting – then very audible with accompaniment to the big theme.

2:03 Guitars KM	In Steve Howe's first solo spot, he plays with the timing of his runs – they phase across the rest of the band's rhythm.	
2:16 Keyboards KM	The keyboards take over from the guitar line and play 2 counter-melodic lines of strong structure culminating in a reiteration of the main theme.	
2:41 Guitars KM	The guitar part is low now, providing a contrast to the main synth line.	
3:09 Theme HBP	"Talk to the sunlight caller" is a variation of "out in the city" in 'The Remembering' at 06:08 PLUS repeated in 'Ritual' at 00:48	
– Vocals KM	Some of the most beautiful Yes choir harmonies.	
3:11 Backing Vocals KM	Is Alan providing some of the backing harmony low vocals again or is this Chris?	
– Bass KM	Dramatic, fast line with bass pedal(?) underneath – In perfect, laid back unison with drums against the big theme.	
– Keyboards KM	Around this point – and for several minutes – the keyboards are in accompanying mode, providing some interesting rhythm to contrast with the bass, drums and guitars. Part of the rhythmic effect is produced by an echo or delay effect.	
3:39	Anderson's vocals here provide a link back to the earliest days of the band. A beautiful tune, sung brilliantly – soft, subtle and tender.	
3:43 Theme HBP	Very similar to the end of Ritual from around 20:02	
4:00 Drums KM	Clearly not Bruford's approach but fits the character of the music perfectly – accents in all the right places to fit with the bassline where the pattern repeats	
4:29 Vocals KM	A classic sing-along vocal melody – catchy and sublime.	
4:30 Guitars KM	Answering phrases from the guitar (with a second part) 'in conversation' with the main vocals.	

4:33 Guitars KM	The upwards runs have 2 guitar parts playing in harmony – I wonder how this was replicated live, if at all.
5:00 Bass KM	Quite low in comparison with a lot of his lines – does start to climb 5mins – and stays there playing elaborate counter-melodic line.
5:04 Drums KM	Great feel - perfectly in time but gives a loose, free feel – then ramps up the mood for 'What happened to this song we once knew so well' – a proper part of the instrumentation – not 'playing along' at all.
5:07 Bass KM	Crashes back in after "moment, moment" – a wonderful 'moment'.
6:00 Bass KM	Around here and elsewhere this seems like a classic Rickenbacker sound.
- Bass KM	Continues to play counter melodic bass line – "What happened to".
- Drums KM	Fills creative round the kit – not straight, '4 on the floor' at all.
- Vocals KM	' ... What happened to this song, we once knew so well? ... ' – spine-tingling prog rock genius.
7:00 Keyboards KM	Strange sound that I think is keyboards creates an undulating line beneath the other parts. It shifts in tone so I think it's Rick playing with the Moog filters Remarkable effect!
7:11 Guitars KM	Under 'Starlight, movement', Howe uses a much more distorted guitar sound to fit the ramped-up mood. Quite an aggressive sound.
- Drums KM	Change of feel 'Starlight movement' – shifts to lots of toms and creative pattern changes between toms part and hi hat.
7:58 Guitars KM	The guitar still has a touch of the distortion but the effect is calmer due to the line being played and the use of the volume pedal – a true Howe hallmark.
8:15 Keyboards KM	Piano adds a different timbre to the guitar line. Rick uses a classical approach to the chords at the end of the pattern and also ascends to higher octaves and doubles the part.
8:30 Drums KM	White brings the motion back in.

8:45 Keys SS	RMI Electric Piano "sounds more like an organ vamp than a piano".	
8:58 Keyboards KM	The reiteration of the first theme is much softer but still provides a familiar link.	
9:12 Keyboards KM	Mellotron takes over providing a beautiful basis for improvised-sounding Howe electric guitar, bass and drums.	
9:08 Guitars KM	Howe moves to a much softer, bluesy, improvised-sounding solo style for a long passage.	
9:50 Drums KM	Another change to feel under Howe calm guitar and piano.	
– Keyboards KM	Under 'They move fast', Wakeman adds superbly-chosen Mellotron solo strings sounds. Perhaps a cello? Then swaps this a few times with a lovely high Moog solo sound through the section.	
– Guitars KM	Howe uses harmonics here in the accompaniment – to great effect.	
10:00 Bass KM	Lovely, front of mix, wide-spanning pitched lines against a sparse texture. Shares main theme answering phrase.	
10:28 Guitars KM	The mood of the music is intensifying so Howe moves to some chords and an increased use of delay.	
– Drums KM	Getting over overhanging trees ramps up the mood again via louder and more intense playing – variation and touch remarkable in his playing in this one piece.	
10:57 Drums KM	The main theme returns – synth and bass – with gentle percussion this time. It provides a contrast to the previous, strident version. The drum pattern is interesting again using toms as well as hi hat.	
11:20 Guitars KM	More up-tempo, choral strumming at the change of mood. This sounds like the Coral Sitar Guitar.	
11:24 Vocals KM	The arrangement of the vocals across the stereo image is wonderful here.	

11:25 Keyboards KM	Piano takes over, providing momentum and a great contrast, complete with fleet-fingered, virtuosic runs, at times almost turning into the King Crimson 'Cat Food' approach.	
12:03 Guitars KM	Dramatic solo electric playing. It sounds like it is doubled with 2 different guitars or 2 different tones.	
12:29 Guitars KM	Steve Howe embarks on a surprisingly atonal guitar solo, bending notes and striding ahead in epic style. The strumming approach returns as well, a little later.	
13:14 Guitars KM	By way of sudden contrast, Howe lightens the mood, still using the electric guitar but playing a slightly haunting new melody, repeated with the addition of the Coral Sitar guitar after a time.	
13:48 Keyboards KM	After a softer, undulating Howe line, the Mellotron plays a beautiful, counter-melodic, haunting flute solo, intertwining with Howe.	
14:03 Vocals KM	This segment is fascinating to listen to in comparison to the original version of 'All Fighters Past'. This is tender and delightful singing from Anderson.	
14:04 Keyboards KM	Wakeman displays his total mastery of the Minimoog by inserting a lovely, tender, high-pitched solo – he makes it sound easy but listen to the way he shapes the sound – that's difficult. A completely different type of Moog solo to the normal, fast, flying-fingered approach. This is repeated later more than once.	
14:14 Keyboards KM	Back to a beautiful Mellotron flute choir, beneath "And through the rhythm ... "	
- Drums KM	Unusual pattern in unison with bass – "all fighters past". "Young Christians see it" – develops into a groove from the more separated pattern previously – for a while.	
14:56 Guitars KM	Guitars are absent from the 'All Fighters Past' section until this point where Howe adds a volume pedal-shaped line, with counter-melodic beauty.	
14:40 Bass KM	Is the sound here doubled with bass pedals?	
- Origin SSm	'Young Christians' section of The Revealing Science of God dated as far back as the Fragile sessions (re-discovered and issued as All Fighters Past on 2015's edition of Fragile)	

14:56 Keyboards KM	Lovely Mellotron flutes again.	
15:34 Keyboards KM	Mellotron strings backing repeats a theme several times as an accompaniment. This is then taken over in an altered fashion by Hammond organ. The texture in this passage is remarkable – Mellotron choir is added to the Yes choir as well as more Hammond and then Minimoog solo over the top.	
16:31 Guitars KM	Solo Howe again to the forefront.	
17:14 Keyboards KM	After a build up, this is where Wakeman 'cuts loose' with what is arguably the greatest Minimoog solo of all time. Astonishing and over far too quickly for me. It sounds like it's doubled across the stereo.	
– Keyboards DW & SSu	The Mellotron work aside, that Moog solo on side one has to be right up there as the perfect example of everything coming together at once to create greatness. – Though that solo, as heard on the original mix, is an edit. An example of Eddy Offord's genius.	
– Drums KM	Supports Wakeman epic Moog solo with classic rock drumming – lots of fills 3/4 or 6/8 more likely.	
18:34 Drums KM	Ride cymbal	
– Drums KM	Drums help to ramp up again to "We've moved fast".	
18:01 Theme HBP	"We've moved fast" – Guitar solo from Steve in the background mirrors the guitar theme in Ritual at the beginning of the movement.	
18:32 Bass AN	Chris' bass playing into "Getting over over-hanging trees" and the incredible climax buildup back to the main theme of the track!	
18:53 Bass KM	Very high playing and line follows bass drum and melody at times – sometimes answering phrases – is this more likely to be a Squire created or at least embellished line?	
19:03 Guitars KM	Two guitar lines in octaves – a remarkable texture created.	

Tales from Topographic Oceans - Yes album Listening Guide

19:09 Vocals KM	Here, the spine-tingle meter explodes as Yes show their version of an anthemic singalong theme. Astonishing.
19:30 Keyboards KM	Repeat of "What happened … " with fabulous Minimoog soloing spanning octave jumps to ramp up the tension, combining with a complementary bass line.
– Guitars KM	The theme re-appearing is another true spine-tingling moment, particularly in octaves!
To end of song Drums KM	Brilliant rocky end on drums with touches of unusual hi-hat as accents – fade away – then some snare almost military snare drumming.
– Guitars and vocals KM	Volume pedal single notes above the newly-harmonised unison chanting, recalling the opening of the movement.

13

MOVEMENT GUIDE 2 – THE REMEMBERING – HIGH THE MEMORY

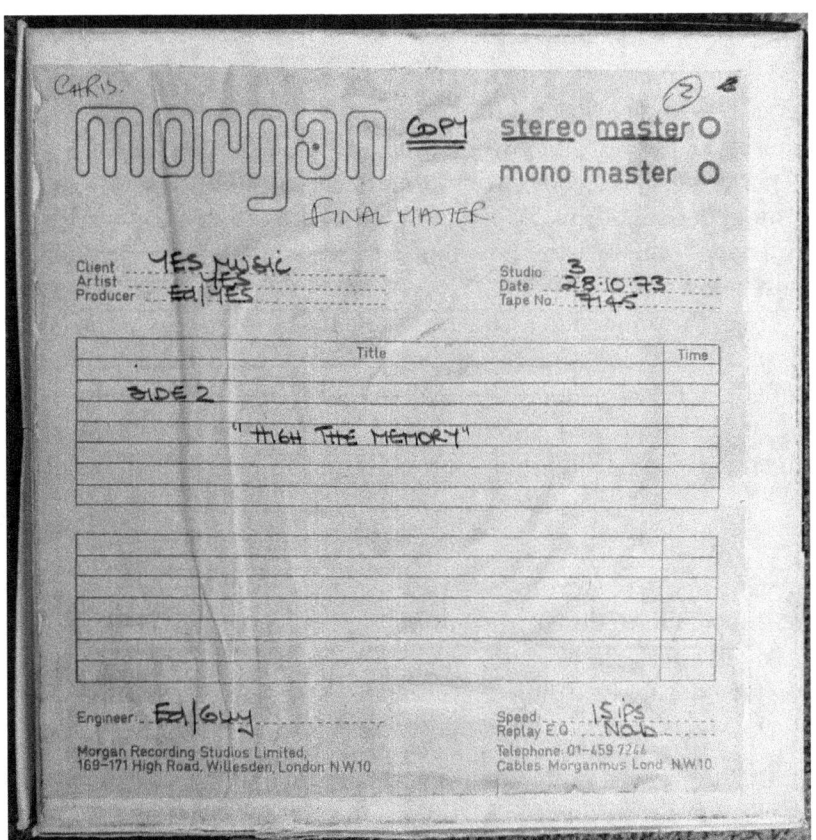

Chris Squire's review copy of 'The Remembering', courtesy of The Clive Ayer Collection, photo by Clive Ayer

"The ingredients are wonderful, the music, the way we're throwing out different ways of actually performing, and you get that walking voice with the guitar playing the same tune. But then lovely things happen in it, and many of them are very significant to me, personally."

"I was a little disappointed that side two wasn't quite at that level. [*Close to the Edge*] It doesn't feel as well crafted, tonally, and in the EQs and the balance."

Steve Howe quoted in the Gottlieb Bros.' tour book for
The Classic Tales of Yes Tour, 2023

"The lyrics of 'The Remembering' are impressionistic and, to me at least, only make sense if you already know what they're talking about. I see this movement as being about the scriptures that hold the memories for humanity. Here are the first lines, for example:

> 'As the silence of seasons on we relive abridge sails afloat
> As to call light the soul shall sing of the velvet sailors course on
> Of the velvet sailors course on.'

And here is what I think it means: "as we live our lives, we re-live other lives and we are called to the light of the cosmic memory that others have traveled before us." The term 'Relayer', appearing later in the movement, is a reference to the Hindu sage who remembers the wisdom of the gods and transmits that to humans. So, no surprise, this is all about memory and how our lives are supported by the wisdom passed down to us through the ages. I am impressed in a number of places in this movement, considered by many to be one of the two "weaker movements" of the album. There are so many good melodies embedded in here, held together by repetition, merging of melodies and motifs and what I call the keyboard theme, which weaves in and out and evokes the lightness and airiness of memory. Well done, Yes."

Robert Keeley

The origins of the music on *Tales* is sometimes uncovered accidentally. At the end of 2024, Paul Hailes spotted an Instagram video[21] by j.j.blair. He analyses studio multitracks from a wide variety of bands. In this example, he plays a 15 min tape of the recording of 'Roundabout' at Advision Studios in 1971. Towards the end, the tape is left running. Yes fan Paul Hailes realised:

" ... that there was some noodling based around what became the 'High The Memory' section of TFTO ... "

Paul Hailes on Facebook

---

21 https://tormatobook.com/instatales

As with the previous example of 'All Fighters Past', the music on *Tales* has deep roots, not only from the Howe and Anderson writing sessions on tour but was also developed from ideas floating around the composers' minds as they worked on other records.

1	2	3	4	5	6	7	8
Kick	Group Vox, Snare	Toms	Toms	Perc, OH	Perc, OH	Bass	Synth, Keyboard Strings
9	10	11	12	13	14	15	16
Keyboard Flute Strings and Choir	Keyboard Strings	Moog, Keyboard Strings	Claps, Perc, Synth	Claps, Perc, Synth, Ld Vox	El Gtr, BG Vox	Leslie El Gtr, 12 String Ac Gtr, El Gtr	Leslie El Gtr, 12 String Ac Gtr, El Gtr
17	18	19	20	21	22	23	24
Piano, El Gtr, Ac Gtr	Piano, El Gtr, Ac Gtr	Organ, Ac Gtr, Perc, El Gtr	Organ, 12 String Ac Gtr, Ac Gtr, Perc, El Gtr	Ld Vox, Bass, Keyboard Strings	Group Vox, 12 String Ac Gtr, Ld Vox, Perc, Cymbal, Keyboard Strings	BG vox, Bass, Ac Gtr, Keyboard Strings	BG Vox, Keyboard Strings, Ld Vox, Moog

Track listing from the analogue to digital transfer, author's version (see chapter 17)

Timestamp – Type – Contributed by	Description
0:00 Drums KM	All sorts of percussion at the start – very subtle though – finger bells/triangle or crotales?
– Keyboards KM	This is where it is easiest to hear the Mander single-manual pipe organ. It's a lovely sound as Wakeman plays lines that curl around each other.
– Bass KM	Is this Chris on the acoustic bass at the beginning?
– Keyboards JL	Rick Wakeman plays on the organ patterns that will be used again in the harp / church organ sequence of Awaken in 1977.
– Instrumentation NK	'The Remembering' starts with Howe on the electric Danelectro 12 string and Wakeman on the Mander Pipe organ, a lovely start to a stunningly lovely track. As the Brits say, "LOVELY, LOVELY, LOVELY!"
– Musical themes and guitar RK	The piece starts with guitar and keyboards noodling for a few moments before launching into the first theme, "as the silence of seasons…," carried by the guitar. I notice that the guitar has a sitar-like sound which I believe purposely evokes eastern thought.

- Vocals KM		For more than five and a half minutes of this movement, the vocals are in a similar style. They move slowly in exquisite harmony. It's like an elaboration of the chanting at the beginning of the record.
0:37 Vocals RK		When vocals come in there is only that melodic line (and a corresponding vocal harmony) going on. There is no counterpoint, the melody is presented strongly.
1:11 Bass KM		There seems to be an additional bass part.
1:27 Drums KM		What I think are crotales add a beautiful, high-pitched background colour to the soft section.
1:30 Bass KM		This is likely to be the fretless bass. There seem to be some glissandi. It's certainly a lovely effect, very appropriate for ebb and flow of the music. A very wide-ranging line, at times holding the beat but up and down the fretboard.
1:33 Musical theme RK		The next theme is built on the first. Bass gives the first three notes of Theme A and then, as the singing begins, Theme B is sung while theme A becomes a countermelody played by bass and guitar. Very nicely done.
- Keyboards KM		Rick doubles the lead vocal theme on Minimoog – adds lovely colour. This approach appears again after 2:15.
- Bass NK		I think Chris Squire said the best bass work of his career was on 'The Remembering – High the Memory'.
2:00 Keyboards CB		Mander organ: a delicate little countermelody perhaps including the principal rank.
2:29 Musical themes RK		There is an abrupt change to Theme C (Ours the story shall we carry on) perhaps in a new key.
- Keyboards KM		Keyboards lead this new theme – Minimoog followed by a long passage of Mellotron.
2:35 Lyrics GB		Steve Howe says of these lyrics " … that gets me tingling a little."

2:54 Musical themes RK	Theme D – One could see themes C and D as one long theme but the parts show up separately later on so I'm choosing to call them separate. C and D are then repeated. Listen to the ascending bass line in the last part of D and then the descending bass line in the instrumental section immediately following.	
3:04 Drums KM	cymbal washes	
3:48 Keyboards KM	Mander organ punctuates the accompaniment for a moment and then Mellotron takes over again.	
3:55 Drums KM	Subtle toms.	
4:20 Structure PC	After the band plays a short, acoustic riff (which is revisited, electrically, in the opening to Ritual...and seems to cut off rather abruptly) Chris's ascending fretless bass slide glides into the majestic sounds of the Mellotron and cymbal crescendos, which, according to Jon Anderson in the liner notes, represents the mind's eye/Topographic ocean. This section is also very similar to Steve's solo after the first section in Ritual, sans the Mellotron. Perhaps, that solo, with its wave effects and cymbals, is also referencing the Topographic ocean, with Steve's guitar "remembering" the themes heard previously on the album?	
– Keyboards CB	Mander organ: another counter-melody.	
4:32 Drums KM	Very obvious crotales.	
4:36 Guitars KM	After a long passage of similar playing, Howe moves to a shimmering tremolo here, like Squire's bass, when the section changes. He returns to the previous approach to accompany another 'verse'.	
4:37 Keyboards RK	Next we have the first in a series of keyboard sections [4:37] that are not melodic but almost serve as a bridge between sections of the piece. They evoke the airy non-specific idea of memory and thought. I believe the chords are the same as the end of Theme D again.	
4:40 Drums KM	Washes of cymbals again – with phasing effects applied.	

5:09 Musical themes RK	Then we are back to Theme A briefly!	
5:33 Musical themes RK	We suddenly find ourselves back to theme C before we come to a new section.	
5:38 Keyboards KM	Possibly the Mander organ adding high, quick notes but could be the RMI Rock-Si-Chord electra-piano 668.	
5:40 Bass KM	Shifts the beat with the drums – from static on the beat.	
5:41 Drums KM	choked cymbals and snare drum with no snare or toms – adding to an exotic feel with the Sitar guitar?	
6:08 Keyboards CB	Mander organ – around this time there is a lot of chirpy countermelody but hard to tell if pipes or Hammond. This organ could add 5th and 3rd pitches like a Hammond, but no vibrato.	
– Musical themes RK	Theme E twice followed by Theme F.	
6:50 Drums KM	More rhythmic but still an unusual sound – More motion – adding handclaps later.	
6:55 Musical themes RK	Themes E and F are repeated.	
7:37 Bass KM	Moves into ambient texture – tremolo on bass to fit in – fingers?	
– Musical themes RK	We jump abruptly to another lengthier keyboard instrumental section over the same chords as before and this time there is a melody that comes in near the end that is none of the sung themes – I'll call it the Keyboard theme.	
8:10 Keyboards KM	Again, Wakeman's mastery of the Minimoog is highlighted with this theme. A slow, finely-crafted melody over Mellotron strings accompaniment.	
8:39 Bass KM	Spread chords.	

9:11 Lyrics GB	Steve Howe: "The 'Don the cap' section also has some very lovely moments."
- Guitars KM	Acoustic guitar accompanying passage. Combines with the bass line beautifully.
9:13 Drums KM	Light drumming with the acoustic guitar- offbeat ride – 6/8 with fretless bass? Hemiola? Quite jazzy – not known for, allegedly.
9:15 Instruments SE	Steve, Alan and Chris... perfection but especially the growling bass.
- Musical themes RK	We then jump to a new section, Theme G sung once, played on guitar once and then sung again ending with 'other skylines'.
10:19 Musical themes RK	The steel guitar plays a new theme (I'll call it steel theme) which leads into Theme H (relayer!), one of the more memorable themes in this movement with a wonderful counterpoint guitar figure.
- Bass KM	Great chance to hear bass line against high electric line.
10:36 Bass KM	Is this still the acoustic bass? It's more raspy rocky sound – faster Relayer section – doesn't sound like the Rickenbacker – sounds more fret-like, less swooping.
10:38 Drums & vocals KM	Brings the band into the Relayer section – vocals and drums seem to phase across the rhythm.
- Guitars KM	The 'Relayer' section includes unusual-sounding fast electric guitar from Howe which moves between octaves.
- Theme HBP	"Relayer" – Drum pattern and melody reminiscent of the one at 01:46 in Ritual.
11:20 Keyboards KM	That great combination of Mellotron strings and MiniMoog soloing returns.
11:51 Musical theme RK	Back to Theme F (like a dreamer) and there is a great moving bass line against the guitar theme that we heard previously.

11:54 – 14:39 Structure KJ	This 2 minute 45 second passage distils down and encompasses much of the essence of what Yes is. It starts with only Steve on acoustic guitar, Jon singing and Rick on organ. Then Chris joins in gently on (acoustic) bass and the band begins to harmonize. Alan joins the fray and the tempo picks up to a roar, as the band kicks it into high gear with Steve's electric guitar and Chris's thunderous bass paving the way to Rick's magical sounding keyboards.
– Keyboards KM	This is one of the best places to hear Rick Wakeman playing the Mander portable pipe organ.
– Guitars KM	The classical guitar blends beautifully with the acoustic bass (with some plucked harmonics) and Jon Anderson's voice – as well as Steve's own voice singing backing vocals.
– Keyboards CB	Mander organ – chords and fragments of melody.
12:28 Guitar KM	Spanish Laud is more obvious – perhaps doubled.
12:49 Guitars KM	Is this a Gibson BR9 steel guitar solo?
13:08 Drums KM	Back to 'Relayer' again in the same way.
– Guitars KM	Back to the dramatic, fiery electric guitar soloing.
– Musical themes RK	Back to the relayer Theme H once again.
13:10 Bass KM	It sounds like the fretless bass here.
13:13 Keyboards KM	The Mellotron plays the vocal melody but about a bar behind Jon Anderson's line, creating a fascinating, quasi-canon effect.
13:40 Musical themes RK	Instrumental Theme A with the Theme H bass line. Very inventive. Followed by a full on instrumental statement of Theme H.

13 - MOVEMENT GUIDE 2 - THE REMEMBERING - HIGH THE MEMORY

- Keyboards KM	Minimoog reiterates one of the slower themes while the rest of the band scurry around energetically. Mellotron and Mini-Moog combine brilliantly here again.
14:15 Drums KM	Elaborate, complex drum pattern with tambourine on top.
14:40 Musical themes RK	A restatement of Theme F.
- Guitars KM	Several guitar parts around this point, including the Spanish Laud, I think.
14:39 Drums KM	Exotic china cymbals accenting with bass guitar – foreshadow sections of Ritual.
14:40 Keyboards CB	Mander organ – like at 6:00, a lot of chirpy countermelody but hard to tell if pipes or Hammond. This organ could add 5th and 3rd pitches like a Hammond, but no vibrato. Repeated later after 15:00.
15:07 Musical themes RK	Two statements of Theme E.
15:52 Bass KM	For long section Back to tremolo but sounds more like an electric bass tremolo this time.
- Musical themes RK	Another Keyboard theme with guitar improvisation near the end.
- Guitars KM	Some of the fastest, intricate whizzing up and down the electric guitar keyboard, sunk into the background, followed by volume pedal work again.
16:38 Keyboards KM	I assume this is keyboards – there is a dramatic downwards run that gets very low.
16:44 Keyboards KM	Synth line to the fore, in ambiguous tonality.
17:24 Keyboards KM	Another of those downwards runs, this time even more elaborate?
17:35 Musical themes RK	Reprise Theme C moving as it often does to Theme D twice more.

17:40 Drums KM	Resolution of the shifting quiet section – proper section of movement but touches of ingenuity – not straight-ahead drumming.
17:43 Bass KM	Remarkable counter melody to vocal line – strong loud and obvious going on for quite a time. Quieter to end.
17:56 Keyboards CB	Mander organ – from an isolated chord at this mark, there seems to be a lot of organ in the wash now including the principal rank so slightly brighter- up to here it seemed mostly flute rank. But much of it is hidden in the general mix – need the master!
18:29 Band JM	For a fraction of a second it sounds like the whole band starts playing Revealing Science of God again. It's as if they 'remembered', get it?
– Guitars KM	Howe cuts loose with spectacular solos, in his own inimitable style(s).
19:26 Keyboards KM	Mellotron chords with the choir sound – gives a dramatic, choral feel.
19:52 Keyboards KM	An amazing combination of Mellotron, MiniMoog and possibly other keyboards finish the movement off.

14

MOVEMENT GUIDE 3 - THE ANCIENT - GIANTS UNDER THE SUN

Eddie Offord's review copy of 'The Ancient', courtesy of The Clive Ayer Collection, photo by Clive Ayer

"The Ancient (Giants Under the Sun) spans side three and finds Yes at their most avant-garde. Chris Squire's galloping bass and Alan White's extraordinary drum part is accompanied by some of Rick Wakeman's most textural rhythmic playing, while Steve Howe delivers a stunningly emotive and plaintive wail across the top, hinting at what was yet to come with Relayer."

From the Gottlieb Bros.' tour book for *The Classic Tales of Yes Tour*, 2023

Steve Howe told me that some parts of the album were easier to conceptualise than others, for example 'Leaves of Green' which could be recorded just by Anderson and Howe and then, " ... other people could add to it."

Steve added:

"I was very excited to use ... what I call the 'guitar cadenza'. In fact, I've released it as 'Ocean's Cadenza' on my album *Motif Volume 2* because I felt that by re-titling it, I was allowed to present it in a form without the song, without any reference to any Yes ideas, just as a guitar thing that could have been like my version of 'Classical Gas'. It was in that kind of area and I felt this is really one of my best pieces."

Steve also mentioned the use of his Gibson BR9 steel guitar on side 3 of *Tales*: " ... we're doing that strange thing where they're playing in one time, see, and somehow I've got to time my tune to arrive at a certain point ... So the arrangement was really kind of stupidly complex because we could have missed the goal, you know, when you get to bar 24 or something, you're supposed to be somewhere. I think the adventurism on side three is quite admirable ... it proves that British bands don't mind being strange and unusual or weird."

1	2	3	4	5	6	7	8
Kick, Ld Vox	Snare, Ld Vox	OH, Tom	Perc, OH	Tom, OH, Perc, Strings	Tom, OH	Wah Bass, Ac Gtr	Bass, Ac Gtr
9	10	11	12	13	14	15	16
Slide Gtr, El Gtr, Nylon Gtr	Slide Gtr, El Gtr, Nylon Gtr	Fuzz Gtr, Organ	Keyboard Strings, Organ	Vibes, Keyboard Strings, BG Vox	Moog, BG Vox	Gong, Strings, Perc, Moog, Organ, BG Vox, El Gtr	Gong, Perc, Count off, BG Vox, El Gtr
17	18	19	20	21	22	23	24
Synth, Slide Gtr, El Gtr, BG Vox, Nylon Gtr	Synth, Slide Gtr, El Gtr, BG Vox, Nylon Gtr	Toms, BG Vox, El Gtr, Nylon Gtr	Toms, BG Vox, El Gtr, Nylon Gtr	BG Vox, Harpsicord, Harp, Nylon Gtr	BG Vox, Harpsicord, Harp, Nylon Gtr	Gong, BG Vox, Keyboard Strings, Organ, Harp, Ld Vox	Gong, BG Vox, Keyboard Strings and Choir, Organ, Harp, Ld Vox

Track listing from the analogue to digital transfer, author's version (see chapter 17)

Personally, I can't hear any harpsichord (spelled 'Harpsicord' above) in this movement. Maybe it was mixed out completely.

Timestamp – Type – Contributed by	Description
– NK	'The Ancient' is about the sun as a divine consciousness worthy of worship. The music is about Stravinsky-Rite-of-Spring-like experimentation. Count me in on both!
0:00 Drums KM	One of the most important percussion sections – The dramatic percussion opening includes tam-tam (gong) then hand-held orchestral crashes plus crotales or another pitched bell-type instrument. It's very exotic sounding before accompanying Wakeman's fast Double Mellotron marimba sound. I think I can hear what sounds like drum sticks on a hard surface plus dampened tom or bass drum.
– Bass KM	The Line under Mellotron part is ostinato-like (repeated) in sync with the drum part. There is an interesting 'squelch' effect that becomes more noticeable, especially after 3mins.
– Guitar KM	This is likely to be the BR9 Steel.
0:30 Keyboards KM	This amazing, fast texture turns out to be not a marimba but the unique Double Mellotron (see chapter 5), played like a percussion instrument.
1:23 Keyboards KM	Is this a Minimoog sound? – a little interjection every few beats. I think a version of the opening marimba Mellotron reappears as well.
2:12 Guitar KM/GB	Possibly the guitar soloing rhythm Steve is referring to when he says it is repeated by the percussion in Ritual at 14:59.
3:16 Keyboards KM	Slowly-moving Mellotron strings chords, possibly making a connection to the previous movement.
3:41 Bass KM	Squire starts the dramatic, stabbing double octave notes in sync with the drums to accompany the vocal line.
– Drums KM	The dramatic punctuation with bass stabs continues under "as one with the knowledge" section.

4:16 Vocals KM	The first vocals of the movement. Anderson's voice in layered harmony – a lovely effect.	
4:33 Drums KM	One of my favourite grooves of the whole album – tuned gongs used very unusually as a pulse or 'bed'. Kit is there as well.	
– Keyboards KM	A gorgeous Mellotron cello solo that is joined by Minimoog later, an octave up.	
5:05 Keyboards KM	At the band stabs, the Mellotron is left hanging on longer than the rest of the instruments, as if in some cavernous place like a huge cave or a cathedral. Truly a 'Giant' effect.	
5:22 Keyboards KM	This time the slow solo is played on the Minimoog with Mellotron beneath, giving it a different feel.	
6:10 Keyboards KM	I'm not sure this is the first time it's used but the very low bass note is clearly audible here. As the next part of the song features what sounds like a low cello Mellotron sound, I think the very low notes are also on the Mellotron. It's an amazing effect and the Mellotron line complements the high guitar line beautifully, often doubling the line.	
6:23 Lyrics KM	Sol – Sun god in Germanic mythology Dhoop – Hindi for sun Sun – English Ilios – Ancient Greek for sun Naytheet – possibly Elamite sun god ('Nahiti' or 'Nahhunte') Ah Kin – Mayan sun god Saule – Latvian sun goddess Tonatiuh – Aztec sun god Qurax – possibly Somali for beauty ('qurux') Gunes – Turkish for sun Grian – Irish for sun Surie – Sanskrit for sun Ir – Hebrew for sun Samse – possibly Sumerian sun god ('Shamash')	
6:32 Bass KM	Odd tremolo – very fast.	
6:39 Structure PC	After Jon Anderson name-checks a few names of ancient civilizations, a Mellotron riff is played by Rick (which echoes the Minimoog melody played about a minute before), and the chaos and eclectic nature of the song seems, for a moment, give away to a sweet and peaceful, yet majestic moment.	

6:40 Drums KM	Sounds like brushes maybe.
6:45 Keyboards KM	Here we can hear two Mellotrons (or the Double Mellotron) played simultaneously. It's debatable whether they are in tune with each other, or anything else.
7:03 Drums KM	Another change to a creative beat.
7:04 Keyboards KM	Keyboards, guitars and other instruments share the theme around. Some spindly, high, atonal lines add a lot of interest.
– Bass KM	Offbeat with bass drum in sync.
7:30 Drums KM	Another change – more percussive with reverb.
8:25 Drums KM	Another change – again with bass in unison. This percussion sounds like something metallic beneath the soloing Howe guitar.
9:00 Drums KM	Change to kit – toms and perhaps splash cymbals.
– Bass KM	Squire plays a fiendishly complex part, integrating with electric guitar soloing.
– Theme HBP	Guitar solo quotes the guitar theme in Ritual at 00:19
10:00 Drums KM	Back to blasts and then another tent pole groove. Keeps the interest up underneath Howe's mad, screeching soloing.
10:15 Keyboards? KM and CD	I thought the harp sound here might have been on the Mellotron but Chris Dale (see chapter 5) tells me there was no harp Mellotron sound. Chris goes on – " ... The harp sweeps here sound very 'old world' a bit like something you'd hear in a very old Disney cartoon. It sounds more like Jon's harp, and I think Jon would probably end the piece of music like that anyway. It's in his playing style, and it's more of a Jon thing to do."

Tales from Topographic Oceans - Yes album Listening Guide

11:06 Drums KM	Almost *Larks' Tongues in Aspic* (King Crimson) twinkling percussion for a few moments.	
12:00 Drums KM	More strident toms.	
12:09 Keyboards KM	One of several Minimoog sci-fi sounds around this point.	
12:30 Drums KM	"So the flowering creativity" – no drums – just acoustic guitar and vocals – turns into a Howe flowing, classical guitar solo – and then 'Leaves of Green'.	
– Bass KM	Is that acoustic bass with acoustic guitar or is it all Howe's guitar – bass doubling vocal melody in octaves with guitar?	
12:50 Guitar KM	Steve Howe's beautiful classical guitar solo is one of the most affecting moments in the whole album.	
– Guitar GB	"I was actually playing a guitar from 1810 at that point. It had such a lovely lute-like sound." Steve Howe	
– Guitar GB	Steve Howe – "I was very inspired by Julian Bream [legendary classical guitarist] when I wrote that."	
14:40 Guitar and vocals GB	Just when the proceedings couldn't get any more esoteric, and let's call it 'challenging' for the uninitiated, it all gives way to one of the warmest and most beautiful acoustic guitar and vocal duets in the Yes canon.	
– Guitar and vocals GB	Steve Howe – " … everything is just magical from the moment we go acoustic. Just thinking of the opening line, there's a lovely moment when you sort of feel like you enter into a medieval place."	
14:41 Bass KM	'Leaves of Green' – the bass is absent.	
14:50 Keyboards KM	Often seen – and performed – as a duet, Rick Wakeman's lovely counter-melodic line elevates the pastoral beauty of the music.	
14:59 Guitar GB	Steve Howe – "I did something I saw flamenco guitarists do, where you cross your bass string and hold it down at some high fret, and when you hit it, it sounds a bit like a snare drum. So there's a bit in there that's a pulse. It goes doying, doying, doying, and Jon's singing."	

15:56 Bass KM	The acoustic bass returns, giving a beautiful extra dimension to the music.	
16:35 Drums KM	Castanets very quietly add to the acoustic feel.	
17:45 Drums KM	A comical, vamping percussion accompaniment before the return of the dramatic, stabbed accents.	
– Guitars KM	Electric guitar reappears for the concluding passage or epilogue. The upwards spiralling effect combined with the tinkling percussion is mesmerising.	

15
MOVEMENT GUIDE 4 – RITUAL – NOUS SOMME DU SOLEIL

Steve Howe's review copy of 'Ritual', courtesy of The Clive Ayer Collection, photo by Clive Ayer

Tales from Topographic Oceans - Yes album Listening Guide

"['Ritual'] is a sprawling masterwork covering a wide range of tempos and moods, encompassing a delightfully bonkers, extended drum section where, led by Alan White, Yes get to pound out what feels like an ancient rhythm before giving way to Steve's soaring guitar, ushering in the light, and a celestial vocal, with Jon Anderson trading earlier Sanskrit and Aramaic chants in for French, but his message is still on point, 'We are from the sun.'"

From the Gottlieb Bros.' tour book for *The Classic Tales of Yes Tour*, 2023

"The moods that ... ['Ritual'] moves through are quite similar to side one, but bigger. We're not playing a smoother way. We're kind of building this up."

Steve Howe from the Gottlieb Bros.' tour book for *The Classic Tales of Yes Tour*, 2023

1	2	3	4	5	6	7	8
Kick	Snare	Tom, Room	Tom	Tom	OH, Steel Drum	OH, Steel Drum	Drum Fill, Conga, Snare, Log Drum, Metal Sheet, Perc, Vibes, Moog
9	**10**	**11**	**12**	**13**	**14**	**15**	**16**
Drum Fill, Kick, Metal Sheet, Celli, Bass, Perc, Moog	Bass, Drums	Moog, Piano	Mellotron (Choir, Strings, Horns), Piano	Bass, El Piano, Mello Choir, Moog, Organ, Mello Strings	Rev Piano, Clavinet, Bass, El Piano, Congas, Whistle, Organ, Moog	Bass, Room, Ac Gtr, Ld Vox, Mello strings, Crashes, Muted Gtr, Drums, Ac Gtr, Bomb	El Gtr, Bass, Drums
17	**18**	**19**	**20**	**21**	**22**	**23**	**24**
Synth, Sitar, El Gtr, Muted El Gtr	Synth, Sitar, El Gtr, Muted El Gtr	Synth, Mello Strings, Chris Vox, El Piano, Steve Vox, Bass & Vox, Bombs, Jon Vox, Gong	Synth, Mello Strings, Chris Vox, Organ, Steve Vox, El Piano, Perc, El Gtr, Bass Bomb, Jon Vox, Gong	Synth, Jon Vox, Cymbals, Room, Piano, El Gtr, Moog, Gong	Synth, Jon Vox, Cymbals, Room, Piano, El Gtr, Moog, Drums, Gong	Bass, Chris Vox, Drums, Gong, Piano, Moog	Room, Bass, Chris Vox, Drums, Piano

Track listing from the analogue to digital transfer, author's version (see chapter 17)

Timestamp – Type – Contributed by	Description
0:00 Drums KM	White creates china cymbal and gong accents in the iconic opening.
– Keyboards KM	Sounds like some backwards piano sunk into the mix, followed by Mellotron textures.

15 - MOVEMENT GUIDE 4 - RITUAL - NOUS SOMME DU SOLEIL

– Bass KM	It sounds like a bass part playing the theme over the top with another joining in with the accents below. There is also some kind of delay in operation.
0:18 Guitars KM	Howe appears with the sublime theme, soaring over the top of the accompaniment.
0:20 Bass KM	A wide-ranging, typical Squire part emerges – lots of octave range-spanning below the Howe soloing. I love the rasping, buzzing tone – brilliant.
0:49 Drums KM	Cross rhythms alternating with huge beat.
– Guitars KM	Accompanying, offbeat, picked part from Howe, alternating with the epic theme again.
– Keyboards KM	High synth solo with unusual-sounding harmonies from the Mellotron.
1:31 Keyboards KM	Mellotron doubles the wordless vocal theme and on the 2nd repeat, (at least) two MiniMoog parts take over.
1:45 Guitars KM	Howe doubles Jon Anderson's wordless vocal part which is used like an instrumental line here.
1:52 Drums KM	There is a great freedom of rhythm here with a wonderful feel under the wordless melody. Fast, rolled fills fit perfectly.
2:13 Keyboards, Bass and Guitar KM	Keyboards combine with bass and guitar to play a theme pretty much in unison that moves in pitch when it repeats.
2:23 Keyboards KM	The Minimoog doubles the vocal line again – repeated several times.
2:42 Keyboards KM	Vamping keyboard chords hold the beat.
2:50 Bass KM	A variety of picking styles here – finger picking gives a soft feel which alternates with the rasping pick.
3:00 Guitars KM	Howe takes centre stage for a great strumming break before the theme returns.

3:13 Drums KM	Around this point, congas are heard deep in the mix.	
3:39 Bass & vocals KM	In unison with Anderson – 'scat' line. An amazing combination.	
4:00 Bass KM	Some very obvious tremolo again under the 'Nous Sommes' guitar solo pre-melody.	
– Bass & Guitar RN	The beautiful atmospheric break, four minutes into Ritual, has Chris Squire playing fast, single notes in the background, while Steve Howe plays a recapitulation of the album's melodies. Steve's signature use of both volume pedal swells (fading each note in) and glissando (sliding from note to note) is masterful ... but especially charming is that he adds a callback to the prior album with the main melody from the song Close To The Edge ... and even teases a bit of 'Born Free', a popular song (and film) of the time!	
– Guitar PC	Over the cymbals, waves, and Chris's fast staccato bass picking, Steve's electric guitar solo glides on the ocean of sound (the mind's eye/Topographic Ocean?), and revisits themes from the album, including bits of The Revealing Science of God, The Ancient, and Ritual.	
4:08 Theme HBP	'The Revealing' quoted by Howe.	
4:23 Theme HBP & JM	'Close to the Edge' quoted by Howe.	
4:29 Theme HBP	'The Revealing' again quoted by Howe.	
5:10 Theme HBP	"Out in the city" melody from 'The Remembering' quoted by Howe.	
5:24 Vocals KM	Like movement three, the vocals with lyrics only appear after five and a half minutes. When they do arrive they are exquisite.	
– Guitar & vocals GDR	The transition from the guitar parts to the main vocal theme, "Nous Sommes du Soleil" builds up to this point from about 4:03. This point is so satisfying after the 5-minute build up. A beautiful musical moment and the resolution of some beautiful guitar work.	

15 - MOVEMENT GUIDE 4 - RITUAL - NOUS SOMME DU SOLEIL

– Guitars KM	Listening carefully to Howe's part in 'Nous Sommes' reveals a clever and precise mixing of different snippets of theme as accompaniment to the glorious vocal line.	
5:26 Keyboards KM	Touches of synth add texture in this passage before becoming more of a 'bed'.	
5:28 Drums KM	Nous Sommes Du Soleil – loose beat under melody – feeling of peace – gets more energetic.	
5:31 Bass KM	The bass part is sublime in 'Nous Sommes' proper – fits the lilt of the music perfectly, leaving gaps. It sounds almost like a reggae bass line.	
6:49 Guitars KM	Howe's use of the Coral Sitar Guitar is beautiful here, adding a touch of spice to the change of feel.	
6:56 Keyboards KM	Pipe organ chords but sounds more like a synth RMI Rock-Si-Chord electra-piano 668 organ to accompany the vocals.	
– Bass KM	The subtle swoops and tone of the Guild Jetstar II short scale fretless bass is the perfect accompaniment for this mood.	
7:17 Lyrics KM/GB	"Life seems like a fight" is a line added by Steve Howe – "The 'Life seems like a fight' lyric and section was particularly important to me. A lot of things happened because that was there, and we lead off to do some really interesting things, playing off of it."	
8:29 Bass and Guitars KM	Theme returns from Side 1- bass line soars beautifully but this time its colour has changed due to the instrumentation, including Howe's Coral Sitar Guitar.	
– Drums KM	Driving the reprise of the theme from side 1 – snare on the beat.	
– Keyboards KM	Minimoog carries the epic theme.	
9:29 Lyrics KM	" ... our music's total retain" – reference to 'Close to the Edge – II. Total Mass Retain'	
10:03 Guitars and vocals KM	Howe moves back to the Les Paul Junior from the Sitar Guitar here, after singing some clearly-noticeable backing vocals.	

10:42 Drums KM	Ramps up with more insistent drumming.
11:07 Drums KM	Return of the choked china and percussion with Squire solo calm until:
– Keyboards KM	After a long passage with simple, atmospheric Mellotron chords, the Mander pipe organ is back at the start of the percussion/bass solo section playing undulating, arpeggiated runs.
– Bass KM	Solo – soft this time – lead bass.
12:04 Percussion SE	The whistle – and the next 1 minute and 40 seconds of sheer brilliance!!
– Guitars KM	I think Howe's Sitar guitar is in this new texture but it's difficult to discern how it is made up.
– Drums KM	Energetic workout with squire and kit – feels semi-improvised – brings in extra percussion – metallic – maybe stick with bells type thing plus congas.
12:06 Bass KM	Faster section hits – turns into a fast and furious, wonderful bass solo.
12:32 Keyboards KM	Some snippets of synth deep in the mix – or perhaps it's electric guitar?
12:50 Guitars KM	Howe is certainly back now with a rocky line.
13:12 Drums & Bass KM	Plays in unison with Squire – almost replicating his melody on snare.
13:27 Drums KM	Ramps up and up due in part to kit drumming.
– Percussion KM	Sounds like congas here.
13:34 Guitars KM	Towering electric solo from Howe with added reverb later on.

15 - MOVEMENT GUIDE 4 - RITUAL - NOUS SOMME DU SOLEIL

14:13 Drums KM	A sudden stop after the preceding maelstrom.	
– Keyboards KM	Although difficult to hear, the sustain of the keyboards make it the only audible instrument in the hiatus.	
14:20 Drums KM	Percussion passage extravaganza – a 'kitchen sink' parallel to 'The Gates of Delirium' battle on *Relayer* – metallic percussion punctuated by tom patterns, breath noises and amazing toms. Timpani joins in for a repeated pattern with growing intensity – this is the part in concert where all the band (apart from Howe) play percussion.	
– Percussion NK	The percussion focus is more of an arranged percussion movement with only minimal soloing by Alan White. Squire plays timpani on and three of them were banging on metal triangles.	
14:59 Guitar/Drums/ Percussion KM/GB	Steve Howe – "It is the same tune, or just the rhythm of the same tune that I play on side three." Possibly the guitar soloing at 2:12 in 'The Ancient'.	
15:13 Keyboards KM	Although known as a percussion extravaganza, the mood is heightened by keyboards – here, Mellotron comes in and plays progressively higher chords.	
15:53 Drums and Keyboards KM	Synth squeaks along with toms in unison – amazing effect – almost 'talking'. This sound and approach foreshadows what was to come on *Relayer*. You could be forgiven for thinking this is actually a Patrick Moraz line.	
15:57 – 16:02 Structure JL	Alan White and Rick Wakeman reformulate rhythmically the theme played by Steve Howe on Revealing Science of God from 1:58 to 2:02.	
16:08 Drums (timpani) JM	During this frantic buildup towards the last ballad section, the timpani arrangement is very noteworthy. You can rhythmically discern several patterns that are also played on guitar by Steve Howe in the first three minutes of 'The Ancient', including a pattern that sounds very much like a Morse code for 'YES' (but it's probably a coincidence). [-.-- . ....]	
16:10 – 16:15 Percussion JL	The percussion ensemble reformulate the sequence played by Chris Squire on 'Ritual' from 13:12 to 13:17.	
16:18 Keyboards KM	Is this wildly oscillating effect created by a strange setting on the Hammond organ with the Leslie speaker whizzing round?	
16:56 Guitar & Drums KM	After the percussion maelstrom, the return of a guitar solo, recalling the theme of 'Nous Sommes' as the percussion fades away.	

17:15 Guitar theme GB	"I had that tune," recalls Steve, "Going back to when Jon and I were jamming around in hotel rooms on the previous tour."	
17:21 Guitar KM and GB	Steve uses the Les Paul Special for this accompaniment. " ... it was a simple guitar and it just allows me lots of expression."	
17:33 Piano KM	Alan adds a beautiful piano part to add to feeling of return of 'Nous Sommes du Soleil' order out of the chaos – fits perfectly with guitar line – piano doesn't last long but great – a few sustained cymbal atmospherics.	
- Keyboards SSu	"The pretty piano part after the drum solo in Ritual was written and played by Alan White ... according to Alan. And for a fact it doesn't sound like Rick's style."	
- Keyboards KM	I asked Rick Wakeman – "Alan White famously provided some piano in Ritual – what did/do you think of his contribution?" He replied, "I had no idea ... but nothing as regards Yes ever surprises me past, present or future."	
17:41 Vocals KM	Who else could have made the repeat of the 'Nous Sommes du Soleil' passage so beautiful. Anderson's voice is a transport of delight here.	
17:42 Keyboards CD	Rick very likely did use a single Mander pipe organ because you can hear it in Ritual as little pipe organ chords and it's a definitely single manual setting. You can hear little, fleeting high-pitched organ chords here in the background, following Jon's lyrics of "Hold me my love, hold me today, call me round".	
18:10 Bass KM	A soft bass sound again – it sounds like the acoustic again.	
19:08 Piano KM	Piano back – longer and more far-ranging in pitch.	
19:50 Guitars KM	Howe ramps up the mood towards the end of the album.	
19:56 Drums KM	The kit back as theme returns.	
- Keyboards KM	Mellotron chords reappear.	
20:30 Drums KM	Emphatic, rocky passage as an epilogue to the movement and the album.	

20:59 Drums KM	Ebbs away to quiet end of the album.
21:06 Keyboards CD	You can hear the single manual Mander pipe organ as the highest last note in 'Ritual' just under the slightly out of tune Mellotron strings. I think Rick did a great job of using very tastefully and using it in a high range where it 'sings' the best.

PART 5 – ALBUMS AND SINGLES

16
ALBUM ARTWORK AND RELEASE FORMATS

US first pressing *Tales from Topographic Oceans* cover signed by all band members and Roger Dean, photo courtesy of Doug Curran

In a 2002 *Rolling Stone* magazine readers' poll, *Tales from Topographic Oceans* was chosen as the best album cover of all time. Roger Dean often explains that the story of the artwork began as he accompanied the band on the *Close to the Edge Tour* while they flew from London to Tokyo via Anchorage. His most recent work had been illustrations for the John Mitchell book, *The View over Atlantis*. Mitchell was a leading figure in the pseudo-scientific Earth mysteries movement and, among other controversial ideas, championed ufology, crop circles and doubt over the authorship of Shakespeare's plays. (Incidentally, I remember my late father, a Shakespeare scholar, being interviewed on BBC television in the early 1980s about this theory.)

> "Michell believed in the existence of an ancient spiritual tradition that connected humanity to divinity, but which had been lost as a result of modernity. He believed however that this tradition would be revived and that humanity would enter a Golden Age, with Britain as the centre of this transformation."
>
> Wikipedia

It sounds like Jon Anderson and Mitchell could have had some enjoyable conversations. It's no surprise that Jon was keen to discuss with Roger Dean what he had learned from the book. Dean was already in the process of developing a vision for not only cover art for Yes but also tour merchandise and live stage design. He envisioned, " ... a sort of magical landscape ... "

> "We did probably the first States-wide merchandising, for *Tales From Topographic Oceans* (1973), which eventually became 'Brockum', a 400 million dollars' worth business when it was sold. Up until that time, different promoters in different parts of the States ran the merchandising. Brian Lane, Yes's manager at the time, was very angry with me for putting together all of the merchandising, as he said it was going to cost him $1,000 a night, but I did it because I hated the look of the stuff that was out there. I wanted my stuff to look as good as it could, so we designed it all. The band was of the same view; they didn't think there was enough money in it to worry about anything other than the quality. We had no experience of doing it and we did everything the wrong way around; we shipped in tonnes of posters from England, whereas most people in America wanted t-shirts, and even the t-shirts we made in England and reshipped to the States, but even so I think they netted something like $250,000 so it was still five or six times as much as they usually did. It was an interesting process but the driving force, the driving motivation, was not to make money, but to do it properly."
>
> Gilmour Design website, 2007[22]

---

22 https://tormatobook.com/gilmour

Roger Dean's previous Yes album covers had been entirely imaginative, some featuring the loose concept of a planet splitting up and travelling through space to a new home. This story featured on artwork for *Fragile* and *Yessongs*. However, everything in the painting for *Tales* exists in the real world. Dean mentioned this in 2025 when he pointed out on social media that the path through the rocks on the right-hand side of the painting is based on a real location in Devon, UK. Dean was to return to the science fiction planet theme for 1980's *Yesshows* but the idea for *Tales* was to complement the collaborative approach being aimed for in the construction of the music. This meant including as many of the band members' ideas as possible. Some of the choices they made are recorded in Roger Dean's book, *Views*. Jon Anderson wanted the pyramid-shaped Maya temple at Chichén Itzá in Mexico and Alan White suggested ancient markings from the plains of Nazca in Peru. The 'monkey' design from Nazca can be seen just in front of Jon's temple on the front cover.

> "Roger Dean arrived clutching his artwork, under wraps and waiting inspection. Roger wondered whether it was cool for me to be present at this secret showing, and I murmured 'de gustibus non est disputandum,' adding a quick 'vita brevis, ars longa' beneath my breath."
>
> 'Do you think,' Jon said at length, 'we could have an Inca temple down here in this corner. Just a small one?'"
>
> Jon Anderson speaking to Chris Welch for *Melody Maker*, 4th August 1973, courtesy of Doug Curran

For some of the landscape, Dean drew inspiration from a set of postcards collected by his collaborator, the late Dominy Hamilton. She was the daughter of the legendary Richard Hamilton, often known as 'the father of pop art'. Amongst other talents, Dominy was a photographer whose band shots were used on the inner sleeve of *Demons And Wizards* by Uriah Heep. Roger Dean's photos were also used on that album and he was the cover artist. Dominy wrote an article about Roger's technique in his 1975 book, *Views*, and was also involved with later volumes of Dean's work. She collaborated on the *Album Cover* books with Dean and Hipgnosis co-founder, Storm Thorgerson (of *Going for the One* and *Tormato* fame). Dominy worked with Dean on the staff of the publishing house Paper Tiger, set up by Hubert Schaafsma, Roger and his brother, Martyn. She 'moved to Brighton' with Roger in 1973, according to the biographical note in *Views*.

The English scenes depicted in Dominy's postcards used by Dean included Brimham Rocks in Yorkshire, Land's End and Logan Rock in Cornwall and single stones from Avebury and Stonehenge in Wiltshire. Dean later said, " ... the result is a somewhat incongruous mixture, but effective nonetheless."

Chichén Itzá

Photo courtesy of Paul Laue, taken while on Cruise to the Edge, with Yes headlining

Chichén Itzá is a ruined Maya city in Mexico, once home to 35,000 people. It occupied over 25 square kilometres at its height, but was abandoned in the 15th Century. The whole city was swallowed up by the surrounding jungle and only excavated 400 years later.

The spectacular central pyramid, named 'Kukulkan', appears on the horizon in the centre of the front cover of *Tales*. Commonly known as 'El Castillo', 'the castle', amongst its remarkable features are 365 steps to match the solar year and snake-like shadows that appear at the equinoxes.

There is also the possibility that the pyramid contains the earliest example of 'recorded' sound in the world. When visiting the site, tourist groups are invited to clap in time with each other near the base of the pyramid. The stone steps produce echoes that resemble the chirping of the sacred quetzal bird. This effect is said to have been deliberately designed into the structure by the Maya architects. As the messenger of the gods, the quetzal is said to be transferring sacred messages via the echoes. Although this might seem far-fetched, it is known that Maya architects also constructed whispering galleries similar in effect to that at St. Paul's Cathedral in London and there are other examples of 'chirping' staircases as well.

The fabulous quetzal bird, photo by Francesco Veronesi from Italy, CC BY-SA 2.0, via Wikimedia Commons[23]

Coincidentally, one would assume, Jon Anderson released a solo album in 1996 called *Toltec* (although this was not its original title). The South American Toltec culture may have been influenced by the Maya, leading to some of their architecture being similar in design to 'El Castillo'.

Nazca Lines – Monkey

Alan White's suggestion, a monkey image is one of the most surprising geoglyphs created between 500 BC and 500 AD by the Paracas and Nasca peoples of southern Peru. Other geoglyphs in the same area include geometric designs, spirals, a bird, a spider and flowers. The drawings are huge man-made engravings, carved into the desert floor. Some cover more than a square mile and may have been used in processional religious rites. The designs remain visible due to the natural wind action of the desert that blows debris out of the grooves.

---

23 https://tormatobook.com/bird

One of the mysteries of the drawings is that they seem only to be viewable from high above. Perhaps they were created to be seen by celestial entities, millennia before manned flight was invented. How appropriate for the cover of *Tales*!

Photo by Markus Leupold-Löwenthal, CC BY-SA 3.0, via Wikimedia Commons[24]

The image is made up of just two continuous lines and, clearly, created without the aid of modern surveying tools. Remarkably, the Nasca artists were able to create light and shadow in their designs by varying the thickness of the lines

Land's End

Land's End is the most Westerly point in England, famous partly for being the starting or ending point on the traditional journey across England and Scotland, 'Land's End to John o' Groats'. A distance of more than 550 miles, this has become an epithet in the UK meaning 'a very long way'. Rather than specific rock formations, Roger Dean perhaps used elements he saw in the postcards to construct the middle and right-hand side stacks of rock in his paintings.

Another Yes-related co-incidence is the appearance of a piece on the band Bruford's 1980 album, *Gradually Going Tornado* named 'Land's End', written by keyboardist Dave Stewart. Ex-Yes drummer Bill Bruford's band also featured Jeff Berlin who stood in for the ailing Tony Levin on the *Anderson, Bruford, Wakeman, Howe Tour* in 1989 and also worked with ex-Yes keyboardist Patrick Moraz.

---

24 https://tormatobook.com/CCby

16 – ALBUM ARTWORK AND RELEASE FORMATS

Land's End, photo by Balon Greyjoy[25], Public Domain CC0 1.0[26]

Logan Rock

The rock formation at the far left of the cover painting is based on Logan Rock, which is located on sea cliffs near the village of Treen in Cornwall, UK. The rock has a fascinating story. Before the 1820s, it was famous for being a naturally-created moving rock. Visiting tourists pushed it to make it sway and it developed a legendary status, rumoured to be impossible to tip off its perch.

Left – Logan rock, photo by Jim Champion[27] dual-licensed under the GFDL and CC-By-SA-2.5[28], 2.0, and 1.0, right – author's collection

---

25 https://tormatobook.com/balon
26 https://tormatobook.com/CCpub
27 https://tormatobook.com/Jim
28 https://tormatobook.com/CCby

In 1824, a group of sailors led by Lieutenant Hugh Goldsmith decided to test the theory. They did indeed manage to tip the stone into the sea, to the dismay of the locals. Such was the outcry that Goldsmith was forced to pay for the stone to be replaced and the remnants of the iron lifting gear can still be seen attached to the stone.

Avebury and Stonehenge

Avebury Stone Circle at the Summer Solstice, photo by William Mulryne

The Neolithic and Bronze Age monuments at the tiny village of Avebury have been recognised as a World Heritage Site because of their historic significance. Avebury Henge dates from around 4,600 years ago and its outer stone circle is the largest prehistoric example in the world. Numerous other sites of significance are close to the henge, but it is the colossal standing stones that Roger Dean featured on the cover of *Tales*.

As you can see from the highly atmospheric photograph by my son, William, the standing stones are particularly impressive at the summer solstice. The main stone in this image could be the one Dean places on the back cover of the album, above the fish. The other stone he painted is likely to be from Stonehenge, one of the most well-known monuments in the world. Also a World Heritage Site, not far from Avebury and probably also a spiritual centre, the stone circle at Stonehenge is around the same age as the one at Avebury.

Brimham Rocks

This naturally beautiful place near Harrogate in North Yorkshire, UK is a popular tourist attraction. The weirdly-shaped rocks, reminiscent of those on the cover of *Tormato*, were formed by the weathering effects of a gigantic river and then wind and rain once the river disappeared. The process began around 320 million years ago. More recently, some of the groups of rocks have been given names such as the Dancing Bear, the Gorilla, the Eagle and the Turtle. Like Logan Rock, there are stones here that move when pushed.

Brimham Rocks, photo by Geertivp[29] CC-BY-SA-4.0[30]

As Dean said, the elements he included on the *Tales* cover are nothing if not eclectic!

Structural elements

A 2009 blog post by Scott M. McDaniel[31] suggests several interesting structural aspects to Roger Dean's painting.

The way in which gatefold sleeves are used means that the art has to work both as a square record cover and as a double-width painting when opened out. This is particularly important with a cover like *Tales* because there is hardly any text on the back cover so the intention is clearly that the whole painting should be viewed.

The format gives Dean the chance to present a puzzle to the viewer. After reading the title, there's a mismatch with the painting. Oceans do not seem to feature at all. There is topography (assuming the viewer knows what the word

---

29 https://tormatobook.com/Geer
30 https://tormatobook.com/CCby4
31 https://tormatobook.com/scot

means!) but no large bodies of water to be seen. Opening up the gatefold to show the whole painting reveals fish that are clearly swimming but apparently in the air. The shadows beneath the aquatic creatures emphasise their mode of locomotion.

Dean has always been a master of this kind of surreal juxtaposition. Examples include his aeroplane image for the band Budgie[32] with its bird skull cockpit, the inexplicable waterfalls of the inside cover of *Close to the Edge* or the tiny world and wooden spaceship on the cover of *Fragile*. These and many more images are intended to warp the mind.

Roger manages to turn the difficulty of the *Tales* gatefold format into an advantage. He presents the viewer with a different focus of attention when the cover is folded to when it is opened out. As a 12 inch square image, Dean has placed the Maya pyramid at the intersection of two of the 'golden section lines'. If you are interested in the mathematics behind this principle, McDaniel provides a useful explanation on his blog but here is what he noticed on the *Tales* front cover:

Golden section lines, after Scott M McDaniel, 2009, photo author's collection

---

32 https://tormatobook.com/budgie

The general layout of the painting (both folded and unfolded) follows the golden section lines, with the horizon close to the lower, horizontal line. The formation of the rocks and even some of the stars lead the eye towards the pyramid on the horizon, making it the focus. Here's how McDaniel shows this:

Front cover shapes leading the eye, after Scott M McDaniel, 2009, photo author's collection

To add an observation of my own, there appear to be several triangle shapes identifiable on the cover that reinforce the effect of the eye being led to the pyramid. These create a kind of path from the triangular visual echoes, encouraging the viewer to 'walk into' the painting towards the pyramid. This idea of a journey into the painting is reminiscent of what Simon Barrow mentions when talking about the concept of the album in chapter 2.

The smaller triangle formed by the rocks at the bottom of the waterfall is slightly bigger than the pyramid in the background, which adds to the effect (see first image on p. 206). Roger Dean seems to have been keen on this waterfall, as it reappears in his painting for the retrospective box set *Yesyears* in 1991 (see second image on p. 206).

'Triangles' on the front cover, photo author's collection

Left, *Yesyears* box set (1991), right, *Tales* cover, author's collection

Geomancy

20 years after painting this cover, Roger Dean's artwork featured in a set of trading cards by FPG Cards in the US, with a cropped version of the *Tales* cover due to the shape restrictions of the trading card format. 90 cards were produced, one of them featuring *Tales*. On the back of this card, Dean explained feeling a little unsure why this image was so popular. He goes on to say that all the symbols contained within it have " ... a geomantic significance."

Roger Dean trading card and outer sleeve, author's collection – a gift from Ken Jonach

Geomancy means 'earth divination' – the practice of using geographical features, markings on the ground or patterns in materials like soil, rocks or sand to gain insight into a question or situation. One example of this is the early 20th century concept of 'ley lines' that are supposed to link together historic structures or geographical features. Jon Anderson believes in this idea and included many references to ley lines in his 2016 collaboration with Roine Stolt, *Invention of Knowledge*. One of these features is Yes Tor in Devon – the inspiration for the name of the 1978 Yes album, *Tormato*. Another type of divination coincidentally makes an appearance on the cover of *Tormato* in the form of a water diviner (see *Yes – The Tormato Story* for more).

Clearly geomancy was a highly appropriate concept to embed into the artwork for *Tales*, given its topographic title. Presumably, Dean was referring to aspects such as the various line drawings, patterns and fossils in his painting, as considered below, but perhaps there is another example of the geomantic art at work in his painting. We have already seen above how keen Dean was on his waterfall so how could this be linked to divination? Here are the 16 geomantic figures:

Image by Tascil[33] – Own work, Public Domain

These figures have names and are divided by their 'ruling class' – fire, air, water and earth. Some of the names will be familiar to millions of Harry Potter devotees. 'Caput Draconis' (Latin for dragon's head) is the Y-shaped symbol on the bottom row and also the first password for the Gryffindor common room during Harry Potter's time at Hogwarts School. 'Fortuna Major' (Latin for 'the Greater Fortune') is the Y-shaped symbol on the second row and was the password in Harry's third year. 'Albus' (White) is the third symbol on the first row and Hogwarts headmaster Professor Dumbledore's first name. 'Rubeus' (Red) is the fourth symbol on the second line (interestingly the inversion of 'Albus') and Hogwarts groundskeeper Hagrid's first name.

---

33 https://tormatobook.com/Tascil

Photo – author's collection

In Dean's painting, could the waterfall be meant to echo the 'Cauda Draconis' (tail of a dragon)? This idea would be more compelling if the meaning of this symbol was connected with water or something appropriate but, unfortunately, it is one of the fire figures. It is also considered to be one of the 'bad' figures, associated with nothing good or positive. As with Jon Anderson's use of the Shastras for the concept of *Tales*, Roger Dean may be making a loose association between the elements of his painting and the practices and beliefs of geomancy.

Perhaps appropriately, when the sleeve is opened to reveal the complete painting, the focus switches to that central water feature.

Golden section and leading lines, after Scott M McDaniel, 2009, photo author's collection

The crossing point of the golden section lines is a little to the right of the waterfall itself but McDaniel thinks this is to ensure the right-hand side of the picture isn't too crowded. Some of the same lines leading the eye can be seen when the cover is opened but these are joined by new ones. We need to ignore the motion line of the fish because that wasn't Dean's idea and he removed it in later versions, as mentioned below.

Motion lines, after Scott M McDaniel, 2009, photo author's collection

McDaniel is keen to point out that the approaches he has noticed in the painting may have been entirely intuitive on Dean's part. At this stage in the artist's development, perhaps it's unlikely that he thought consciously about where to position the elements so that they coincide with the golden section. There is a parallel to this in writing music – once you have written many songs, do you plot out the structure as deliberately as you did when you started or does it become more instinctual? That's an interesting concept to grapple with when we consider the construction of *Tales*. It's arguable that Jon Anderson and Steve Howe's plan for the music was too detailed and deliberate, and that the best Yes music comes from a freer, less scaffolded approach.

Band Personalisation

In addition to taking their suggestions for graphical elements into account, the cover art may also have been personalised to the band in two other ways. Firstly, according to a Japanese music blog[34], each of the band members' star signs is represented in the constellations drawn by Roger. When Roger was asked about this at a live event back in 2018, rather than confirming or denying the theory, he told the story of the flight to Japan, as mentioned above. Of course, he is fully entitled to keep some secrets and perhaps fans' speculations are more entertaining without specific answers.

Fish Tales

Secondly, there are 5 fish on the bottom left of the original cover image. Again, many believe these animals to be symbolic representations of the five band members. I am indebted to palaeobotanist and Yes fan Chris Berry for his expert knowledge of this facet of the cover art of *Tales*.

---

34 https://tormatobook.com/starsigns

Chris told me that four of the fish are similar, and in the foreground. They notably have a spiny front dorsal fin, a less rigid rear dorsal fin, small paired pectoral and pelvic fins and a single anal fin. They belong to the ray-finned fishes, the most familiar group of fishes to most of us, and are likely bass. It is not clear if they are fossil or living bass, or if they are freshwater or marine.

The fifth fish is largely obscured from view but is of greater significance. There is speculation that this one is intended to represent Chris Squire. This theory is supported by Squire's 'fish' nickname and his song on Fragile 'The Fish (Schindleria Praematurus)'. Unfortunately, the fish in question on the cover of *Tales* doesn't look anything like *Schindleria praematura* (the correct name of the creature). Schindler's fish, as it is known in English, isn't blessed with beauty so maybe it just wasn't attractive enough to be a cover star.

From the bones of the head, and the shape of the tail, this fifth fiah can be confidently identified as the fossil fish *Eusthenopteron*, known from the early Late Devonian (c. 380 million year old) estuarine rocks of Miguasha, Quebec, Canada. It is a lobe-finned fish which has been intensively studied over the last century. Dean's drawing seems to be based on a reconstruction drawn in 1954, published by the Swedish paleontologist Erik Jarvik. Notably we see two large bony plates covering the gills towards the back of the skull, known as the opercular series. Only partly visible are the four lobe fins, the front pair of which contain bones recognizable as being the humerus, ulna and radius present in our own arms.

Immediately to the left of the *Eusthenopteron*, on the front of the rock which it is partly obscured by, is a fossil skeleton. This is clearly a close copy of the skeletal reconstruction of *Ichthyostega* published by Jarvik in 1955. An amphibian of late Late Devonian age (about 365 million years old) from Northeast Greenland, *Ichthyostega* has limbs with toes rather than fins. In comparison with the closely related *Eusthenopteron*, the opercular bones have disappeared, leaving a neck, and the rearmost bone of the skull visible in *Eusthenopteron*, the cleithrum, forms the prominent shoulder girdle in *Ichthyostega*. (The scapula, now our own shoulder blade, was small and located at the joint of the humerus and cleithrum in these animals).

Although *Ichthyostega* is now regarded to have only limited locomotion on land, in the 1970s it was widely regarded as the archetypal first terrestrial vertebrate during the Devonian period. Given the theme of 'the Ancient' in *Topographic*, it is interesting that Dean chose to go back beyond the dinosaurs to the very beginnings of vertebrate life on land, and very carefully chose two closely related animals that represent the transition from water to land, a lobe-finned fish and an early form of amphibian.

To confirm that this was no accident, in the Steve Wilson remix artwork, *Eusthenopteron* is replaced by two coelacanths. Coelacanths are also a type of lobe-finned fish closely related to land vertebrates. Although known from fossils going back to the Devonian period, a rare living type of coelacanth (*Latimeria*) was famously discovered fresh in a fish market in South Africa in the 1950s, and has now been found more widely in the southern oceans. Coelacanths are easily recognized from their distinctive three part tail. In this later illustration, Dean shows us the paired fins with their bony lobes much more clearly than in the original.

In more recent versions of the *Topographic* cover art, such as the presently available limited edition print, some of the details which allow us to definitively recognise these fossils has been lost. It seems likely that Dean has redrawn his artwork rather than return to the original, then accurate, sources he used in 1973.

Changes

Despite its iconic status, the original *Tales* cover did change a little over time, even before Roger Dean re-imagined it in 2016 (see below). On the cover of the first releases of the album, the imagined path the fish have taken can be seen as a 'slipstream' motion line originating from next to the pyramid on the horizon. The line goes around the back of the central waterfall and one of the standing stones. Roger confirmed to me when I met him in Birmingham that this was something he discussed with Jon Anderson, who was keen on the idea. Roger wasn't as keen (possibly due to the motion lines interfering with his composition, see above) and so it was removed from later versions, including on posters and other advertising. The effect had been added on a piece of clear cellulose after the painting was finished, so it was easy to discard:

Two versions of the *Tales* cover, as seen in the 2016 Steven Wilson remix CD box set – left with motion line, right without, author's collection

Another difference was mentioned to me by Doug Curran. There appears to be a Roger Dean signature in the corner of the front of his original US cover which is missing from other copies. Roger doesn't know how this ended up in the printed version.

Left – original (US only?) cover, courtesy of Doug Curran, right – updated cover, author's collection

Is it a bird? Is it a plane? Is it just a tree trunk?
Author's collection

The colouration in the 2 versions is also significantly different and some of the details as well. This may have been down to the reproduction techniques used at the time or Roger Dean may have re-touched his original at the same time as the motion lines were removed. As usual, the exact chronology of changes is difficult to follow.

One of the most intriguing parts of the painting

is on the left of the central rock structure. I have often imagined that it could be the skeleton of an enormous, winged creature or maybe some kind of surreal part-animal part-flying machine device.

On closer inspection, I think it's actually supposed to be vegetation of some kind but it serves to remind us that part of the joy of listening to this record and other Yes albums with Roger Dean artwork is poring over the cover at the same time. This is precisely why Dean's work has become inextricably linked with the music of Yes in the minds of fans.

Decades after the initial release in 1973, Roger Dean decided to create new versions of the iconic *Tales* artwork. In an email conversation with Yes and Roger Dean fan Paul Denham (see below), Roger said " ... there are two other painted experiments of the original painting. One used on the Steve Wilson re-mix and the other on a Disc Union Japanese box set." In fact, both of the alternative versions are used on the vinyl version of the Steven Wilson remix of *Tales* (front and back of the gatefold sleeve) and they also both appear in the booklet of the first Steven Wilson releases – the CD/Blu-ray/DVD versions of 2016. A 2019 Japanese UHQCD also used both new paintings and the Disc Union box set referred to by Roger was actually an empty CD display container that featured his new *Tales* artwork.

The new version on the front cover of the Steven Wilson remix vinyl version features the different fish discussed above while the back cover omits the fish and the temple entirely. I don't know if the new paintings are the same shape as the original, but I suspect they are not, as they are both presented on the Steven Wilson remixes in square format, not the wide format that wraps around the whole of the 1973 double album.

Perhaps the most interesting development in the new paintings, apart from the varying painting/drawing techniques, is what is depicted behind the central rocks. The greenery from the original version is gone, leaving bare rock. This makes the tree trunk look much more like a fossilised wing or the wing of a part-animal, part-machine hybrid, perhaps Roger Dean's 'Space Ark' that first appeared on the cover of *Fragile*? The story of the *Fragile* (1972) planet breaking up and the Space Ark shepherding the pieces to a new planet is continued on *Yessongs* (1973), so is it too fanciful to suggest that the Space Ark was always intended by Roger Dean to be glimpsed, abandoned and covered in vegetation behind the *Tales* cover rocks? The part of the structure just visible on the right hand side of the rocks on the front cover of the Steven Wilson remixed vinyl *Tales* is too dark to be identified but the version on the back reveals a solid structure in black and grey. It looks just like the cockpit window of the Space Ark to me. Knowing Roger Dean's mischievous sense of humour, I think this is highly likely.

Details from the 2 new *Tales* paintings on the Steven Wilson remix vinyl version, photos author's collection

A version of this flying machine does appear on the inner sleeve of *Tales*, used like a trademark. Dean has used this image throughout his career to denote his work on album sleeves. This machine is rather different to one on the cover of *Fragile* but in a recent box set of Space Ark illustrations, Roger Dean includes both. See the photo below and make your own mind up:

Detail from a Roger Dean drawing of the ornithopter (reversed), photo author's collection

Another difference between versions is the trademark Dean lettering of the title (see p. 216).

There is more variation in colouring than I had expected. (See the *Tales Listening Guide* colour supplement for details.)

1 original US pressing 2 UK CD version 3 Steven Wilson CD 4 UK 1980s vinyl
5 Alternative Steven Wilson CD 6 Steven Wilson vinyl,
author's collection and courtesy of Doug Curran

Again, some of this could be attributed to differences in printing. For example, images 1, 2, 4 and 5 seem very similar in intention but vary in shade and concentration of colour while 3 and 6 are definitely differently coloured. Some fans have commented that these versions with only the first 3 or even just the first letter brightly coloured look 'unfinished', despite their appearance on official releases.

Dean has stated that the lettering for his album covers is always added after the painting is complete. For the different iterations of *Tales*, the general lettering design stays the same but on some versions the title is displayed at a larger size than others. When the artwork started to be reproduced in CD format in 1988, the lettering became very small, so it tends to be enlarged and the Steven Wilson vinyl box set version also has an enlarged (and differently coloured) title.

The size of the text on the inner gatefold also becomes illegible when reduced for CD. This can lead to packaging that is attractive, for example the Steve Wil-

1994 UK CD version with larger lettering, author's collection

son 'definitive' CD/Blu-ray version, but not at all practical. Interestingly, the booklet that comes with the 'definitive' box set does not reproduce the inner text at all, which is a shame. My 1994 2-CD set does feature the entire text in its booklet as well as another variation of the title colouring.

The original 1973 consistency of design Roger Dean was keen to develop across all aspects of the album and the *Tales Tour* was carried through to elements such as the vinyl record labels.

Before *Tales*, Yes albums had featured some wonderful design elements such as the paper lyrics and credits sheets in *Yes* and *Time and a Word*, the colour, magazine-style insert in *Fragile* with some great Roger Dean paintings and the calligraphic inner bag of *Close to the Edge*. On all these releases, however, the record labels were of generic Atlantic Records design.

Tales from Topographic Oceans - Yes album Listening Guide

Labels for *Yes, Time and a Word, The Yes Album, Fragile* and *Close to the Edge*, author's collection

For *Tales*, the label became part of the overall packaging approach and featured the whole Roger Dean painting, cropped to fit the round format. Even when the listener pulled the record out of its sleeve, the sense of a complete package was now preserved.

German manufactured version, 1980s, author's collection

This attention to detail in the design of Yes records continued with *Relayer* and even the compilation *Yesterdays* in 1974. Roger Dean had set the standard for years to come.

Albums released in the 1970s relied heavily on radio play for promotion. Clearly, this was an issue for *Tales* as there were very few – if any

16 - ALBUM ARTWORK AND RELEASE FORMATS

– radio stations prepared to play 20-minute songs as part of their regularly-scheduled programming. Hit albums of the day almost always contained at least one single that was played frequently on the radio. It was standard practice to send physical promotional copies of albums to radio stations and these were delivered with advice for DJs. This practice was, somewhat surprisingly, followed for *Tales*. So what was the advice for DJs when they were deciding which parts of the album to play and, more importantly, how were they to identify literally 'where to drop the needle?' In order to solve this problem, Atlantic produced 'spiralled' copies of *Tales*. Yes fan Ken Jonach kindly sent me photos of his copy:

Promotional 'spiralled' copy of *Tales*, photos courtesy of Ken Jonach

Where other albums had clear 'bands' and silence between tracks (i.e. songs), *Tales* had none so the suggested portions of each movement were split up by creating grooves that were spaced out to make visual cues of where to place the needle. As can be seen in the image above, each side was split up into 4 or five sections. The longest section is 9 mins 19 secs ('The Ancient') and the shortest 1 min 45 secs ('The Remembering'). I wonder how many times those were played.

While some versions of *Tales* maintain the gatefold aspect ratio of the original 1973 vinyl version, others cannot. This is most apparent in cassette tapes. With the cassette's portrait format and often 'J'-shaped inlay card, it is impossible to replicate the *Tales* artwork appropriately. This led to some creative solutions. Perhaps amongst the least satisfactory is Atlantic's own 1973 cassette that features only a square version of part of the painting, negating a lot of the features built in by Dean.

1973 UK cassette, author's collection

16 – ALBUM ARTWORK AND RELEASE FORMATS

This view of the painting is not a particularly effective one. The fish feature on this version but not the pyramid on the horizon. Also completely missing from cassette versions are the sleeve notes. As with many Roger Dean covers, the design of the inner parts are important in understanding the band's intentions for the music. This is accomplished not only through text but also via graphical items. Sadly, cassette versions tend to omit almost all the content of the inner sleeve, leaving fans who only had the tape scratching their heads even more, perhaps.

1973 UK cassette, author's collection

Yes albums from the first (1968) to *90125* (1983) can be found in 8-Track format. In 1973 when *Tales* was released, 8-Track cartridges were fairly common in the US (partly due to the practice of fitting 8-Track players into all new cars) but rather less so in the UK and elsewhere. Earlier in 1973, the triple album *Yessongs* had been released on 2 8-Track cartridges.

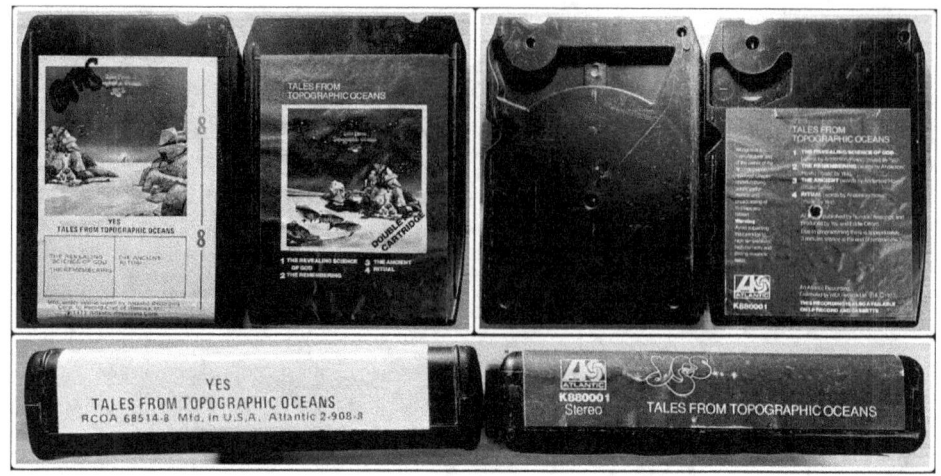

Left images – Record Club of America (RCOA) version, right images – UK 1973 first release, author's collection

Owing to how the technology works, 8-Track cartridges are split into 4 'programs'. Record companies aimed to have 4 programs of as equal length as possible so that there would be no long gaps at the end of any of them. This led to some strange anomalies such as additional songs being added to use up the time. For example, the 8-Track version of *Classic Yes* from 1980 has the 2 live songs that accompanied the vinyl version as a 7 inch single included at the end of 2 of the programs.

Tales' 4 sides fit the 8-Track format rather well but side 3 is only 18 mins 32 secs while side 4 is 21 mins 31 secs. I listened to the RCOA version on my 8-Track player. The sound reproduction is rather good for a 41 year old tape. However, the 4 program system causes some issues.

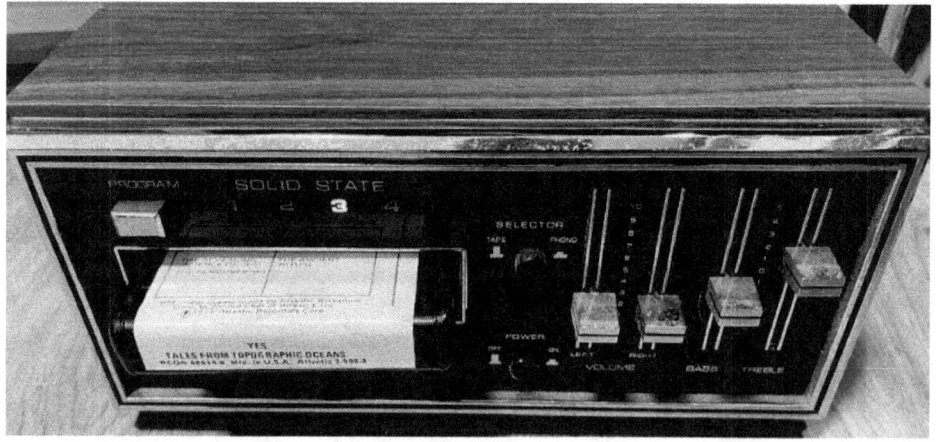

Here is what I discovered:

Program 1 – The whole of Side 1. End – 10 secs gap.
Program 2 – The whole of Side 2. End – 2 secs.
Program 3 – The whole of Side 3 PLUS 1 min of Side 4! End – fade out.
Program 4 – Fade in from 1 min of Side 4. End – 30 sec gap.

A final, obscure but not short-lived format for releasing music was reel-to-reel tape. Consumer reel-to-reel players used basically the same technology as recording studios did from the 1950s to the mid 1980s.

> "Tape is the superior analog format for fidelity. At speeds of 7.5" per second the waveform has a lot more space to be stored for playback. It's the same with a 45rpm 12" sounding more dynamic and have better soundstage than the same 33rmp 12". 15ips is the speed master tapes are recorded at and what most professional analog recording is done at because of the superior fidelity.
>
> Reel to reels are a beautiful machines usually but the tapes are very impractical for casual listening. They can require a lot of maintenance to keep them functioning optimally too. I have one but it never gets used. It's a great conversation piece though."
>
> LongLiveAnalogue on Reddit[35]

Major record companies seem to have released 'selected albums' on reel-to-reel from the 1950s until the 1980s. The superior quality of sound reproduction came at a high retail price and, as other more convenient formats started to emerge, even fewer albums were released on reel-to-reel. Often, only those releases that were supposed to be attractive to audiophiles were produced and, anecdotally, by 1978 around two thirds of all titles were not considered for this format. As with other discontinued audio formats, pre-recorded reel-to-reel tapes have recently been made available again via specialist companies.

Yes' record label, Atlantic, did use the reel-to-reel format, releasing several albums by Led Zeppelin, *In The Court of the Crimson King* by King Crimson and even *Genesis* by Genesis, released in 1983. The usually fairly accurate Discogs website only lists 2 reel-to-reel releases for Yes – *Tales from Topographic Oceans* (1973) and *90125* (1983). Presumably *Tales* was chosen for this format because of its 4-movement structure and the grand nature of the music (see p. 224).

Although reel-to-reel was a specialised format aimed at discerning listeners, its approach to the *Tales* artwork was a little disappointing, compared with the 12 inch vinyl. The 7.5 inch box features the same front cover as the 12 inch record but, because of the format of the box, it doesn't wrap around to the back. The comparatively wide spine of the box interrupts the painting and,

---

35 https://tormato.com/analogue

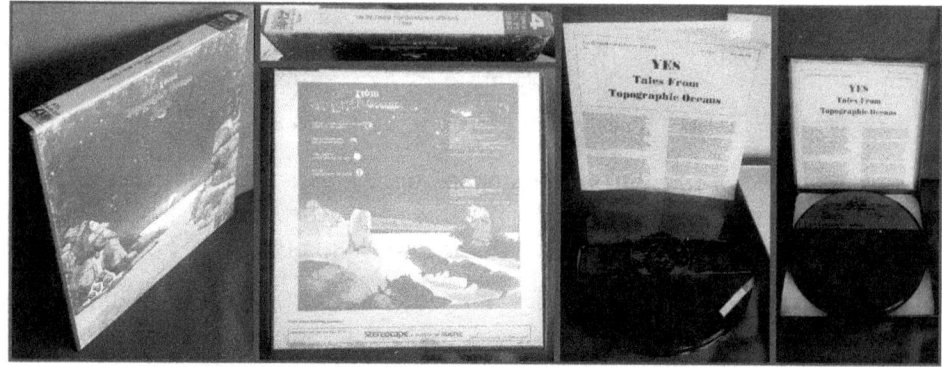

The rare *Tales* reel-to-reel edition, photos courtesy of David Watkinson

even worse, the back is in black and white with lots of text, unlike the vinyl version. The inner gatefold artwork is also missing with just the text included in a black and white card format. This version was manufactured by a company called Stereotape in North Hollywood, California in 1973. Other albums released in 1973 by Stereotape include *Brain Salad Surgery* by ELP, *A Passion Play* by Jethro Tull, *Selling England by the Pound* by Genesis and *Houses of the Holy* by Led Zeppelin. After being sold to other companies and finally ending up being owned by Magtec tape duplication, Stereotape became defunct in 1979 when more modern tape formats had taken over. The small numbers of reel-to-reel copies produced means that this version of *Tales* is difficult to find and usually very expensive.

The contents of Jon Anderson's explanation of how *Tales* came about is covered in chapter 2, but the inner gatefold sleeve contains other graphical aspects that are just as interesting. 11 photographs illustrate the 'movements', each one contained in a typically Dean-esque frame. Roger confirmed to me when I met him in Birmingham that he took the photographs himself and chose them simply because of their appropriateness to the movement. The tale he has re-told many times about discussing the artwork with Jon Anderson on an aeroplane journey to Japan (see chapter 2) sometimes includes the recollection that the views out of the window of the aircraft provided inspiration for the artwork to come. Perhaps some of the photographs on the gatefold were actually taken out of the window on that very flight.

Another intriguing aspect of the inner sleeve are the icons or symbols that accompany the lyrics of each movement. Here is a useful definition of these terms:

> "There is a simple way to define what an icon or a symbol is. It goes like this:
>
> **An icon** is a simple image that represents a real thing. For example, a shopping cart icon.

A symbol is a simple image whose meaning must be learned. For example, most traffic signage is made of symbols. A "no parking" sign with a P crossed out with red needs to be learned to be understood."

flaticon.com[36]

Unfortunately, Roger has no recollection of exactly why he chose the symbols so our own interpretations will have to suffice.

Dean's image to represent 'The Revealing Science of God' appears to be an embryo. Perhaps the idea was to suggest beginning of life to tie in with the beginning of the album. The subtitle 'Dance of the Dawn' also refers to the beginning of the day. The icon's connection with 'Shrutis' is a little more difficult to fathom. 'Shruti' is a sanskrit word meaning 'that which is heard'. Other meanings such as 'listening' and 'hearing' are referred to by Anderson in his explanation of the movement: " ... the song that has been left to us to hear."

'The Remembering' has an almost cartoon-like depiction of a seascape for its image. Roger confirmed this to me when I spoke to him in Birmingham in June 2024. In his explanation of the movement, Jon Anderson talks about Wakeman's keyboards, " ... which bring alive the ebb and flow and depth of our mind's eye: The Topographic Ocean." This makes the seascape an appropriate choice. The movement is also referred to as 'Smritis', which is a class of sacred Hindu text based on human memory – hence 'High the Memory'.

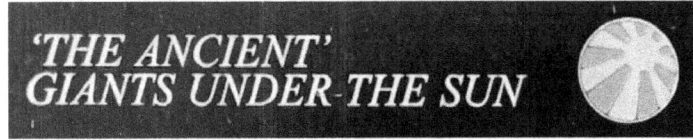

This movement is tagged by Anderson with the Sanskrit word 'Puranas' meaning 'ancient'. Once again, this refers to a vast genre of Indian literature, this time including beliefs, mythology and traditions – cultural heritage handed down the ages. In his explanation, Anderson widens the concept to include the knowledge of all sorts of ancient civilisations – Indian, Chinese, Central American and 'Atlantean'. These, I assume, are the 'giants under the sun' of the title. The image of a stylised sun might seem obvious but I wonder if it is meant

---

36 https://tormatobook.com/icons

to evoke other connections. This sun's simple shape and just two colours is reminiscent of the Rising Sun Flag used in Japan, the country Dean was flying to when he discussed art ideas with Anderson. 'Nippon', the pronunciation of the Japanese word for the country, literally means 'origin of the sun'. The 8-ray version created by Roger Dean echoes the ancient emblem of the Japanese Kikuchi clan:

Emblem of the Kikuchi clan, image public domain

This pattern is also used in the design of the current flag of the Japan Self-Defense Forces and the Japan Ground Self-Defense Force, although that has a more complex shape:

Flag of the Japan Self-Defense Force and the Japan Ground Self-Defense Force (JGSDF), image public domain

The Rising Sun Flag is controversial among certain countries who see it as emblematic of Imperial Japan's wartime atrocities from various historical periods, including World War II. In the 21st Century, certain sports tournaments have either banned its use or have been asked to by other countries. These issues were probably not in the public consciousness at the time *Tales* was created.

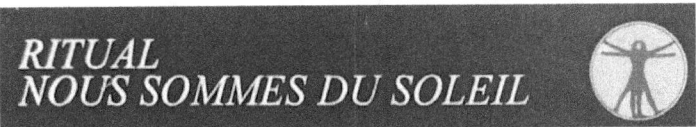

Finally, for the fourth movement, Dean uses a simplified version of Leonard Da Vinci's drawing, 'The Vitruvian Man' in a bright yellow circle, perhaps to represent the sun in order to tie the symbol in with the title – 'nous sommes du soleil' – 'we are of the sun'

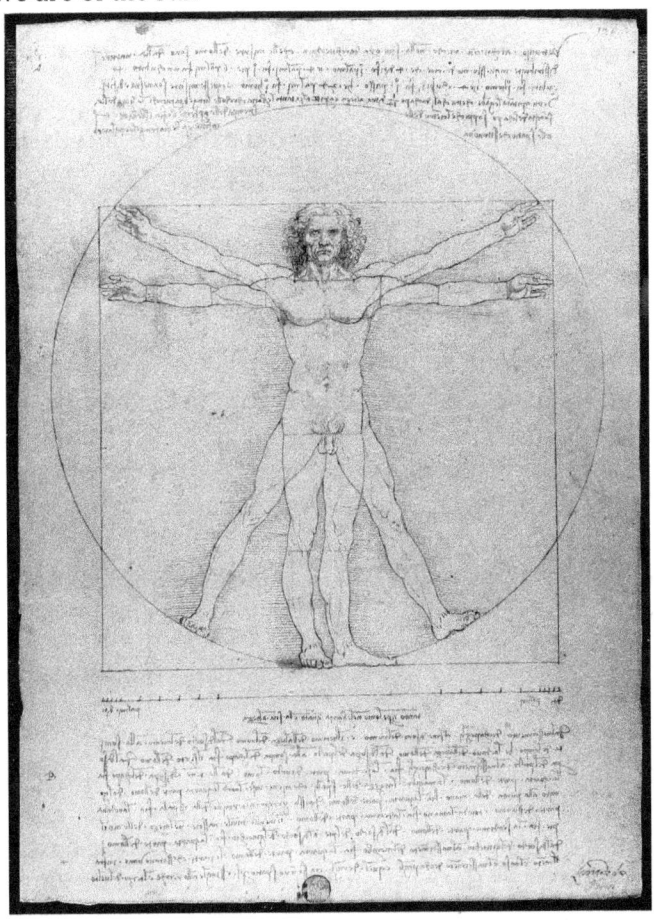

The Vitruvian Man by Leonardo Da Vinci, photo public domain by Luc Viatour
https://Lucnix.be[37]

---

37 https://tormatobook.com/Luc

Interestingly, the basic shape of Da Vinci's drawing features similar elements to Jon Anderson's 'Olias' symbol. This famous image appeared first on the artwork to his solo album *Olias of Sunhillow* in 1976:

Left – *Olias of Sunhillow* symbol, author's collection, right – Da Vinci's *Vitruvian Man*, public domain, showing the similarity in shape

Clearly, it doesn't quite match up but perhaps there is a conscious or unconscious link.

Various combinations of concentric squares, circles and triangles have been used across cultures and throughout time but a description can be found linking the Olias symbol to some large concepts:

> ' ... combining the circle, square and triangle (the specific version of the symbol appears to be the work of the artist David Roe who designed and illustrated the album cover and gatefold sleeve) – the symbols of the fundamental dimensions of consciousness from oneness to diversity. They are all actually part of the same oneness. There are many paths back home, all unique to the individual who finds their way back, but all have one thing in common – the way back home is through TRUTH, as it was the distortion of TRUTH that made us seem lost and away from home."
>
> City of Grove website[38]

The *Vitruvian Man* drawing dates back to around 1490 and takes its inspiration from the Roman architect Vitruvius. Both Vitruvius and Da Vinci developed ideas on the 'ideal' human body proportions. Other artists had previously attempted to draw their own depictions of the human body, based on the same mathematical principles. Here is how the explanation of the formula begins:

> "The length of the outspread arms is equal to the height of the man. From the hairline to the bottom of the chin is one-tenth of the height

---

[38] https://tormatobook.com/olias

of the man. From below the chin to the top of the head is one-eighth of the height of the man. From above the chest to the top of the head is one-sixth of the height of the man ... "

> *The Vitruvian Man of Leonardo da Vinci as a Representation of an Operational Approach to Knowledge*[39]

In his notes, Da Vinci describes the drawing as 'The Proportions of the Human Figure after Vitruvius'. Some scholars link the style chosen by Da Vinci to some of his earlier works such as the painting of an angel in *Annunciation*. Perhaps Da Vinci was intending to weave together the human and the divine, as biographer Walter Issacson puts it. This would add to the appropriateness of its use to represent the fourth movement of *Tales* with its link to 'Tantras'.

'Tantra', is derived from the Sanskrit verbal root meaning 'to weave' or 'to compose'. A Tantra is a type of instructional text that first emerged in India in around the sixth century. Often taking the form of a dialogue between a god and a goddess, the texts outline rituals for invoking or calling upon one of the many powerful Tantric deities. Normally, a teacher or 'guru' is required to guide the person reciting the tantra, to gain the use of worldly or supernatural powers. These might include long life, flight or spiritual transformation. Many of the tantras are controversial because they involve rituals that go beyond social norms and contravene taboos. Some entail sexual rites, the use of intoxicants of various kinds and even interaction with human remains.

Jon Anderson was certainly influenced by the impact Tantra had on the UK and US in the 1960s and 70s. It was seen as a movement that could inspire the ecological and free love ideas prevalent at the time – themes that Anderson was known for incorporating into his music and art.

Dean's symbols were also incorporated into Yes' stage show. The 'sails' or 'wings' at the sides of Alan White's drum setup were used as screens onto which various symbols were projected including the ones from the sleeve notes (see p.230).

I have managed to identify (or guess) 7 different images, numbered in the photos above, that were projected during the Tales Tour:

1. A star field or the aftermath of an explosion like the Big Bang?
2. A South American Inca mask?
3. The sea image from the sleeve notes to side 2 – 'The Remembering'
4. The rising sun image from the sleeve notes to side 3 – 'The Ancient'
5. Spartan warrior helmets

---

[39] https://tormatobook.com/daVinci

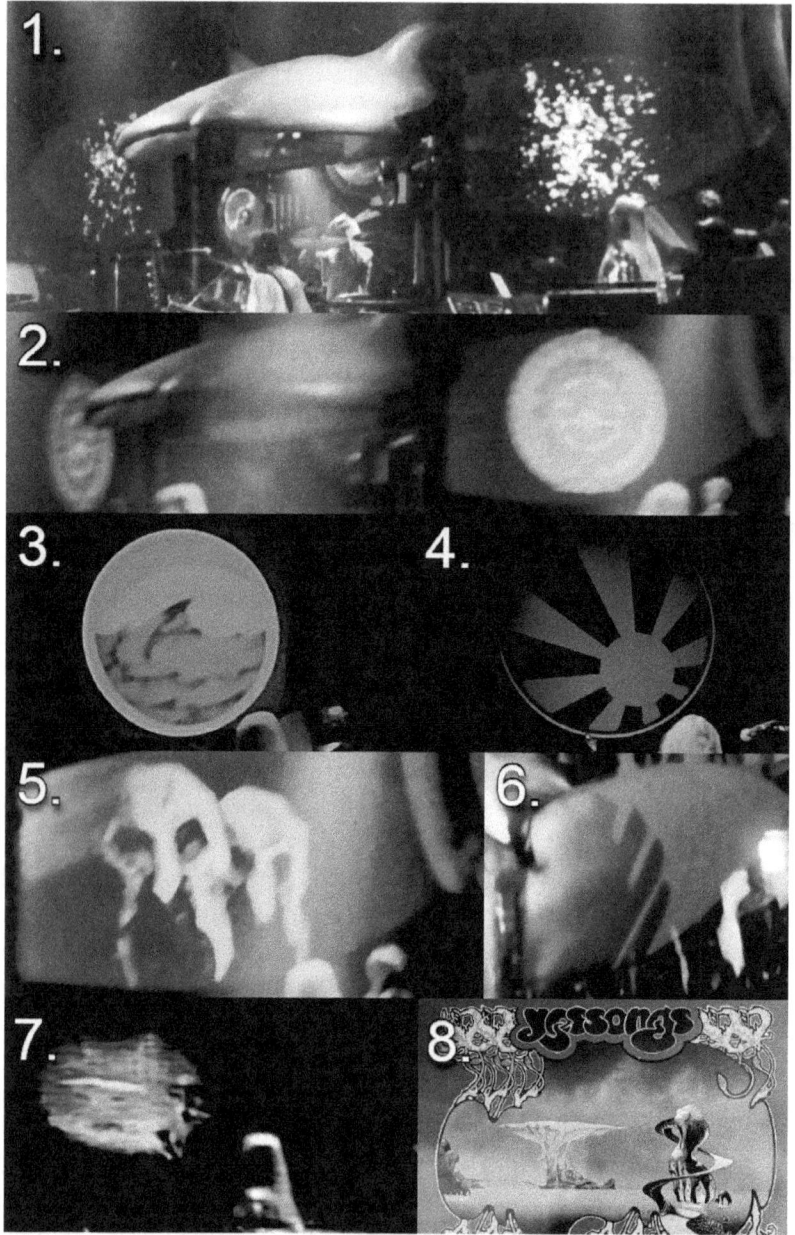

Details from photos uploaded to Forgotten Yesterdays[40] by RDZK, Michael Mayer, Larry Butler and (top) courtesy of David Cohn[41]

6. A geometric, interlocking pattern
7. (As pointed out by YMP listener Peter Corda) 'Pathways' painting by Roger Dean, as used on the front cover of *Yessongs*
8. Cover of *Yessongs* for comparison (author's collection)

---

[40] https://tormatobook.com/forgottentales
[41] https://tormatobook.com/cohn

16 – ALBUM ARTWORK AND RELEASE FORMATS

Although I've never seen any of the other *Tales* movement images in live shots or videos, it seems reasonable to assume all the movements were accompanied by their symbol – or perhaps all the images used were simply on a loop. Michael Tait couldn't remember this detail when we spoke to him on the Yes Music Podcast, but he did remember a variety of different tools being used to project lights and images, including basic slide carousel technology, which seems a likely candidate for this effect. (See chapter 20.)

Finally in our examination of the cover art, there is a small drawing at the bottom of Jon Anderson's lengthy explanation of the concepts of the record. Roger agreed that the drawing was supplied by Jon (hence his signature at the bottom right) when I asked him and he also took the opportunity to remind me that Jon was responsible for the movement line behind the fish in the original cover (see above). Roger still prefers the scene without that addition.

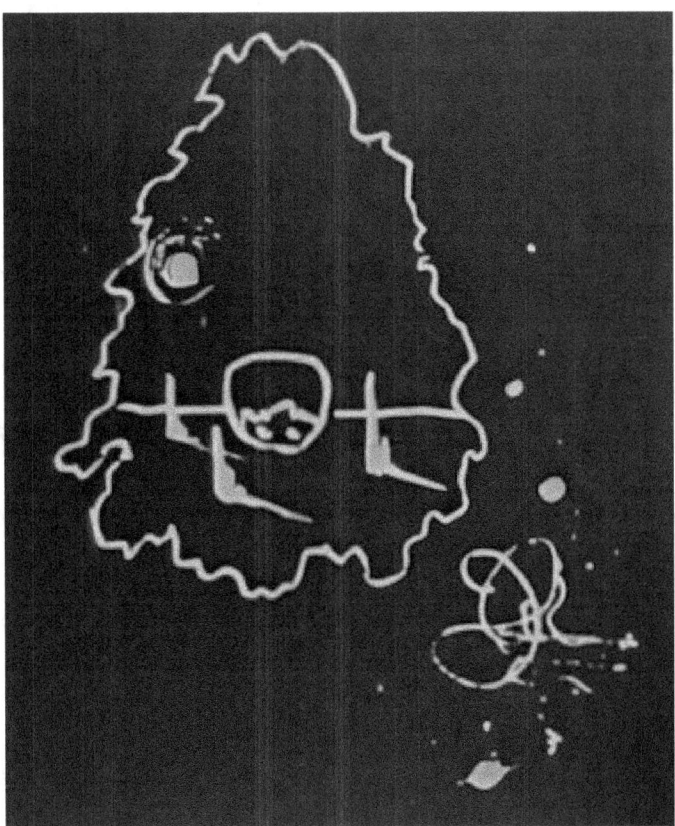

Jon Anderson's sketch at the bottom of his concept explanation in the gatefold sleeve, author's collection

What is the sketch supposed to show? Your guesses are bound to be different to mine but no less worthy. The horizontal line is presumably meant to be the horizon with the moon or (perhaps more likely) the sun in the sky – nous sommes du soleil. The central oval could be a stone or maybe even a cooking pot. It doesn't seem to have a shadow like the 3 slender objects around it so maybe it is actually a doorway of some kind, showing what lies beyond. The vaguely triangular border around the image might be a gap in a forest through which the viewer sees the scene. Whatever the case, the image is, perhaps, suitably mysterious to support the general feel of the concepts evoked by the music.

The popularity of the *Tales* artwork has never waned since it first appeared in 1973. Roger has produced limited edition versions in glorious quality and has begun to make these prints unique by adding new details onto some of them. Yes and Roger Dean fan Paul Denham kindly sent me photos of him picking up his print from Roger as well as a larger version of the added fish. This fish even made it onto the front cover of Prog Magazine's *Tales* special edition.

Left – Paul Denham picks up his *Tales* print from Roger Dean, painted by and © Roger Dean 1973, used by kind permission, painting behind this © Freya Dean www.rogerdean.com, right – the additional fish and the cover of Prog Magazine, photos courtesy of Paul Denham

In the decades since *Tales* was released, its artwork has been featured in many publications but perhaps my favourite was as part of a stamp collection. First released in 2016, six paintings were chosen by Dean to be converted into stamps by the Isle of Man Post Office (The Isle of Man is technically a self-governing British Crown Dependency in the Irish Sea). He created a new work called 'Meeting Place' inspired by the landscape of the Isle of Man and the others were the *Tales* cover, a painting called 'Blind Owl Late Landing' allegedly intended for a never-released Yes album, 'Pathways' from the cover of *Yessongs*, 'Green Parrot Island' used for the 2013 Yes box set *The Studio Albums*

1969–1987 and 'Sea of Light' which appears on the cover of the 1996 Uriah Heep album of the same name.

In 2018, three of the stamps were re-issued to commemorate the 50th anniversary of Yes and made available in a limited edition pack. The *Tales* cover, 'Pathways' and 'Green Parrot Island' were presented in a beautiful, signed package. It is one of my favourite Yes-related items.

Isle of Man limited edition Roger Dean Yes 50th Anniversary stamps, author's collection, plus a rare, full page of Roger Dean *Tales* stamps, courtesy of Doug Curran

Five years after the 50th Anniversary of the band, *Tales* itself celebrated its own half century. This seemed like a great opportunity for a new version of the album to be released, maybe as a box set with lots of extras. I have no proof of this but I wonder if one of the reasons there wasn't one is because of the legal wranglings over the sale of the Yes back catalogue to Warner Bros. This was finalised in January 2023 so maybe it was too late to put a package together. More recently, in 2024, a Rhino records representative confirmed that the next Super Deluxe Edition Yes release will be *Tales from Topographic Oceans*. The set will contain multiple discs.

Spurred on by the lack of any release to celebrate the milestone (at the time), Yes fan and collector Ian Hartley made the surprising decision to create his own. He is keen to point out that this was a personal project and only one copy of the box set exists. There are no other copies for sale but, as can be seen below, what he produced was remarkable.

Ian Hartley's bespoke *Tales 50th Anniversary* box set, images courtesy of Ian Hartley

17
STEVEN WILSON REMIX

Vinyl and CD/Blu-Ray versions of the Steven Wilson Remix of *Tales from Topographic Oceans*, author's collection

"Topographic Oceans was a particular challenge, with these huge 20-minute pieces of music which were recorded on 24 tracks — because what Yes were reaching for was something way beyond the capabilities of 24-track tape."

Steven Wilson, Sound on Sound interview[42], 2019

In 2013, modern progressive rock legend Steven Wilson embarked on the

---
42 https://tormatobook.com/sostales

most significant reworking of Yes albums to date. Wilson was already a veteran of the remixing art, having begun this journey with two albums that must also have been challenging, King Crimson's In *The Court of the Crimson King* and *Lizard*, both released in 2009. To date, Wilson has produced new versions of more than 75 albums, including a lot of those regarded as progressive rock classics.

Jon Anderson (left) and Rick Wakeman (right) at the Morgan Studio 3 mixing console, photo credit: Laurens Van Houten / Frank White Photo Agency

To accompany the digital sound files for the remix, Rhino (part of Warner Music) sent the following image files to Steven. He kindly arranged with the record company for me to include them here (see below and next page).

The box of the master tape of 'The Revealing Science of God' digitised by Rhino for the remixes

17 – STEVEN WILSON REMIX

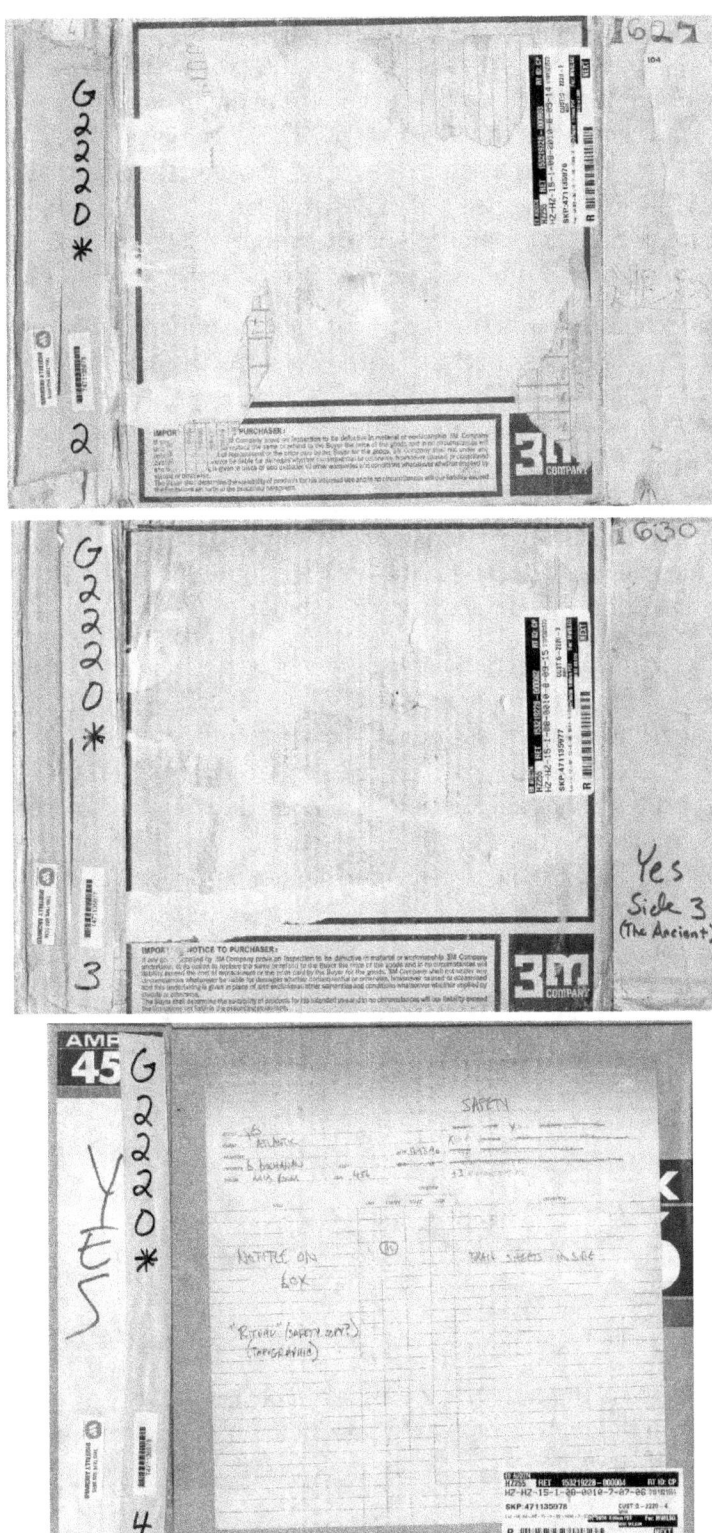

It seems that the concept of 'safety copies' was rather important in *Tales'* case. 'Ritual' has been digitised from an Ampex safety copy rather than the original 3M tape. This copy is dated December 1990 and engineered by B. Buchanan. It isn't clear whether this is the date that the safety copy was made (this seems unlikely) or if this is the date the tape was checked. The fact that it says 'NO TITLE ON BOX' would suggest that all the information we can see was added later than the tape was created. Keyboard expert Chris Dale (see chapter 5) adds some detail on the Ampex tape used for the safety copies of *Tales*:

> " ... some of the Birotron [forthcoming Rick Wakeman instrument renovated by Chris] master tapes are in boxes like this, and all of them need to be baked for 4-6 hours before playing them. The tape formula was one of the best at the time – its strength was giving one of the best sounds recording tape could possibly give, but the sacrifice was in the longevity and durability of the tape. It was not made to last. That's why this tape formula is always of suspect condition in today's age. To not bake it means possibly destroying both the tape and the tape playback equipment. Baking is mandatory with Ampex 456."

Fortunately for us, the safety master tape of 'Ritual' appears to have been appropriately treated in the analogue to digital conversion process, leaving Steven Wilson with top quality sound files to work with.

The labels of the 3M tapes are in poor condition and only a small section of the track listing is legible on the 'Revealing Science of God' tape box. However, Steven also received the following original, hand-written tracks lists (see below and following page):

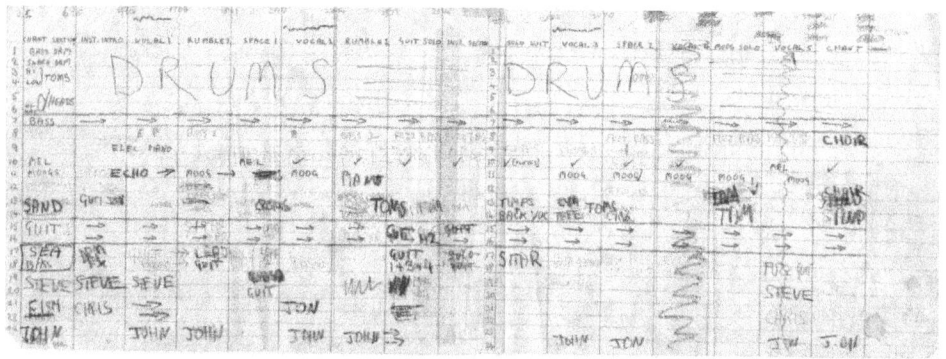

The original track list for 'The Revealing Science of God'

These appear to be the only track lists available, so it was essential to create new ones, from the master tapes. On pp.239 and 240 are the ones Rhino created and sent to Steven:

The *Tales* remixed album was released in October 2016 on the Panegyric label.

17 – STEVEN WILSON REMIX

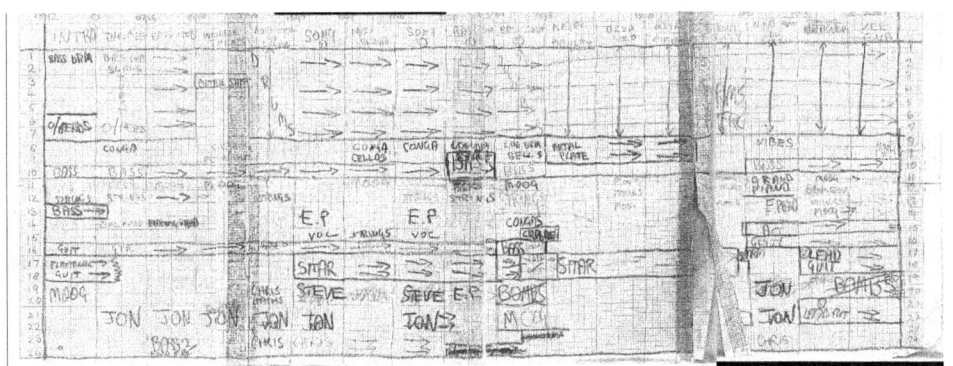

Probably a photocopy of the original track list for 'Ritual'

Track Sheet Song: **The Revealing Science Of God / Dance Of The Dawn** Source Reel: G-2220 Reel: 03

Artist: Yes   Album: Tales From Topographic Oceans   Original Recording Date: 1973   Label: Atlantic   Sel.# SD-2908   ARCMT-1004296

1	2	3	4	5	6	7	8
Kick	Snare	Hi Tom	Lo Tom	OH	OH	Bass	Ocean FX, Mellotron & Moog Speaker, El Piano Dly, Bass, Group Vox
9	**10**	**11**	**12**	**13**	**14**	**15**	**16**
Ocean FX, El Piano, Ac Piano, Mellotron(Strings, Flute, & Choir), B3,	Mellotron(Strings, Flute, & Choir), El Piano, Ac Piano.	Moog, El Piano, Ac Piano	Moog, Toms, El Gtr, Room, Organ, Group Vox	Perc, Piano, Hi Hat, Timp, Cymbals, Toms, Kit, Gong	Perc, El Gtr, Hi Hat, Toms, Timp, Cymbals, Kit, Gong	El Gtr, Sitar	El Gtr, Sitar
17	**18**	**19**	**20**	**21**	**22**	**23**	**24**
Sound FX, Drum FX, El Gtr, Sitar	Bass, Drum FX, El Gtr, Sitar	Jon Vox, Steve Vox, Moog, Piano, Mello Strings, El Gtr, Rev Cymbal	Ac Gtr, Steve Vox, Piano, El Gtr, Mello Strings, Jon Vox	Chris Vox, Jon Vox, Sitar, Piano, Mello Strings	Jon Vox, Chris Vox, Piano, Mello Strings	Jon Vox, B3	Jon Vox, B3

Tape: 2" analog   Speed / 15ips   Dolby / Yes/A   SMPTE / N/A   Slave Reels: N/A   Tones from Reel: MRL(+3/355nWb/m

This track sheet was created during analog to digital transfer due to inaccurate or incomplete original track sheet documentation on this date: 06-20-2011

Track Sheet Song: **The Remembering / High The Memory** Source Reel: G-2220 Reel: 03

Artist: Yes   Album: Tales From Topographic Oceans   Original Recording Date: 1973   Label: Atlantic   Sel.# SD-2908   ARCMT-1004296

1	2	3	4	5	6	7	8
Kick	Group Vox, Snare	Toms	Toms	Perc. OH	Perc. OH	Bass	Synth, Keyboard Strings
9	**10**	**11**	**12**	**13**	**14**	**15**	**16**
Keyboard Flute Strings and Choir	Keyboard Strings	Moog, Keyboard Strings	Claps, Perc, Synth	Claps, Perc, Synth, Ld Vox	El Gtr, BG Vox	Leslie El Gtr, 12 String Ac Gtr, El Gtr	Leslie El Gtr, 12 String Ac Gtr, El Gtr
17	**18**	**19**	**20**	**21**	**22**	**23**	**24**
Piano, El Gtr, Ac Gtr	Piano, El Gtr, Ac Gtr	Organ, Ac Gtr, Perc, El Gtr	Organ, 12 String Ac Gtr, Ac Gtr, Perc, El Gtr	Ld Vox, Bass, Keyboard Strings	Group Vox, 12 String Ac Gtr, Ld Vox, Perc, Cymbal, Keyboard Strings	BG vox, Bass, Ac Gtr, Keyboard Strings	BG Vox, Keyboard Strings, Ld Vox, Moog

Tape: 2" analog   Speed / 15ips   Dolby / Yes/A   SMPTE / N/A   Slave Reels: N/A   Tones from Reel: MRL(+3/355nWb/m

This track sheet was created during analog to digital transfer due to inaccurate or incomplete original track sheet documentation on this date: 06-20-2011

Tales from Topographic Oceans - Yes album Listening Guide

Track Sheet — **Song: The Ancient** — Source Reel: G-2220 Reel 03

Artist: Yes   Album: Tales From Topographic Oceans   Original Recording Date: 1973   Label: Atlantic   Sel.# SD-2908   ARCMT-1004296

1	2	3	4	5	6	7	8
Kick, Ld Vox	Snare, Ld Vox	OH, Tom	Perc, OH	Tom, OH, Perc, Strings	Tom, OH	Wah Bass, Ac Gtr	Bass, Ac Gtr

9	10	11	12	13	14	15	16
Slide Gtr, El Gtr, Nylon Gtr	Slide Gtr, El Gtr, Nylon Gtr	Fuzz Gtr, Organ	Keyboard Strings, Organ	Vibes, Keyboard Strings, BG Vox	Moog, BG Vox	Gong, Strings, Perc, Moog, Organ, BG Vox, El Gtr	Gong, Perc, Count off, BG Vox, El Gtr

17	18	19	20	21	22	23	24
Synth, Slide Gtr, El Gtr, BG Vox, Nylon Gtr	Synth, Slide Gtr, El gtr, BG Vox, Nylon Gtr	Toms, BG Vox, El Gtr, Nylon gtr	Toms, BG Vox, El Gtr, Nylon Gtr	BG Vox, Harpsicord, Harp, Nylon Gtr	BG Vox, Harpsicord, Harp, Nylon Gtr	Gong, BG Vox, Keyboard Strings, Organ, Harp, Ld Vox	Gong, BG Vox, Keyboard Strings and Choir, Harp, Ld Vox

Tape: 2" analog   Speed / 15ips   Dolby / Yes/A   SMPTE / N/A   Slave Reels: N/A   Tones from Reel: MRL(+3/355nWb/m

This track sheet was created during analog to digital transfer due to inaccurate or incomplete original track sheet documentation on this date: 06-20-2011

Track Sheet — **Song: Ritual** — Source Reel: G-2220 Reel 03

Artist: Yes   Album: Tales From Topographic Oceans   Original Recording Date: 1973   Label: Atlantic   Sel.# SD-2908   ARCMT-1004296

1	2	3	4	5	6	7	8
Kick	Snare	Tom, Room	Tom	Tom	OH, Steel Drum	OH, Steel Drum	Drum Fill, Conga, Snare, Log Drum, Metal Sheet, Perc, Vibes, Moog

9	10	11	12	13	14	15	16
Drum Fill, Kick, Metal Sheet, Celli, Bass, Perc, Moog	Bass, Drums	Moog, Piano	Mellotron (Choir, Strings, Horns), Piano	Bass, El Piano, Mello Choir, Moog, Organ, Mello Strings	Rev Piano, Clavinet, Bass, El Piano, Congas, Whistle, Organ, Moog	Bass, Room, Ac Gtr, Ld Vox, Mello strings, Crashes, Muted Gtr, Drums, Ac Gtr, Bomb	El Gtr, Bass, Drums

17	18	19	20	21	22	23	24
Synth, Sitar, El Gtr, Muted El Gtr	Synth, Sitar, El Gtr, Muted El Gtr	Synth, Mello Strings, Chris Vox, El Piano, Steve Vox, Bass & El Gtr, Bass, Bomb, Jon Vox, Moog	Synth, Mello Strings, Chris Vox, Organ, Steve Vox, El Piano, Perc, El Gtr, Bass, Bomb, Jon Vox, Gong	Synth, Jon Vox, Cymbals, Bass, El Gtr, Moog, Gong	Synth, Jon Vox, Cymbals, Room, Piano, El Gtr, Moog, Drums, Gong	Bass, Chris Vox, Drums, Gong, Piano, Moog	Room, Bass, Chris Vox, Drums, Piano

Tape: 2" analog   Speed / 15ips   Dolby / Yes/A   SMPTE / N/A   Slave Reels: N/A   Tones from Reel: MRL(+3/355nWb/m

This track sheet was created during analog to digital transfer due to inaccurate or incomplete original track sheet documentation on this date: 06-20-2011

Originally, it was available either as a CD and DVD Audio box set or a CD and Blu-Ray audio box set. The sets included new, 'definitive' mixes by Steven Wilson, Dolby 5.1 Stereo mixes by Wilson, a wide variety of original versions of the album, converted into digital format and extras including 6 'single mixes' and alternate takes. The Blu-Ray version contains more content than the CD/DVD version, presumably due to the greater capacity of the format. New, extensive sleeve notes were also included in a separate booklet, with Sid Smith providing historical insights and perspective (see chapter 1). The sets contained 2 mini replica record sleeves, the booklet and a cardboard slip case. 3 of these

4 covers are identical and feature the original 1973 record artwork, complete with the motion trail behind the fish. This was suggested by Jon Anderson but Roger Dean subsequently insisted on it being removed (see chapter 16). The fourth cover doesn't have the motion trail, is lighter in colour and has differently-coloured (and slightly unfinished-looking) title lettering.

Steven told me that he was keen also to remix both *Going for the One* and *Tormato* but was told that the master tapes for those later albums were 'unavailable', so when he had completed his Yes album remix project, a vinyl box set of all 5 was released in 2018. Roger Dean was enlisted to refresh the covers of each album for this box set. His new versions had varying approaches, with *Fragile*, *Close to the Edge* and *Tales from Topographic Oceans* all being given brand new cover paintings, based on the originals. While *Fragile* and *Close to the Edge* seem to have been created specifically for the vinyl box set, the *Tales* front and back covers had already been seen in the booklet for the CD/DVD/Blu-Ray box sets. Perhaps the reason the vinyl Steven Wilson remix of Tales does not feature a full-width painting that wraps around the front and back of the package is that the paintings produced for the CD-sized booklet were square in shape. This means that the proportions of the painting as originally conceived and discussed in chapter 16. The front cover has the pyramid shifted significantly to the right on the horizon compared to the original placement and the central rock structure is shifted in relation to it as well. It's as if the viewer has moved to their left and altered the perspective of the scene. This also has the effect of revealing 2 of the fish that are on the back cover of the original album cover. The fish have been dramatically re-designed. They are now blue and a different species. These look like *Latimeria chalumnae*, a species of Coelacanth. Interestingly, these fish are closely related to tetrapods, an example of which appears in fossil form on a rock on the original album cover (see chapter 16).

The back cover of the vinyl Steven Wilson remix features another different version of the original cover, this time without either the pyramid or the fish. Just the central rock formation is pictured. The style of the painting is a little different as well. The rock is lighter in colour and the shadows make it seem to be a different time of day to the front cover, despite the sky being dark and full of stars in both versions.

In January 2019, Sound on Sound Magazine published an in-depth article on Wilson's approach to remixing, including his work on 5 Yes albums, *The Yes Album, Fragile, Close to the Edge, Tales from Topographic Oceans* and *Relayer*. At the time, he was clear that he will not be attempting any other Yes albums, based on his stated principle:

> " ... I've only ever wanted to remix things that I have an affinity with,

whether it's an album I grew up listening to, or one that I can genuinely say I love — and with nearly all the projects I've taken on, both are true."

This now needs to be seen in the context of what I learned from Steven above.

It's also important to remember what Wilson intends to achieve with his remixes. As he points out, " ... on the surface, it's not supposed to sound different." He is trying to create an enhanced version of the original, not a new experience. Despite this, not all fans are keen on the Steven Wilson remixes of their favourite albums. Even some of the original artists would rather their historic works are not 'touched up' in this way. When we asked Steve Howe about Tales on the Yes Music Podcast, he said:

" ... it's all very well, you know ... remastering and all that. And we should do that occasionally. But you know, what the band did together, particularly with Eddie Offord ... in that period, in a way, there isn't a better version ... the original imprint, if you like, of Yes, is definitely there. It's not ... possible to make it better. There's nothing about it that needs making better."

In order to discover more about what experienced and expert Yes fans think of the Steven Wilson remix of *Tales*, I assembled a roundtable for a discussion. The panel comprised:

- Simon Barrow, author of *Solid Mental Grace, Listening to the Music of Yes* and contributor to this book
- Geoff Bailie, regular contributor to 'The Prog Report' and contributor to this book
- Mark Anthony K, co-host on the Yes Music Podcast
- Stephen Lambe, author of *Yes – Every Album Every Song* and *YES – 90125*

Although not everyone believed that *Tales* benefited from being remixed at all, there was general agreement that Steven Wilson was the best choice to attempt the process because of his genuine feel for and knowledge of the music. Above all, he has a musician's sensitivity and is unlikely to do anything just because it can be done. He also goes to great lengths, where he can, to involve the original artists in the process. After completing a draft new stereo mix, he says, "Hopefully, then the artist will come up and listen, and maybe they'll have some more feedback based on listening to it in my studio." In a number of his remixing projects, Wilson has had extensive interaction with the original artists. For *Tales*, however, this wasn't the case. Apparently, Steve Howe did visit him but only for about an hour – not even long enough to listen to the album all the way through. That's entirely Howe's choice of course. As mentioned above, he would prefer all Yes albums from the 1970s to be left as they are.

To emphasise that Steven Wilson didn't want his remixes to sound entirely different to the originals, he points out that several of these projects began not with a request for a new stereo version but to produce a Dolby 5.1 surround sound mix to re-imagine the album in a new, spatial version. A stereo mix was created from the original master tapes as a necessary part of that process and was never intended to be released. Often, the record labels decided to release the new stereo version, not Steven Wilson himself. In the case of the *Tales* CD/DVD/Blu-Ray box sets, several different mixes of the album are included, including 'needledrop' versions taken directly from original records. Clearly, there is no attempt to make either the new stereo mix or the new 5.1 surround mix the 'definitive' one. They are presented as alternatives, alongside the originals.

> "[The Steven Wilson] remixes offer you the opportunity to discover things that you've missed, to re-hear things in a different way."
>
> Simon Barrow

Owing to the complexity and length of the 4 movements on this album, even Morgan Studios' brand new 24-track tape machine was pushed to its limits, as Steven Wilson found when he received the digitised files:

> "So a 24-track tape ended up being maybe an 80-channel session, because I've given every little piece its own track."
>
> Steven Wilson, *Sound on Sound* Magazine, 2019

Steven told me he received photographs of the original track sheets but they were incomplete or inaccurate so new versions were made during the analogue to digital transfer process. This took place, interestingly, back in June 2011.

It's important to remember that where a track is labelled with more than one instrument or voice, this doesn't mean they are playing or singing throughout 'Ritual'. The band had 24 tracks that could be used simultaneously but sound was normally only active on a few at a time. Tracks 1-5 above were used exclusively for Alan White's drum kit, presumably either because it was the first element to be recorded or because it was present almost all the way through the 20 minute piece and there was no room for anything else on those tracks. However, track 8, for example, is labelled 'Drum Fill, Conga, Snare, Log Drum, Metal Sheet, Perc, Vibes, Moog'. This doesn't mean all those instruments are playing all the time. When there is no drum fill in the song, that track is vacant so congas or one of the other instruments can use it. This made the construction of Tales enormously complex.

Once all the recording had been done, a plan was made for how the tracks should be mixed together and the final mix down was done 'live'. Eddie Offord, Chris Squire, Steve Howe, Jon Anderson and Alan White were all seated around the mixing console with their hands on the controls. Genarro Rippo (who was there but not taking part in the mix) told me that Eddie was in charge and also mixed the keyboards in Rick Wakeman's absence. According to Genarro, "Basically Rick just let them get on with it. He wasn't mad or anything. He … just … had a lot of other things to do. Which he did." Interestingly, Rick spoke about the basis of his attitude towards mixing on his podcast in March 2025 – he was influenced by what David Bowie told him. The pair had worked together extensively in the years before *Tales* was recorded. Bowie was well-known for leaving the studio as soon as the last take of a record was completed. He advised Rick never to attend mixing sessions because the best time to hear a record was when it was finished – that way, it could remain fresh. The mixing process for Wakeman and Bowie would 'tarnish' the connection they had with the music. Rick also mentions that the Yes mixing process was even worse than the others he had experienced because of the way the whole band would literally have their hands on the mixing controls, as can be seen in the photos in chapter 4.

Although more active in the process, Alan White, " … was very low profile because he knew Eddie who got him in the band would be looking after his drum sound as well as all the other sounds."

Left to right – Chris Squire, Alan White and Eddie Offord at the mixing board in Morgan Studio 3 working on *Tales*, photo by Martyn J Adelman

The 24-track tape was played back through the mixing desk and a separate, 2-track recording was made – this is the 'mix down' process. The controls for each track were tweaked to balance the sound of the final 2-track recording.

17 – STEVEN WILSON REMIX

So the coordination of all the changes to the individual tracks was crucial. Even more complexity must have been added by the fact that 'Ritual' (in this example) was 21 mins 31 secs long. Controlling the sound of, for example, the piano track on a 3 minute pop song was rather different to looking after, for example, track 22 of 'Ritual' that changed between 'Synth, Jon Vox, Cymbals, Room, Piano, El Gtr, Moog, Drums [and] Gong' – all in the same song! Presumably each participant in the mix down process also had to look after multiple tracks simultaneously.

The track sheet for 'Ritual' also gives us lots of extra information on exactly what instruments and voice parts were recorded for the song, regardless of whether they are audible on the original record or in the Steven Wilson remix. Unfortunately, there is no way to know when each instrument or voice is present on the tracks, unless we could look at Steven Wilson's Logic Pro files (the software he uses to edit and remix). However, it gives us a chance to listen out for some instruments perhaps we didn't realise might be in the original or the remix:

Metal Sheet
    Celli (presumably synthesised, perhaps by the Mellotron?)
    Steel Drum (the Caribbean instrument?)
    Conga
    Log Drum
    Vibes
    Mellotron choir, strings and horns
    Electric Piano
    Clavinet
    Whistle
    Organ
    Bomb(!)
    Sitar
    Gong
    Perc (could be anything!)

Steven Wilson Remix Mini Listening Guide

We compared the *Tales* 2003 remaster to the Steven Wilson 2016 Stereo Mix. Generally, the remixed version of the album seems to have greater separation of instruments. It's easier to hear, for example, what a keyboard is doing when a guitar is playing a dominating part. Whether this is a positive feature in terms of overall enjoyment of the music is up to the listener.

Perhaps unsurprisingly, considering that Jon Anderson and Steve Howe are the originators of the music, the original album mix seems to be weighted towards vocals and guitar. Incidentally, the inclusion of instrumental versions in the Steven Wilson remix sets provide some remarkable insights into aspects of the music hidden by the vocals (see below).

As he has mentioned in interviews, Steven Wilson is not keen on techniques like compression. This is a process by which the quieter parts of the music are made louder and the louder parts quieter in order to have an overall listening experience with more consistency. This makes sense if, for example, music is being prepared for playing on the radio. Radio listening conditions in a car may be noisy, so making the volume of the music throughout a song more consistent will help. However, compression also means that the dynamic range of music is reduced. Where the band's original intentions might have been to have some dramatic volume contrasts between sections, compression will lessen the effect. In classical music and a lot of progressive rock, huge differences in dynamics are common, so Wilson's preference to mix the music without compression is understandable. This does mean that Steven Wilson remixes are often 'quieter' than those that have been mixed and mastered by other technicians. This is certainly true in the case of the 2003 remastered version of *Tales* and Wilson's.

'The Revealing Science of God (Dance of the Dawn)' – 2016 Stereo Mix

> 00:00 The introduction restored on the 2003 CD reissue and released on the 2002 box set *In a Word Yes (1969 –)* is missed out.
> 10:50 The increased clarity of the new mix highlights the Moog solo.
> 11:05 The piano reference to 'Heart of the Sunrise' is clearer.
> 13:35 'Orchestral' percussion interjections are more prominent.
> 16:30 The Moog solo seems to be a different take to the original album mix – it is clearer and sounds more expansive although it doesn't necessarily deviate from the original notes. Some of the original additional parts are less audible or even missed out completely.

'The Remembering (High the Memory)' – 2016 Stereo Mix

Wilson seems to have kept the majority of the content of side 2 identical to the original mix. Some of what Rick Wakeman refers to as 'padding' has been brought forward in this new version, however. This includes Wakeman's more supportive and textural material. It ebbs and flows and creates a beautiful, perhaps more symphonic atmosphere.

> 00:00 – 02:28 and 17:38 – end The Guild Fretless bass, which plays a significant part in anchoring the material is heard more clearly.
> 01:20 The fretless bass seems to have more resonance.

'The Ancient (Giants Under the Sun)' – 2016 Stereo Mix

Again, Wilson appears simply to have accentuated existing aspects of the mix for side 3, rather than adding anything obviously new. He has certainly altered the stereo feel, however. Also, in the first half of the song, a synth and a Mellotron often play together and Wilson has brought the Mellotron up slightly in the mix so it can be heard more easily. Likewise, the large amount and variety of different percussion instruments in the movement are accentuated.

> 00:00 The opening tam-tam moves from left side to right side in the stereo of the original mix whereas it stays dead centre in the Steve Wilson version.
> 3:15 – 4:15 A percussive rattle can be heard that is absent from the original mix.
> 8:57 – 12:20 The bass guitar is much clearer including passages of bass duet practically inaudible on the original mix.
> 10:00 – 11:00 The harp sweeps are a lot more obvious than on the original and a 'trumpet' sound present in the original at the same time is almost mixed out.
> 12:35 The doubled Yes choir of Anderson and Squire is differently mixed with Squire more audible and moved further into the middle of the stereo image.
> 16:24 – 16:50 The castanets in the background of the 'Leaves of Green' section are much more prominent than in the original.

'Ritual (Nous Sommes du Soleil)' – 2016 Stereo Mix

Wilson appears to have made Steve Howe's guitar smoother-sounding than in the 2003 version and the drums seem to have much more reverb and be softer – perhaps a surprise considering how important the drums are in 'Ritual'. As noticed in previous comments, panning across the stereo image is less dramatic in the Wilson version and Jon Anderson's vocals tend to be louder. Squire's bass seems strangely quiet as well.

> 1:45 The wordless vocals seem louder and Howe's guitar tone sounds much smoother.
> 3:39 Anderson's vocals doubling the bass part are louder.
> 11:02 The metal sheet sound effects are quieter.
> 12:07 Surprisingly, Squire's bass seems to be quieter than in the original and the percussion and sound effects are lower in the mix.
> 12:20 The background electric guitar line has been made more noticeable.
> 17:00 The electric guitar solo has been made less brittle, smoother and easier on the ear.
> 17:42 An effective new reverb has been applied to Jon Anderson's vocals on the 'Nous Sommes du Soleil' section. Howe's acoustic guitar has

also been EQd to sound a little more delicate than the original.

Blu-Ray Extras

Some of the most interesting additional items included on the Blu-Ray version of the Steven Wilson remixes of *Tales* are the studio run throughs and the instrumental mixes. The titles below are as they appear on the sleeve notes.

Dance of the Dawn (studio run through)

This version has very good sound for what is supposed to be a studio run through. The original extended opening that was reinstated in the 2003 remastered version of *Tales* is included and it seems to give the opening chanted lyrics from Anderson a little more context. I prefer this extended approach. There are clearly overdubs here, so the mix had definitely been worked on. I could be convinced this was the original version from the album! Overall, I think this would be better termed an alternative mix, rather than a formative run through.

High the Memory

The next track doesn't seem as complete as 'Dance of the Dawn' and the quality is less pristine. There are even a few millisecond drop-outs which may be due to my Blu-Ray player. The mix is fairly rough in places with triangle and Mellotron sticking out inappropriately. Interestingly, the pipe organ sounds rather different and it's even possible to hear Steve Howe counting into the 'Don the cap' section. Some of the instruments are a little out of tune and some seem entirely different to me, for example additional acoustic guitar parts. There is even a very different Moog part towards the end. It's dramatic and surprising in an otherwise 'floaty' section.

Giants under the sun

This movement is dramatically different from what appears on the record. The accompaniment sounds raw and there doesn't seem to be any of the Mellotron marimba sound. That part is played on a different synth and it sounds like Steve Howe is trying out different parts. As you would expect from a run through, Jon Anderson's vocals are more of a place holder and lack actual lyrics, particularly the different sun names. Where the Mellotron does appear, it is possible to hear it reset itself at the end of the tape loop and the tubular bells are untreated.

Perhaps the most startling difference is the electric guitar accompaniment to the 'Leaves of Green' section. The song also has more of a percussive feel with various untuned instruments that were to be omitted from the final version. Finally, the ending is familiar but lacks the ascending electric guitar.

Ritual (live in Zurich April 1974)

The final movement does not have a studio run through for an undisclosed reason. Instead, we are offered a live recording of 'Ritual' from Zurich on the final, European leg of the *Tales Tour*. I have read that this recording comes from Steve Howe's personal collection. This begs the question – does Steve have recordings of all or at least some other concerts on the *Tales Tour*? If he does, then, on the evidence of this one, perhaps a *Progeny II* could be constructed along the same lines as the *Seven Shows from Seventy-Two* collection. Certainly I think the quality of this rendition of 'Ritual' is excellent. Presumably, this recording is from the reel-to-reel tape machine mentioned by Peter Greenwood in chapter 22. However it was made, it is far better than any bootlegs I have heard.

After an introduction from Jon Anderson, the performance is remarkable. The mixing is not great with Squire's bass, particularly in his solo passages far too loud and Howe's guitar also sticking out at times. The Yes choir are beautifully matched reminding us of how talented the three singers were as is the band's control of the contrasts in the music.

Squire's bass soloing is epic and towering with some ferocious drumming complementing his performance. The percussion section comes over superbly. It must have been hugely exciting to hear this live at the time and the speed and rawness of Alan White's playing foreshadows the 'battle sequence' of *Relayer*.

The second 'Nous Sommes du Soleil' section features what is presumably Rick Wakeman playing Alan White's piano parts and he adds his own touches which are a joy. The ending, with some clearly audible guitar strumming from Jon Anderson, is beautifully conveyed and the listener is left with the feeling they have experienced something special.

2016 Instrumental Mixes

Obviously, the instrumental mixes allow you to hear everything except the vocals so you can discover parts you have not heard – or not heard so clearly before. Instrumental versions of *Tales* movements are rather different to typical 3 minute pop songs, of course, because there are already large expanses of material without vocals. So perhaps there is less to discover in these tracks than one might hope. However, here are just a few of the aspects I noticed when I listened to them.

The Revealing Science of God

There is a distinctive rhythm on the keyboard that is more difficult to hear on the original version. Drum fills and the figures that they contain are also more noticeable and the careful shading of guitar parts to make room for the vocals is noticeable. This combination of production and arrangement shines through when one element is taken away. Intriguingly, Jon Anderson's voice is heard in a few short passages, presumably because it shares a track with an instrument.

One of the textures that is noticeable is created by multiple guitar parts. With only Steve Howe playing these kinds of parts live in concert, it's surprising the band managed to reproduce the right atmosphere for some of these sequences. Also much clearer is a very low bass note. It sounds like some kind of a bowed instrument like a double bass but perhaps it's the bass pedals speculated about in chapter 8.

The Remembering – High the Memory

The second movement has a relatively sparse texture but despite this plenty of interesting aspects are uncovered in this instrumental version. It's possible to hear the swoops of the fretless bass and even the key action of the Mander portable pipe organ. I'm not sure that was intentional – maybe they were trying out different ways of recording the instrument. However, the little counter-melodic lines played on the organ are heard more clearly so that's a real bonus, even if it's also easier to hear that the instrument is slightly out-of-tune as suggested in chapter 5!

Another noticeable keyboard effect is the Moog doubling. This creates the impression of a polyphonic instrument and shows why Rick Wakeman's live set-up always featured at least 2 MiniMoogs at this time. Other doubling is also audible – or rather one half of it. The missing vocal lines are sometimes doubled on guitar to create a different colour and I'm sure there is a Mellotron choir in the mix at some times as well.

The Ancient – Giants under the sun

There is another example of very low bass notes at the beginning of the third movement and the opportunity to distinguish the myriad different percussion instruments in the gong-led section. One example of this is the appearance of several harp 'swoops'. I wonder if these are created by Jon Anderson on his real harp or if it's a harp sound from the Mellotron.

Once again, Anderson's voice can be heard in the introduction to the 'Leaves of Green' segment and it's a delight to be able to concentrate on the picked guitar accompaniment which turns out to be another lovely counter-melodic line.

Ritual – Nous Sommes Du Soleil

There is an electric piano sound I hadn't noticed previously and the timing of some synth lines are more syncopated than I had realised. It's also possible to hear the way the bass line leaves large gaps to break up the rhythm to create an amazing flow to the music. I love the sound of the Coral Sitar guitar line that includes a quotation of one of the main themes of the album.

It's much easier to hear the synth organ part on the RMI Rock-Si-Chord electra-piano 668 and notice the stark difference in sound quality between it and the Mander pipe organ. This synth line includes the 'we sing our music's total retain' vocal line. It's a shame that Squire's Guild Jetstar II short scale fretless bass part is rather sunk into the mix, making it difficult to hear but it is obvious where he returns to the Rickenbacker 4001S.

Overall, it's surprising how much detail of the arrangement of the instruments is uncovered from listening to these instrumental mixes, despite the fact that there are long stretches of music on the album without vocals. It serves to reinforce the brilliance of the arrangement and production of the record and raises questions around how the band were able to play this music live. Gennaro Rippo was on hand with his tape machine of course, but I'm unsure how much that was used to fill in parts in the performances of *Tales*.

Single edits

A final set of extras on the Blu-ray set are the single edits. It's not clear to me exactly what these are. I assume they are experiments by Steven Wilson rather than actual edits made at the time. There were no singles released from *Tales* and many fans are grateful that the practice of cutting up long Yes songs for 7" versions was not even attempted here.

> "We feel that there is no singles market for our type of music in this country [UK] so we think it is better to stick with albums here."
>
> Chris Squire interview, October 1973, *Harrow Observer and Gazette*

The last single to be released before *Tales* was 'And You And I' from *Close to the Edge*. The song was split up into 2 parts over the 2 sides of the single which was perhaps a better idea than fading out a longer song, but the resulting record only achieved chart positions in the 40s and 50s on both sides of the Atlantic. Perhaps the label realised the futility of trying to promote Tales with shortened or cut up versions of the epic songs.

However, there are 5 of these edits on the Blu-ray.

'Revealing Science of God'

This 'single' starts with Minimoog and bass before the lyrics 'And through the river ... ' The words make it seem an odd place to begin but the segment chosen is the 'All fighters past' part which does make some sense as it could be viewed as its own section, a little like 'Leaves of Green' but less of a coherent 'song'. The origins of this section lie in the abandoned song 'All Fighters Past' – see chapter 12.

It does include the masterful Wakeman Minimoog solo so I would buy the single just for that but the fade out after this is an uncomfortable ending for those who know the whole movement.

'The Remembering'

Here, the 'Don the cap ... ' moment is chosen as the starting point. Again, it does feel plucked out of nowhere, especially as the vocals are short and then an instrumental section takes over. However, the 'Relayer' section is included so that provides an exciting section to the 'single'. The ending is disappointing again with dark Mellotron tones leading to a fade out.

'The Ancient'

It would be reasonable to expect a single from this side of the album to be simply the 'Leaves of Green' section. This is as close to a complete, short song as there is on *Tales*. Obviously, this is why it was played so many times over the decades on its own by the band (see chapters 20, 23 and 24). It is surprising, then, when this edit actually begins at 'So the flowering creativity' and leads into Howe's extensive preamble before the introduction to 'Leaves of Green'. It is undeniably a lovely song once it gets going but I'm not sure this could have worked as a single.

'Ritual' (single edit 1)

The first of the 2 edits from the final movement of *Tales* begins with the words 'Open doors we find our way'. Once again, this is in the middle of the movement. This part of the song goes with a swing and includes the lovely sounds of Steve Howe's Coral Sitar. There is also the wonderful main theme from 'The Revealing Science of God' but the edit fades out during an exciting build up which is a shame.

'Ritual' (single edit 2)

Finally, the second edit of 'Ritual' begins with the guitar and Alan White's piano introduction to the second iteration of 'Nous Sommes du Soleil' – 'Hold me my love'. This is possibly the best of all the single edits due to its proper introduction. The Mander pipe organ is great to hear but this version does include the loud section at the end of 'Ritual' which sounds a little out of place. Perhaps fading before this point might have worked better.

5.1 Mixes

One of the (presumably) unintended consequences of including Dolby 5.1 Surround Mixes in the Steven Wilson sets is that the music is split up into different tracks in order to create the surround sound effect. With the appearance of more advanced and now AI-based music tools in recent years, this has meant that creative approaches can be taken to the *Tales* songs. Bruno Samppa is one of the intrepid individuals who has tried out different approaches to producing something 'new' from these tracks. In 2020, he published on Facebook[43] what he called, 'Chris Squire – The Remembering (Yes)'. He told me that this was constructed from the 5.1 mix tracks, with Chris Squire's backing vocals brought to the front. It has an introduction and then contains the 'Relayer' section of the movement.

At the start of this 9 min 56 sec excerpt, Chris appears to be singing the lead vocal line of 'The Remembering', rather than Jon Anderson. In fact, this is what Chris sings on the original version of the song, but doubling the Jon Anderson line, hidden in the mix. Later in the clip, what we can hear is Squire's harmony vocal line, presented as if it is the lead vocal. Even later, Jon Anderson's part is included and the original balance is restored – even if this isn't the same mix or take as is used on the record.

This 'new' version is very interesting and shows us what it could have been like to have Squire singing lead vocals here. There are some odd aspects to the clipped part, for example missing guitar parts, which have presumably been omitted due to the choice of tracks used to assemble this version.

---

43 https://tormatobook.com/sampaatales

PART 6 – PROMOTION AND RECEPTION

18

ALBUM AND TOUR PROMOTION

Left – Dave Watkinson with items from his Trading Boundaries exhibition, photo by Grace Hayhurst, right – author outside Trading Boundaries, photo author's collection

In February 2025, Rick Wakeman played 3 nights at the wonderful music venue/fine art gallery/furniture emporium, Trading Boundaries in East Sussex.

To complement the concerts, Yes author and memorabilia collector Dave Watkinson was invited to create a mini exhibition alongside the Roger Dean permanent exhibition at the venue. I was fortunate to be able to visit Dave and we recorded a video as we walked around and discussed what was on display. There were plenty of Tales-related items including Dave's unique collection of balloon memorabilia:

A report in Philadelphia's *The Drummer* magazine shows the process of inflating the balloon before either the afternoon or evening show at The Spectrum on 16th February 1974, courtesy of David Watkinson Collection

In addition to more traditional marketing efforts, some concerts on the Winter 1974 *North American Tales Tour* featured a unique, spectacular advertisement. David Watkinson stumbled across the story via the comments accompanying an online, live painting session by Roger Dean. Atlantic Records and Yes commissioned a huge hot air balloon to fly above or near to selected venues of the tour. The weather often prevented passengers being accommodated but the sight of the balloon must have been eye-catching. Surprisingly, this unusual idea came from balloonist Donn Miller, not the record company or Yes management. He managed to convince Yes' manager, Brian Lane, that the balloon would be a good idea.

It turned out that the balloon manufacturer couldn't add the intricate detail needed to replicate Dean's artwork. They were able to add massive Yes logos on additional canvas panels and a few other simplified items of iconography, but the full effect of the project seemed to be in doubt. Fortunately, Miller had a plan. He contacted a local student artist, Julie Britton, who had been recommended to him by her teacher. Miller asked Britton, his future and then ex-wife, if she could add the Roger Dean-designed decorations by hand and even arranged for Dean to surprise her with a phone call. She eventually agreed and began work in her family home on gondola panels, the balloon wind skirt and huge canvas additions to the main body of the balloon.

Above, upper section – the painted panels on the ballon gondola, lower section – the gondola panel from Dave Watkinson's exhibition

Roger Dean, who had to rely on Miller and Britton from over 4,000 miles away in the UK, decided to include not only artwork and lettering from *Tales* but also from the recent *Yessongs* live album and even paintings he had created for another band, Osibisa, due to their appropriateness for this project.

After the painstaking process of transferring the painting was complete, and following many technical difficulties, Miller piloted the airborne advert at several concert venues on the Tales Tour and the response of Yes fans was always ecstatic.

Julie wore this specially-decorated jacket when she flew in the balloon before Yes concerts with Donn, courtesy of David Watkinson collection

The balloon was used on Yes' 1975 and 1976 tours as well as the *Tales Tour* and also took part in ballooning events, again piloted by Donn. It was eventually sold and its whereabouts are now unknown. Read much more about this amazing *Tales* story in Dave's article on Yesworld.com[44].

The Yes balloon in action post-*Tales Tour*, courtesy of David Watkinson Collection

44 https://tormatobook.com/daveballoon

More traditional press adverts were created and published in local and national papers and magazines.

US magazine advertisement, photo courtesy of Paul Hailes

19
ALBUM RECEPTION

Eddie Offord's RIAA gold award for *Tales*, courtesy of The Clive Ayer Collection, photo by Clive Ayer

"In classic Yes style, the band hit the road in support of *Tales From Topographic Oceans* more than a full month before the album was released, and proceeded to perform it in its entirety and in order, after first performing all of the *Close to the Edge* album before capping things off with 'Roundabout'.

The immense and unfamiliar material left some fans and even former loyal press allies scrambling to keep up, but the album shipped gold on preorders alone, none-the-less. Once fans could actually hear the album ahead of the concerts, reactions quickly became increasingly exuberant."

Gottlieb Bros. tour book for *The Classic Tales of Yes Tour*, 2003

"On this new album there are a few are quite a few sections which are quite horrific, it depends on the frame of mind you're in when you listen to it, but there's always the answer in the end. We play a heavy piece of music that is frightening, and at the end of that, give them a love song. just to ease their minds, just to make them go through a trip and then bring them back."

Jon Anderson, interviewed by Chris Welch, *Melody Maker*, 29th September, 1973

Newspaper headline, origin unknown, courtesy of David Watkinson Collection

"This LP – I know it's going to get slagged, and I know it'll get enjoyed. We just want to better ourselves musically, and learn more about what we are doing. The audience will have to learn with us."

Jon Anderson speaking to Chris Welch for *Melody Maker*, 4th August 1973, courtesy of Doug Curran

A vast amount has been written in reaction to *Tales* and its associated tour, at the time and subsequently. Rather than attempt to collate all the different viewpoints, which would be impossible, I have collected some of the more interesting articles and reviews I have found that I hope to give a flavour of the feedback the band received in 1973 and 1974.

Yes, they've done it again!

Melody Maker Tales preview headline from 22nd September 1973, courtesy of David Watkinson Collection

As the follow-up album to *Close to the Edge*, fans were hoping for another ground-breaking record. The initial signs were positive. Karl Dallas spoke to Eddie Offord as he emerged from another all-night session at Morgan studios, " ... barefoot and dressing-gowned, looking like a miniature Ghengis Khan ... " Dallas was reporting for the respected magazine Melody Maker, sold both in the UK and the US. Offord, according to Dallas very much a member of Yes, enthused about how good the album was sounding, with the newly-integrated Alan White. Offord also praised the sounds they were getting out of Rick Wakeman's revamped Double Mellotron, featuring new tapes and the ability to play both violins and cellos at the same time. He says the band were currently working on overdubs after spending four weeks recording, " ... the four basic tracks more of less live, with everyone playing and a rough vocal." Eddie says that the plan is to release the album in stereo first and then in a quadraphonic version later on. This never transpired.

> "Though this was a rough recording with many of the solos and all the vocals to be redone, it was a real revelation of what a cooking band Yes can be."
>
> Karl Dallas writing in *Melody Maker*, 22nd September 1973

He describes a 'serene, soaring guitar solo' from Steve Howe that reminds him of a solo on *Close to the Edge*, amid a 'mounting staircase of phrases'. He goes on to describe what he hears in an enthusiastic tone, even referring to a passage sounding like it was written by Lennon and McCartney at the height of their collaboration, but in no way derivative. Clearly talking about 'Ritual', Dallas praises what he calls the 'Aztec sequence' that features all the musicians except Rick Wakeman playing drums and ends the glowing preview with:

> "This is space music for the mind and body, the most head-blowing thing they have ever composed."

Imagine reading this in a music magazine as you wait for the new record from your favourite band. I think it would have whetted my appetite.

Once *Tales* was released, however, the critical reception was mixed.

In the UK, despite its glowing preview above from September 1973, one of Melody Maker's most high-profile critics and friend of Yes, Chris Welch, was rather more reserved in his review on 1st December. He had listened to the record several times and witnessed the press concert at The Rainbow Theatre at the end of the previous month (see chapter 20). The headline to his piece read, "Yes – Adrift on the Oceans." He feels the album is a 'fragmented masterpiece', "Brilliant in patches, but often taking far too long to make its various points, and curiously lacking in warmth or personal expression." Welch does admit that repeated listening to the album makes some of the themes more appealing than they appeared to be in concert. He goes on to describe some of the music as sounding like it comes from a great movie epic and a lot is 'cleverly conceived' but Steve Howe's guitar soloing seems to leave him cold and even the promise of 'Ritual' ends up being, " ... lost once more to the gods of drab self-indulgence." He is particularly concerned that Howe's guitar seems to have been given more prominence than the keyboards and the music album overall, " ... is more of a worry and test of endurance than a transport to delight." He does congratulate the band on setting themselves such high standards but wishes they would make it easy on themselves. As someone who knows the band well, he is clearly missing the more 'basic' music of their earlier career.

Unconventional & arresting
Yes' new album: "Finest marriage of rock & classical"

Tales review from *The Scene* magazine, courtesy of Doug Curran

A more positive reaction is received from some critics in the US. In his review for The Scene magazine, Mark Kmetzko makes the point that Yes have amassed such a following in the US that any record they release is bound to be a bestseller. This, he says, is why they can afford to deliver an album he regards as, " ... so unconventional (for a rock band) ... " He urges the band not to worry about the album's reception because he thinks *Tales* is, " ... for the most part a beautiful and arresting piece of music." He recognises that the new album represents a continuation of and a progression from *Close to the Edge* and it is, as the headline reiterates, " ... the finest marriage of rock and classical musics to date." He does acknowledge that a lot of people will probably find the record boring as it contains few of the usual rock fireworks or constantly repeated melodies. Rather, he highlights the way the band alter and mutate the themes of *Tales* to access their full musical potential. This is a noteworthy comment, given the classical leanings of the arrangement of the music in *Tales* I mention in chapter 9. Kmetzko dislikes the way Anderson writes the lyrics seemingly so that only he will understand them but he says this is really not necessary to enjoy the album. He can treat Anderson's voice as another instrument and not worry about understanding the words. Interestingly, this reviewer favours the intricacies of sides 2 and 3 of *Tales* and ends his glowing review by expressing his sadness that this record will not receive the radio play it deserves due to its structure.

In a similar vein, here is another US review:

> **YES, "TALES FROM TOPOGRAPHIC OCEANS."** If you like Yes and want to hear this album, you'll probably have to buy it as this LP won't get much airplay. In this double-record set, each side contains one non-stop song and instrumental. This album is a total concept, taking eight months from beginning to end to develop. Guitarist Steve Howe is building an excellent 'comping' technique. In his style, *meaningless* guitar playing is omitted, but calling Yes a "group" is becoming *meaningless* as they are now an orchestra of professional stature. The Yes have imparted a positive *feel*, and their music casts no down moods. It's a positive search in the right direction toward universal music. While still containing an element of rock about their music, Yes is evolving a new mixture of many old musical idioms. Then again, like all groups, Yes have many boundaries to break, but unlike many groups, Yes have already broken quite a few. Yes' music ranges from acoustic to ultra-electronic, from classical to jazz, from mellow to exciting. Howe's solos are rare, but always brilliant. Atlantic, SD 2-908.

Howard P. Mosher *Tales* review, courtesy of Doug Curran

Doug Curran interviewed the band for the first time in 1975 for WBBY radio in Westerville, Ohio, which had an AOR (album-oriented rock) format at the time. He made sure he mentioned what he thought of *Tales*:

> DOUG: I have to ask you about the *Tales* album. I absolutely love it, it's a grand work.
>
> STEVE- Thank you, that's nice to hear, especially what was said after it came out! (laughs all around).
>
> DOUG: Jon, I've read that you and Steve wanted to expand on what you had done with *Close to the Edge*, and push the boundaries, to go over the edge, pun intended!
>
> JON: Yes, exactly. We were in a position where we weren't confined by anyone or anything. We thought of the 4 movements of a symphony, with the fourth including a finale. So after I read the book and gave it to Steve, we set about to work up a modern rock symphony of sorts.
>
> DOUG: Well, I think you succeeded quite well, even if Rick didn't see eye to eye on some of it.
>
> CHRIS: I think Rick was caught off guard by Jon & Steve bringing the basics to the rest of us, rather than the 5 of us creating the songs from scratch, as we usually did, with exceptions. And I think he felt that the keyboards weren't featured enough, at least as far as solos go.
>
> ALAN: I should say that Rick's solo on side 1 is fantastic, his work on side 2 is beautiful, the same on the others. Understated and the layering of sounds throughout.

DOUG: I must mention Roger's artwork, the painting, and the photos, the lyrics, the vinyl labels art, are just perfect complements to the music

CHRIS: Thanks. To me, this is Roger's best cover for us so far. The inside of *Close to the Edge* is marvellous, and should have been on the cover, but Roger did a wonderful job of incorporating all of our ideas into one total. We kept adding things for him.

PART 7 – TALES LIVE

"In classic Yes style, the band hit the road in support of *Tales From Topographic Oceans* more than a full month before the album was released, and proceeded to perform it in its entirety and in order, after first performing all of the *Close to the Edge* album before capping things off with 'Roundabout'.

 The immense and unfamiliar material left some fans and even former loyal press allies scrambling to keep up, but the album shipped gold on preorders alone, none-the-less. Once fans could actually hear the album ahead of the concerts, reactions quickly became increasingly exuberant."

Gottlieb Bros. tour book for *The Classic Tales of Yes Tour*, 2003

20

TALES ON TOUR IN 1973 AND 1974

"Do you know that, when we started, we used to play all *Close to the Edge* first, then all *Tales*? I mean, I don't know what we were thinking."

Steve Howe, Yes Music Podcast, 2025

Jon Anderson performing *Tales*, screenshot from 8mm film of the *Tales Tour* concert in Atlanta on 11th February 1974, courtesy of Ron Gerber Films and the Classic Rock Media Archive

RABBIT HOLE TALES – MAKERS OF MELODY

The 10th November 1973 edition of Melody Maker provides a fascinating contemporary snapshot of *Tales* and Yes. This copy of the iconic music magazine appeared 6 days before the start of the UK *Tales Tour*. As can be seen in the Yes *Tales* advertisement, even at that stage all dates were sold out. The advertisement includes the slightly mysterious notes that, "As there is no support at any of the concerts it is essential that all ticket holders are seated prior to the time of performance. Nobody will be admitted after the start of the performance." Classical music concerts may have insisted on this kind of behaviour but this was an unusual departure for rock music in the early 1970s.

The statement that a very limited number of tickets would be available each night clearly predates the 'SOLD OUT' addition and supports Gennaro Rippo's recollections of the quadraphonic sound system taking up a lot of space and the mixing desk setup often having to be positioned in the gallery of the fairly small UK venues. The spectacular auditory and visual production was to the detriment of venue capacity.

Roger Dean's co-ordination of album cover, scenery and merchandise is referenced in the message that official souvenirs will be available and fans

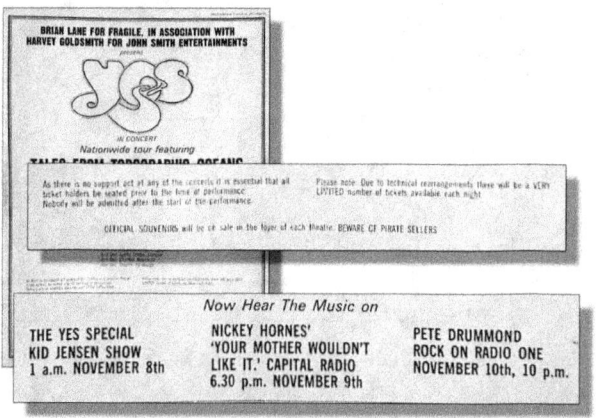

Melody Maker, 10th November 1973, author's collection

should beware of 'pirate sellers'. The bottom section highlights the fact that *Tales* wouldn't even be released for almost another month (7th December 1973). The three radio performances of the album are noted, evidence both of the stature of Yes after their previous album, *Close to the Edge*, and the financial backing afforded to this album by the record company and/or Brian Lane. I imagine it had more to do with Lane's persistence and music business contacts as well as the band's commercial and artistic success at that time.

Alongside this official Yes advertisement, the issue includes other tantalising snippets as well. The Black Sabbath album that Rick Wakeman played on during breaks from recording *Tales* (see chapter 4) is advertised, along with its own radio broadcast:

Melody Maker, 10th November 1973, author's collection

Elsewhere, *Tales* is also featured. Here is a small excerpt from a full-page advertisement from the Express Records Service:

HOT FROM THE PRESS

YES Tales from Topographic Ocean (2LP)	3.49	2.80
ALICE COOPER Muscle of Love	2.45	2.00
EMERSON LAKE AND PALMER Brain Salad Surgery	2.45	2.00
LINDA LEWIS Fathoms Deep	2.17	1.80
OSIBISA Happy Children	2.17	1.80
BACK DOOR Eighth Street Nites	2.17	1.80
PETERS AND LEE By Your Side	2.18	1.80
IAN CARR AND NUCLEUS Roots	2.38	1.95
THE ALEX HARVEY BAND Next	2.38	1.95

Melody Maker, 10th November 1973, author's collection

The other albums 'hot from the press' are an interesting selection, particularly *Brain Salad Surgery*, developed in the same building as *Tales* (see chapter 3).

Finally, there is an unintentional look into the future. Perhaps not a huge fan of *Tales*, music journalist Chris Welch is, however, very impressed with another brand-new band, Refugee. Fewer than 10 months later, Refugee keyboardist Patrick Moraz would be Rick Wakeman's replacement in Yes.

Welch points out the pedigree of Lee Jackson and Brian Davison who were members

Chris Welch's glowing article on the new band, Refugee, author's collection

> of The Nice alongside Keith Emerson, who left to form ELP and the exciting potential of Patrick Moraz, the " ... brilliant young keyboard player who has sailed in from the unknown." Moraz tells Welch that he has already played with such luminaries as legendary drummer Billy Cobham and earned an award for his film score at the Cannes Film Festival. Yes certainly spotted the keyboardist at least partly from his work in Refugee.

" ... [Eddie] noticed that I had stamina because I was at every night in the session. And I was ... accepted by the crew and the band."

Genarro Rippo, Yes Music Podcast, 2024

After he was involved in the Morgan Studios recording and mixing sessions (see chapter 4), Genarro Rippo went on to cement his position as Eddie Offord's right-hand man when he was invited by Eddie to go on the road with the band. His role was to mix the live sound for the vocals and the keyboards and to work the Revox tape machines. Tapes were needed for cues such as Stravinsky's 'Firebird' opening music, the church organ and bird sound for 'Close to the Edge' and various others. This was all coordinated on a brand-new mixing console designed by Eddie Offord himself for a company called MAVIS (Music Augmentation Voice & Instrument Systems Ltd.). Three of these P.A.S. 30/30 machines were made. One was used by ELP on the road, Eddie had another for his own use and the third was for hire. This equipment was being assembled while Yes were recording *Tales* and then, just a week before the first date, Eddie told Genarro that he would show him how to use it – and that he could be in charge of it on the forthcoming Yes *Tales Tour*.

The first job Genarro had to do was at the Yes equipment warehouse (see *Yes – The Tormato Story* for details). Phil Hepple took him along to work on the Yes sound system that they had bought from Iron Butterfly, after touring with them as a support act around Europe and the UK in 1971. This was the first 3-way system in the UK, featuring separate low, mid and high frequency units. Based on systems originally developed for use in cinemas, the setup weighed 500lbs. Iron Butterfly didn't want to pay the exorbitant freight costs to have it shipped back to the US after the tour, so Yes were the beneficiaries of the situation. It was only one of the several huge elements of their stage show that Yes did end up shipping to North America, despite knowing that its previous owners couldn't afford to do the same. Here it is being set up for a *Tales Tour* show on Monday 25th February 1974 in Montreal, Quebec. Note the trademark 'horns' on the top of the stacks for high frequencies (see p.276):

Phil Hepple's idea was to use this system at the back corners of the venues in combination with the front-of-house setup. This would create quadraphonic

Possibly Roy Clair on top of the speaker stack, photo courtesy of David Cohn[45]

sound for the *Tales Tour*. Phil also hired out the system to other bands in the UK and part of it can be seen in videos of T-Rex at Wembley. They used it for stage monitoring – it must have been fairly loud. The cabinets were so large, however, that sound engineers Clair Brothers later built smaller ones for use by Yes, but even then some UK venues were just too small for quad sound. Consequently, the aural experience was different depending on where you saw the *Tales Tour*. Genarro says that the quad setup was used mainly for effects, for example making the keyboard sound seem to spin around the room.

---

45 https://tormatobook.com/cohn

20 - TALES ON TOUR IN 1973 AND 1974

The lower part of the ex-Iron Butterfly/Yes 3-way sound system in use by T-Rex at Wembley, screenshot from the YouTube video[46] of the event

The opening concert of the 1973 *Tales Tour* was on 16th November 1973 at the Bournemouth Winter Gardens on the south coast of England. The original Victorian building on the site was similar to the Crystal Palace in London and was used for classical concerts until its demolition in 1935. Perhaps Jon Anderson felt a spiritual link to the site because the former auditorium hosted composers/conductors such as Edward Elgar, Hubert Parry, Gustav Holst and one of his personal favourites, Jean Sibelius. The replacement building, designed initially as a bowling centre and then converted into a concert venue, was used extensively in the 1960s and 70s by the popular bands of the time. Both The Beatles and The Rolling Stones played there in the early 60s and the early 70s saw top acts such as T Rex, Jimi Hendrix, Pink Floyd, Jethro Tull and King Crimson delighting fans. Other artists who played there the same year included Elton John, David Bowie and Wings. Yes themselves played there in 1971 on *The Yes Album Tour*. The venue closed in 2002 due to its comparatively low capacity, compared with other venues in the town, and was demolished in 2006. Most recently the area has been used for car parking while redevelopment plans are considered.

---

46 https://tormatobook.com/trex

The mixing desk set up and operated by Genarro Rippo for use on the *Tales Tour*, photo courtesy of Genarro Rippo

Genarro says that the mixing equipment was usually set up on the balcony of the venues on the UK *Tales Tour* and he also set up Mike Tait's equipment, which famously included double cigarette lighters in a very 1970s fashion. The balcony was chosen for the technical equipment to avoid disruption from audience members going to the bar during concerts when the back row of the stalls was used. The equipment was in 12 cases and Genarro remembers having to win over the crew hired by the promoter and persuade them to help cart everything upstairs.

During the concerts, Genarro would be sitting in the middle with Mike on the left and Eddie on his right. One of the reasons the equipment worked so well was because Eddie Offord was highly unusual in England at the time – he was a studio engineer and producer who also knew how to mix live sound. Genarro learnt a great deal from him and they rapidly became something of a dynamic duo for Yes with Genarro confirming his role as, " ... Eddie's bodyguard, student, studio manager, [and] equipment man."

20 – TALES ON TOUR IN 1973 AND 1974

The Rainbow Theatre in 1990, photo uploaded by https://cinematreasures.org/members/davidsimpson/photos Attribution 3.0 Unported (CC BY 3.0)

Another of the most memorable venues Yes played at on the UK touring circuit was The Rainbow Theatre in London. After four concerts in 1972 (including those captured for the live concert film and possibly the album, *Yessongs*), the band returned for a 5-night stint between 20th and 24th November 1973. They were the first rock band to achieve such a feat and tried to secure 2 additional

The Rainbow Theatre today, photo author's collection

nights at The Rainbow due to the demand for tickets. Unfortunately, the dates were not available.

Yes played *Tales* in its entirety alongside the whole of *Close to the Edge* and an encore. In fact, the day after this run of concerts, Rick Wakeman decided to leave the group, partly as a reaction to having to play the *Tales* material live. As Forgotten Yesterdays puts it –

> "Saturday, November 24, 1973 – Wakeman quits, but is convinced by the band, Brian Lane and Atlantic's Phil Carson to stick it out until the end of the remaining Tales tours."

Forgotten-Yesterdays.com

Originally a combined cinema and live entertainment venue called the Finsbury Park Astoria, Steve Howe told me The Rainbow wasn't far from where he lived as a child and he used to see films there fairly regularly. In fact, it was the source of his slight unease when in cinemas to this day. As child, he once found himself trapped in the Finsbury Park Astoria when it was closed. He now associates the smell of cinemas (presumably the cleaning chemicals or popcorn) with this scary childhood experience. However, Steve regards it as a fine venue and he played there many times, including with one of his earliest bands, Tomorrow. Proof of this can be seen in the Rainbow Theatre History's Facebook group[47] that includes a poster for concerts there in October 1967. The bands playing included Steve Howe in Tomorrow (featuring the in-vogue Keith West), Traffic, Vanilla Fudge (later cited by Yes as an influence), The Young Rascals (from the US) and Art.

The Rainbow developed a remarkable reputation during the 1960s and 70s. It was here that Jimi Hendrix first burned a guitar live in concert and where Frank Zappa was seriously injured when an audience member pushed him from the stage into the orchestra pit. That incident took place only two years before the *Tales Tour*. Zappa ended up with life changing injuries from the 12-foot fall and a sloped wooden cover was fitted over the pit which can be seen in many concert photos and videos taken at the venue.

Perhaps Yes were inspired in 1973 to 'go one better' than Pink Floyd, who had played 4 nights in a row the previous year. The list of important bands and artists who appeared at the venue from the 1950s until its closure for live music in 1981 is long. The Rainbow was eventually converted into a Church in 1988 and, a little unusually for the locations Yes used around this time, the building still stands and its stunning interior has been restored. This survival is primarily due to a preservation order it was given in the 1970s.

---

47 https://tormatobook.com/facebookrainbow

RABBIT HOLE TALES – AN ATMOSPHERIC RAINBOW

Most photographs of performances at The Rainbow and even films like Yessongs are understandably more focused on the bands than the venue. So unless you have been to The Rainbow yourself, you may be surprised by its amazing 'Atmospheric Theatre' style. Until I delved into the history of the building, I was unaware of this. The style is defined by the Historic Theatre Photos[48] website as follows:

> "The atmospheric theatre style was designed to evoke the sense of being transported to an exotic outdoor location. Far-away places were considered exotic and so in America that often meant European cities, places which most Americans would never have the chance to visit."

This aesthetic movement resulted in more than 150 venues created between 1920 and 1936 across the world. Before the Great Depression prompted more austere and streamlined designs, atmospheric theatres incorporated spectacular 3D Mediterranean or Spanish courtyard or garden settings. These were often decorated with lighting effects creating the appearance of moving clouds and stars. Perhaps Yes staging wizard Michael Tait was inspired by The Rainbow in his burgeoning career. Genarro says that Tait had to " … do some demolition work … " at this venue to make way for follow spots. I wonder if this had to be repaired in the restoration, years later.

Interior of The Rainbow Theatre in the mid 1970s, photo uploaded by https://cinematreasures.org/members/kenroe/photos Attribution 3.0 Unported (CC BY 3.0)

48 https://tormatobook.com/atmos

The Rainbow was designed in the 'Spanish Village' version of the atmospheric style, whereas other remaining UK examples include (using their current names) the Odeon, Streatham in 'Egyptian' style, the O2 Academy, Brixham in 'Italian Courtyard' style and Blackpool Winter Gardens' Spanish Hall in 'Andalusian Courtyard' style. A Chinese style also exists but what might seem like the most obvious example, the TCL Chinese Theater on the Hollywood Walk of Fame, is actually an example of 'Exotic Revival' architecture, according to the US National Register of Historic Places.

The entrance hall of The Rainbow Theatre today, photo author's collection

20 – TALES ON TOUR IN 1973 AND 1974

Yes playing the first night of five at The Rainbow Theatre, London, 20th November 1973 – note the sloped front of the stage, installed following Frank Zappa's fall, photo by Barry Plummer

Chris Welch[49] says that the Rainbow concerts were especially difficult. As mentioned previously, a strange notice appeared not far into the sold-out tour to warn audience members that they must be seated before the performance began and no-one would be admitted after the first notes had been played. As Welch says, this was more like the kind of crowd control you would expect at a performance of Wagner's *Ring Cycle*!

Apparently, it was cold backstage at The Rainbow and Anderson was irritated at having to play for mainly a music business audience. There were also some definite sources of friction between the band members (as always for Yes?) At the beginning of the tour, the rest of the band implored Anderson to stop mentioning God in his frequent introductions to the movements of *Tales*. In fact, the audience was very tolerant of Jon's somewhat spiritual approach. More troublesome, perhaps, were the musical disagreements. Calls for Anderson to play fewer instruments during *Tales* were dismissed by Howe. As he pointed out, there were expansive passages where there were no vocals. Howe asked the others, "What is he supposed to do, read a newspaper?" Brian Lane, Chris Squire and others also advocated for dropping side 3 of the album. As Chris said, "It really is a bit of a drag." Interestingly, 'The Ancient' ended up being performed 55 times in 1973 and 1974 but hasn't been played in its entirety since.

---
49 *Close to the Edge – The Story of Yes*

Of course, Genarro was at these gigs, working alongside the rest of the crew including Howe's guitar technician, Claude Johnson-Taylor, and Alan White's drum technician, Nu Nu Whiting. The friends were part of the load-in crew at The Rainbow. However, band setups weren't the only activity these workers were engaged in:

> " ... me and Claude and Nu Nu. We redid Brian Lane's house, the asphalt driveway."

Lane's role, recalls Genarro, was to 'encourage the band in anything they wanted'. Whether it was a Rolls Royce, a new flat, a blank chequebook for your wife to decorate the flat or whatever was desired. Of course, the money to pay for all this came from the band themselves and a major part of that income was from touring, even in the early 70s.

Genarro's living arrangements at this time also brought him into contact with the Yes setup. Originally staying in a Youth Hostel, Eddie Offord stepped in to help out.

> "After the rainbow shows on that tour, I stayed in the bed and breakfast across the street from the Rainbow Theatre. And when [Eddie] found out, he said, well, you can come live with me."

Eddie's father owned a furniture supply business in Vauxhall Bridge Road called Offco, which shared the building with one of the first mobile phone companies. The penthouse apartment on the fourth floor was where Eddie lived. Genarro moved into a bedroom there that had recently been vacated by Alan White, as confirmed by him in a 1976 Sounds magazine interview:

> "I was living with Eddie Offord, who was Yes' producer, in London, for about a year."

Not only was this a great place to live, it also became a Yes equipment store and workshop. Genarro set up all the equipment in the apartment and worked on it there.

Life on the road with Yes wasn't always plain sailing. Even though they were, at the time, one of the biggest touring bands in the world, their technical equipment wasn't always of the highest quality. I won't name the late Advision Studios engineer in the following story but, as you will hear, the quality of his work left a little to be desired. Apparently, he used metal tobacco tins as housing for the effects pedals he created:

> " ... he tried to make some effects pedals for Steve Howe ... and ... when I was taking down the console, I got it thrown at me ... he ruined a bunch of Steve's pedals ... [he] didn't have much luck making equip-

ment for Steve Howe."

There were also teething problems with the iconic and innovative Roger and Martyn Dean stage sets (see chapter 21).

> "Roger and his brother Martyn, they designed all the sets and then when they ... went to Bournemouth Winter Gardens, they realised that they had to cut the sets to get them into the auditorium, get them through the door ... And he learned that you can design a set, but you have to make sure when you take it on the road, how to pack it, and how to make sure it goes in the door."

Genarro was involved in the 'reconfiguration' of the sets on that first night but Adam Wildi, who had previously worked with ELP on tour, was entrusted with getting them roadworthy for the rest of the tour.

Despite issues with the stage sets, Roger Dean was always keen to get involved with whatever was going on, according to Gennaro:

> "Roger Dean helped me set up the consoles ... the first night of Bournemouth Winter Garden, we're loading in [and Roger] was so enthusiastic to be around. 'Yeah I'll help you, I'll give you a hand'. Yeah, he's a very nice man."

A Mander portable pipe organ – it's unclear whether this is Rick Wakeman's instrument, image source unknown, published in *The Musical Instruments of Progressive Rock* by Gerard Bassols

Another challenge for the team was Wakeman's Mander portable organ (see chapter 5), used for 'Close to the Edge' as well as *Tales*. This instrument had real pipes and was housed in two parts. Genarro and the team had to set the pipes element up in a room backstage due to its size. They then had to position microphones to feed the output back into the mixing desk. The connection between the two units was a 'snake' of 128-way multi-core control cables (one for each organ pipe!) This had to be run from the remote keyboard in Wakeman's rig, making the whole system very complex and time-consuming to set up. Eventually, the setup was simplified by Derek Dearden who developed a pre-midi electronic system that used only a single coaxial cable instead of the multiple leads (see *Yes – The Tormato Story* for details) but, for the moment, that was in the future.

As mentioned above, another innovator in the Yes camp was Michael Tait. Responsible for Howe's remarkable guitar tree and many other aspects of the staging of the *Tales Tour*, Mickey had gained an enviable reputation. He seemed to be able to turn his hand to anything practical that the band needed. As can be seen on *Yessongs*, one of the principal lighting techniques in those days was the follow spot. Amongst many other innovations, Tait was famous for developing a 'zip cord communication' system to keep all the follow spots working together. Like other members of the Yes team from that time, Michael developed into an industry-leader and performed a transition from lighting to staging after the success of the *Tormato Tour* circular, rotating stage (see *Yes – The Tormato Story*). The company he established in 1978 went on to become the dominant player in the live music and event staging industry. Now employing more than 2000 people globally, Tait (the company) has recently worked with artists such as Rhianna (Super Bowl halftime show), U2, Beyoncé (world tour), Taylor Swift (world tour), Ed Sheeran, Metallica and many others.

Michael has now retired from direct involvement in the company, but Yes continues to use the Tait Lititz facility to prepare for US tours, a practice established in the 1980s. Michael had chosen this location after his working situation in the UK had become problematic (in a similar fashion to Gennaro's). Called Tait Towers after the innovative lighting system he had designed, Lititz in Pennsylvania was chosen partly for its proximity to the home of Clair Brothers sound engineers, who also worked with Yes, including on the *Tales Tour*. Lititz is still a small, quiet town so the nearby massive rehearsal and production facilities are appropriately discrete for the world's biggest stars.

Originally, the plan was to record the audio from all the shows on the *Tales Tour*. Unfortunately, the tape machine they needed didn't arrive in time, and when it did finally appear, it wasn't configured correctly. Gennaro and Mike Phillips ended up rebuilding it and putting it into 3 cases. It was only ready to be used when Yes were preparing to record their next album, *Relayer*, so Eddie and Genarro took it to Chris Squire's house, New Pipers, in Virginia Water. It was finally used to record Patrick Moraz, White, Howe, Squire and Anderson, and Gennaro was there once again throughout the process.

> ### RABBIT HOLE TALES – AN ALTERNATIVE YES LOGO?
>
> One of Barry Plummer's photos of Yes in concert at The Rainbow Theatre reveals an intriguing set of what look like flight cases at the back of the stage, one white and one black. They have contrasting versions of a Yes logo I've never seen before, in a style influenced by the Art Deco movement of the early 20th Century. I asked Genarro Rippo about these and he said they were the two-part Leslie speaker set-up for Rick Wakeman's Hammond Organ, inside their flight cases. The usual practice was to position these off-stage, along with the pipe assembly of Rick's Mander portable organ but perhaps there wasn't sufficient space at The Rainbow.
>
>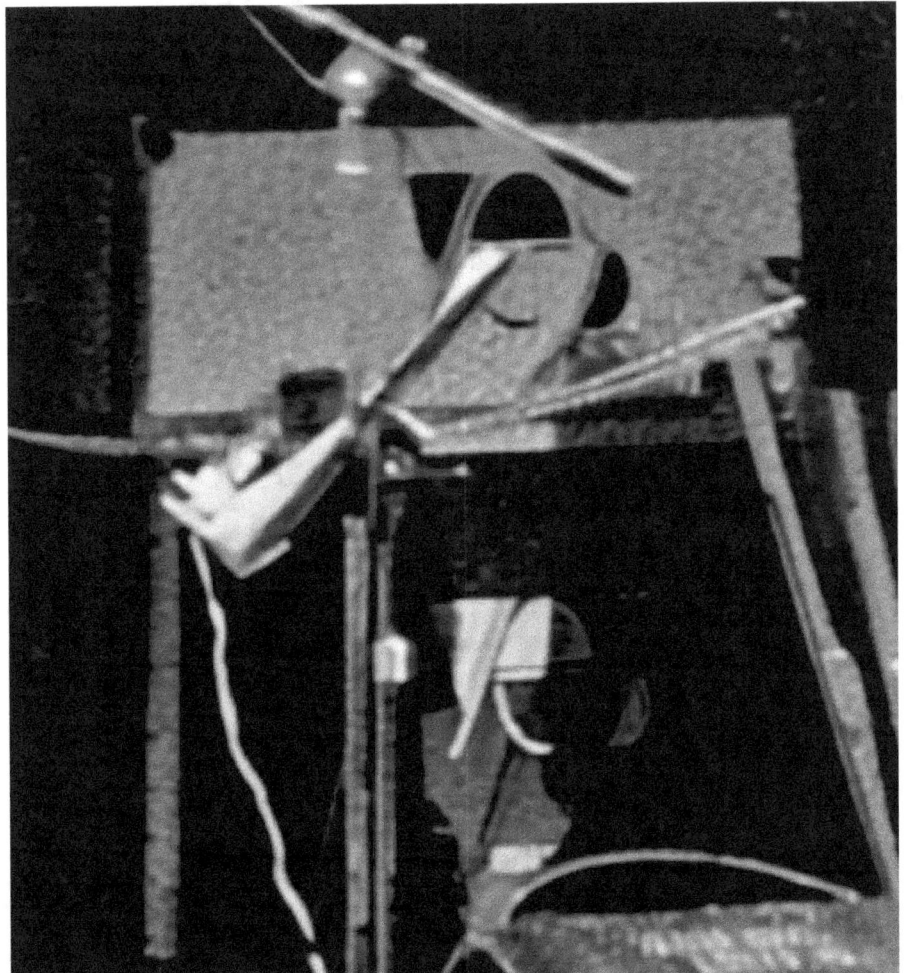
>
> Detail from a Barry Plummer photo of Yes performing at The Rainbow Theatre

In the same photo, just in front of Alan White's drums, is a small Roger Dean Yes logo, as used on the cover of *Tales*:

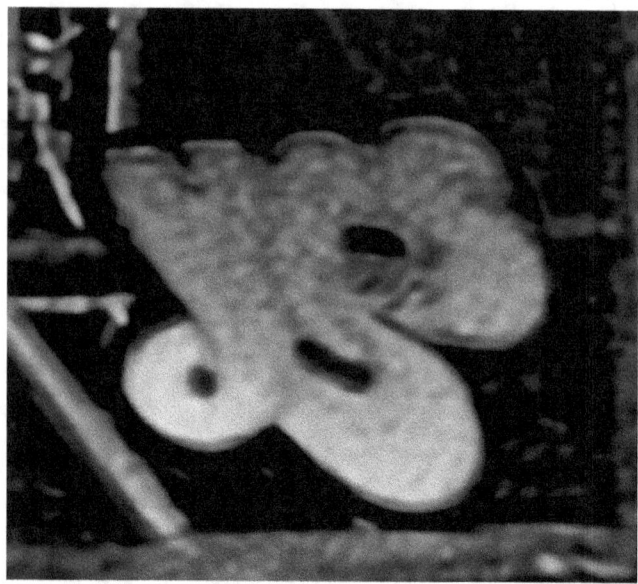

Detail from a Barry Plummer photo of Yes performing at The Rainbow Theatre

Subsequently, I spotted another example of the Art Deco style logo in a photo of the technical setup process at the Montreal Forum on 25th February 1974:

Right – Clair Brothers speaker system, left – Alan White flight case rotated and enlarged, photo courtesy of David Cohn

This logo is slightly reminiscent of the one used for the Madison Square Garden concert of 18th February 1974, below. Early Yes concert posters also used the art deco style.

Image courtesy of Doug Curran

One of the most important insights Genarro shared with the Yes Music Podcast was how the *Tales* album and tour changed the band. Everything seemed to be getting bigger. Roger and Martyn Dean's new set designs (see chapter 21) made the band's physical presence colossal, they (at least initially) played 4 sides of their latest double album as well as all of *Close to the Edge*, and the combination of Tait lights and staging with Clair Brothers sound increased the scale further. At the time, the UK still had relatively small venues, hence the issues accommodating the scenery, but, once the roadshow made it to the US, the era of Yes arena events truly took off. As Genarro pointed out, Michael Tait had the ability to handle that transition in his role as Production Manager.

> "I've never been exposed to so many groundbreaking creative people who later ... became major ... manufacturers of equipment, sound companies, everything. Yes, was a doorway to [the] Premier League."

Rick Wakeman, lost in the live moment, screenshot from 8mm film of the *Tales Tour* concert in Atlanta on 11th February 1974, courtesy of Ron Gerber Films and the Classic Rock Media Archive

The oft-referred-to 'difficulty' of performing (and/or listening to) sides 2 and 3 of *Tales* is reflected in the statistics collected on the amazing Forgotten Yesterdays website:

Side	1973/74 Tales Tour performances	Later performances	Total
1. THE REVEALING SCIENCE OF GOD - DANCE OF THE DAWN	53	172	225
2. THE REMEMBERING - HIGH THE MEMORY	30	3 (1976 only)	33
3. THE ANCIENT - GIANTS UNDER THE SUN	55	0	55
4. RITUAL - NOUS SOMME DU SOLEIL	56	290	346

On the *Tales Tour*, all sides were performed every night until 16th February 1974, a total of 22 times. The 16th February concert where the pattern was broken was the afternoon performance at the Spectrum Arena in Philadelphia, Pennsylvania. This huge venue had a capacity of 19,000 (The Rainbow Theatre had a capacity of 2,500) and yet Yes were able to schedule both an afternoon and evening performance on the *Tales Tour*. Philadelphia is rightly known as Yes' home in the US. It seems that technical problems meant that the afternoon concert had to be cut short and so, in a foreshadowing of what was to come, sides 2 and 3 of *Tales* were omitted. The evening concert featured all four sides of the album once again, as did the next eight concerts, including the two showcase performances at one of the most famous venues in the world, Madison Square Garden in New York City.

Transportation problems caused issues several times on this *Tales North American Tour*. The next time a show had to be shortened was on 27th February 1974 at The Cobo Arena in Detroit. The distances involved between venues in the US and Canada are difficult for those of us who live in the UK to comprehend. The *Tales Tour* required a fleet of huge articulated lorries to transport the equipment and the schedule was punishing, with often only a day between shows. For example, stop 41 of the tour was in San Diego at the San Diego Sports Arena on 21st February 1974, and stop 42 was in San Antonio at the San Antonio Civic Centre on 23rd. The distance between those two cities is 1,275 miles, according to today's online map apps, and the time it takes to travel between them in 2025 is 17 hr 52 min. Conditions were surely less favourable for the crews in 1974 so travelling was probably worse than these modern-day equivalents.

Just some of the dozens of flight cases required to transport Yes' equipment around North America, photo courtesy of David Cohn

As an example of the scale of transportation required, Yes fan Joey Wise has created a list of the gear in Alan White's *'Tales From Topographic Oceans Touring Drum Kit'*. (Adapted from the 1973 UK Tourbook and various interviews.)

Tales from Topographic Oceans - Yes album Listening Guide

All drums by Ludwig: 2 13" × 10" Toms 2 16" × 16" Floor Toms 14" x 5" Supraphonic Snare Drum (either 400 or concert) 22" × 14" Stainless Steel Kick	Gretsch 14" × 5" (likely not used on this tour, but he owned it at the time and it was given to him by Keith Moon)
14" × 6" Timbale	13" × 6" Timbale
Zlidiian 14" A (perhaps new beat) hi-hats	Zildjian 22" A (unknown) Crash Ride
2 zildjian 18" A (unknown) crashes	Paiste 20" 602 black label China
Wuhan 20" china	4 Dresden Tympanum - 23", 26", 29", 32"
1 Set Tubular Bells	1 Cymbal Tree
1 Tenor Pan Jamaican Steel Drum	Compacti Piano
24" × 16" Concert Bass Drum	5 Symphonic Gongs – 14", 20", 22", 24", 32"
Various found percussion including whistles, cowbells, pipes and shakers	Assorted splash and crash cymbals
1 Thunder sheet	Janco Vibraphone
2 African log drums	Fender Twin Reverb
Minimoog	1 Moog drum

Some of these instruments can be seen in these wonderful photos, taken by Barry Plummer at The Rainbow Theatre. I think I can see a set of crotales in addition to the above list (see facing page):

> " ... from my point of view ... it was like being on some kind of insane ... mad journey ... the manager was setting up gig after gig after gig. We did 10 nights on the road ... in a go, you know, doing stuff that nobody had done before. So ... the last thing I was thinking about was the art of it, frankly ... or the experiential element to it ... "
>
> Adam Wildi, Yes Music Podcast, 2025

Inevitably, the constant travelling caused problems, as noted by some fans:

> "The band arrived late and they were still constructing the set when we arrived. It was during the "gas crisis" days and I'm sure that travel was the problem. In any case, they pared down to only the last two sides of Topographic."
>
> classicyesfan on Forgotten Yesterdays[50]

---

50 https://tormatobook.com/classicyesfan

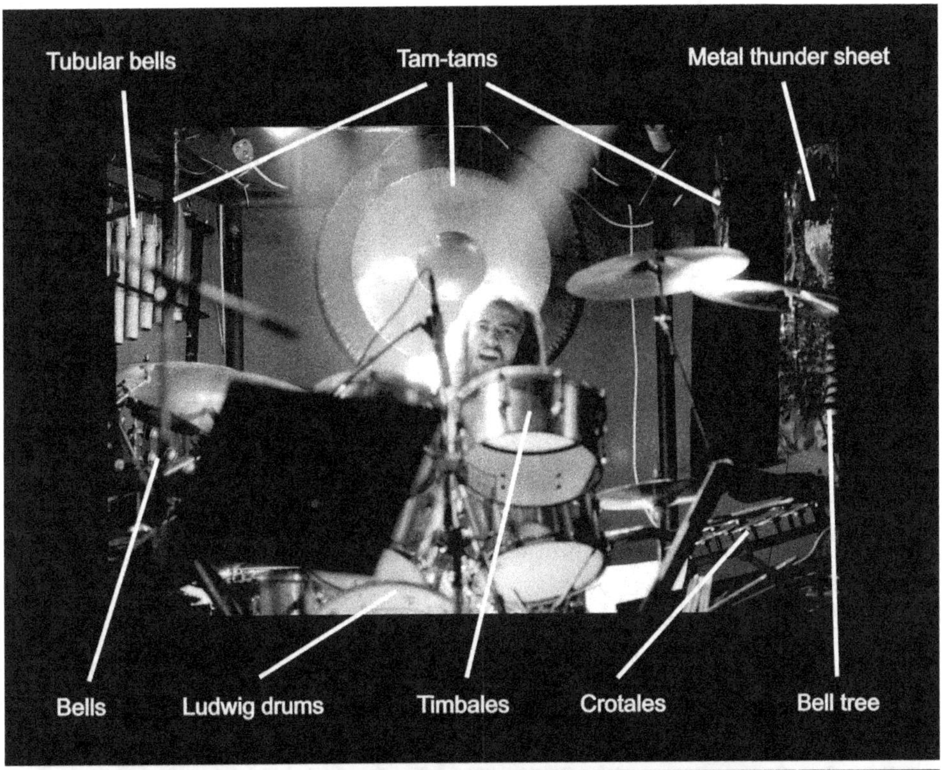

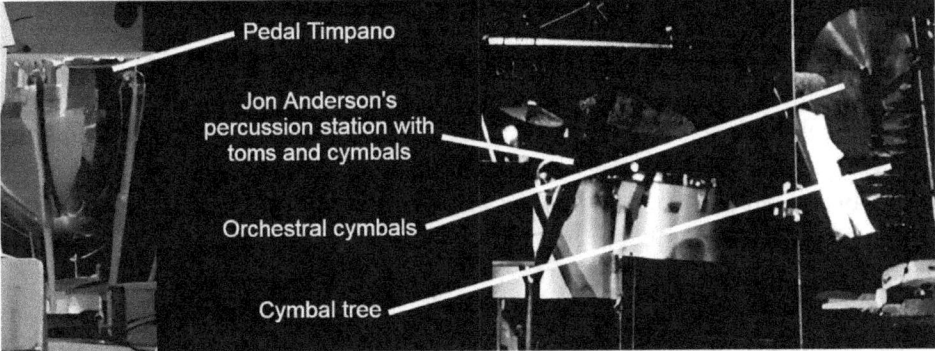

It is intriguing to see that sides 3 and 4 were played on 27th February in Detroit, especially when we consider what happened to side 3 as the tour went on. Once again, there was a second night at The Cobo Arena where all four sides were performed.

The problems that caused the next setlist change were, it seems, precipitated by the venue itself. Apparently, far too many tickets were sold for the 7,225 capacity of the Hersheypark Arena in Hershey, Pennsylvania:

"Yes played in Hershey, PA early March on the Tales tour that year. My first show. Overflow crowd caused a late start and the band only played the Ancient and Ritual."

Greg S on Forgotten Yesterdays[51]

So, the band again chose to leave out sides 1 and 2, as they did at their next show on 2nd March at Louisville Gardens. Unfortunately, the reasons behind the omissions at this venue are more difficult to discover.

Before the next time the band played, something had happened. The decision appears to have been made to permanently alter the setlist for the rest of the tour. From 3rd March 1974 at Cincinnati Gardens until the end of the European leg of the tour on 23rd April at Palazzo dello Sport in Rome, Italy, a total of 22 concerts, Yes did not play 'The Ancient – Giants Under the Sun' again. In fact, as mentioned above, side 3 of *Tales* has never been played since March 1974 in its original, full form.

The road transportation situation was in marked contrast to how the band travelled around North America. Steve Howe told me about their rather more comfortable arrangements:

> " ... it was fantastic because we decided that private jets were just the only way we could do this. ... what we could do was just go straight to where we needed to go because there were private [air]fields all across America. So ... preempting Concorde quite considerably, but ... this felt like Concorde to us."

This wasn't the first time the band had used a private jet. Apparently, there was an occasion when the band had to play a concert in Glasgow (Steve believes) and then be back in London the next day. They took a tiny Hansa jet that Steve describes as 'more like a military aircraft' and recalls that he and possibly some of the other band members were a little nervous about the flight, particularly as it took place after the concert, in the dead of night. He remembers taking off which felt like being propelled upwards by rockets. By the time of the *Tales Tour*, the experience was a lot more comfortable in Gulfstream jets. Steve says it was 'the lap of luxury'. Chris Squire and Steve were more than happy to sacrifice some of their income for the convenience and comfort of traversing North America in this way, even if some other band members were less keen. Steve remembers the shock of his first commercial flight on tour with Asia, a decade later. He really had been spoiled by the private jet experience with Yes and it was at this point that he decided to purchase a car for North American travel. Since the 1980s, he has always driven himself between venues on tour in the US and Canada, whenever possible, and tours are now scheduled to allow this.

---

51 https://tormatobook.com/gregG

20 - TALES ON TOUR IN 1973 AND 1974

I asked Adam Wildi what relationships were like between the band and the crew. He mentioned that the musicians often felt the crew were at fault for problems that cropped up. With hindsight, Adam is not surprised that the scale of concerts and the gruelling schedule caused some of the musicians to behave in less than an accommodating fashion. Alan White is singled out for his relaxed and friendly manner, but the pressure affected the others quite significantly. As Adam explained:

> "[The band] probably had all sorts of views about me, about Clive [Richardson], you know, because we couldn't always get it right. Sometimes things wouldn't work ... Sometimes the scenery wouldn't operate properly. You only had a limited amount of time to set up ... we were all under huge pressure from the management to run these shows day after day after day. They worked out that the maximum mileage they could do and still do one night was 500 miles. So we had a crew to set up the basics and then we would fly in and be the show crew and that's how we did it. But we'd do like 13, 14 nights in a row. We'd be dead at the end of that ... animosity would build up because of the tension and pressure of the whole thing ... I once had to get a car battery out to Mike's lighting ... 18,000 people all completely out of their heads ... he was marooned in a little, like a desert island in the middle of all these hippies ... and I'm carving a way through them with a car battery because his lighting desk is not working ... So no, we weren't a happy go lucky, join together band and crew."

In the US, the political and cultural situation also caused problems. Adam says it felt like the country was still rebounding from the Kennedy assassination, over a decade earlier:

> "The situation in the southern states was really bad with black people. [The local people] regarded us ... as kind of mad people with long hair and f*****g weird clothing, tight jeans, all that stuff ... in Little Rock, Arkansas, [on the *Relayer Tour* in 1975] they wouldn't let us turn out the lights. We had to cancel the show after they let the audience in ... these were high pressure situations."

Similarly to Gennaro, however, Adam now recognises what a huge achievement the *Tales Tour* was:

> "We were all ... really young. I mean, I've been in entertainment all my professional life. And I look back on that time thinking, Jesus Christ, what an achievement given what we were up against, particularly the equipment stuff."

21

THE SCENERY

"They came up with a glowing landscape that looked like the album cover come to life."

Chris Welch, Close to the Edge – The Yes Story

" ... we tried to choreograph an audio visual experience as opposed to just a rock show, you know ... it was pretty innovative in those days. It sounds like meat and potatoes now because everybody does it, but nobody was doing it then."

Adam Wildi, Yes Music Podcast, 2025

RABBIT HOLE TALES – APOCRYPHAL SCENERY ANECDOTES

In his book, *Grumpy Old Rock Star*, Rick Wakeman tells a story that I believe is apocryphal. He claims that Alan White became trapped inside the scenery at a show on the *Tales Tour* and was gasping for air in the air-tight structure. Given the design of the drum canopy, I can't see how this could have happened. When Wakeman goes on to describe the stage crew having to use pickaxes to prize the 'pod' open and a cheer going up from the crowd when he was finally released, I feel we have entered the domain of embellishment and exaggeration for comic effect. Rick is a master storyteller but I wonder how much the *Spinal Tap* film has become merged with his own memories over more than 5 decades.

Perhaps his anecdote about the fibreglass tunnel was more accurate. Apparently, the roadies hated it because it was very difficult to set up and pack away. They asked if the band could stop using it, but they refused because of the spectacular entrance it provided for the musicians – they could emerge from an internally-lit structure, only viewable by the audience in silhouette. Rick says the crew wreaked their revenge by positioning the tunnel one night to deposit the band at a door marked EXIT rather than onto the stage. Even if this didn't happen, it's a brilliant story.

Yes in concert at Newcastle City Hall on 8th or 9th December 1973 with the entrance tunnel at the top of the shot, image courtesy of David Watkinson Collection

"We're just trying to make it more theatrical, and this is what we're getting into. It's something we've talked about before for years. Roger Dean has designed the stage scenery, and he's just in the process of constructing it now and it will work in conjunction with each musician so that he'll have the space that he needs and rest of the space will be developed for the show. We'll try and take it everywhere on tour with us."

> Jon Anderson, interviewed by Chris Welch for *Melody Maker*, 29th September, 1973

With the *Tales from Topographic Oceans Tour*, Yes' stage setting took an enormous leap, thanks to the vision of Roger Dean and his brother, Martyn. It couldn't have been achieved, however, without the skill, dedication and ingenuity of a team of builders including Michael Tait, Adam Wildi, Clive Richardson, Felicity Youette and others.

Before the concert – a still from the YouTube compilation of 8mm films of the *Tales Tour*, by Duke Albert – see below

Previously, Yes tours had featured lighting setups designed and made by Michael Tait but practically no scenery. I asked Michael what he thought of the scenery for the *Tales Tour*. He said:

> "So the scenery, the fibreglass stuff, which was all very artistic. This was in the days when bands didn't take too much in the way of scenery. And it was not designed or built in a way to transport. … But we had to fight with that wretched fibreglass into trucks every night. It was a bitch. And everything was done on a shoestring. We didn't have a lot of money to spend on that. There was no money spent on packaging. You know, it was manpower that made that work. Eventually, technology caught up with the scenery. And that took a few years before people started designing stuff properly.
>
> We were one [of] the first to do that kind of scenery and put on that kind of show."

> Michael Tait, Yes Music Podcast, 2024

Yes biographer Chris Welch says that the huge scale of the scenery envisaged by Roger and Martyn Dean was partly to give the audience in massive US venues something to look at rather than trying to spot the tiny figures of the musicians from a quarter of a mile away. It was also deliberately designed to complement the music and co-ordinate with Roger's overall album artwork, advertising and merchandise plan. Martyn was inspired by stories of the massive amount of scenery and equipment carried around Europe by Richard Wagner in the nineteenth century to stage his operas – surely Yes could do something similar?

I was fascinated to find, however, that Alan White's drum canopy also had another use. Interviewed in an article uploaded to Forgotten Yesterdays, Alan says:

> "The reason I had it built was nothing to do with the stage set or anything, but because in America, with the different size of auditoriums, the acoustics affect the drum sound every night. It really used to hang me up, like I'd get on stage and because the people had come in, the drum sound I'd had in the afternoon had completely changed. So I had this kind of hood built over me so I'd get the same drum sound every night in every place I played. I've got my own acoustics, it's all miked up inside the hood which is made of fibreglass. And then, of course, Roger Dean got into it and designed this thing which opens up."

This makes a lot of sense to me because the photograph of Jon Anderson at the Manticore Studios rehearsals (see chapter 3) for *Tales* shows what looks like a canopy over the drums. This would have been a long time in advance of the Roger Dean scenery being designed and built:

Detail from a photo taken at Manticore Studios by Martyn J Adelman

Welch says that Roger Dean intended the scenery to be ambiguous, an approach favoured by surrealist artists. The curved shapes behind Rick Wakeman could have been interpreted as organ pipes or some kind of a plant and the beetle-like shape over the top of Alan White's drums that was lit up and opened during 'Ritual' was deliberately vague in conception. After the initial design work was complete, Roger's role was finished. He admits being frustrated by the lack of funding, despite the amazing results that were achieved. He says that some other bands at the same time were being given 100 times more money than his team were. Yes' record company didn't contribute at all, so it was left up to the band themselves and the tour promoters.

> " ... we were somewhat surprised when we got on the tour that we also seemed to be responsible for some very, very heavy fibreglass scenery designed by Roger who we'd never me. We were just hired as a lighting crew to put up some lights ..."
>
> Adam Wildi, Yes Music Podcast, 2025

As we heard from Genarro Rippo in chapter 20, there were many teething problems with the scenery, particularly its size. When they tried to use it in the smaller UK venues, it caused problems and ended up being completely rebuilt into a lighter, stronger format for the US leg of the *Tales Tour*. In fact, the scenery used on the UK leg of the tour was just the moulds for the final designs, according to Roger Dean himself, and a lot of the scenery wasn't used at all until the band reached the US.

> "And what was wrong with it was that they just treated them as sculptures. And so they were very heavy and tended to chip quite a lot ... technically speaking, we used ... the fibreglass sculptures that we had [in the UK] as moulds and made lighter-weight fibreglass structures from them and then packed them and took them to the States."
>
> Adam Wildi, Yes Music Podcast, 2025

Yes lighting engineer, electrician and Michael Tait's assistant Adam Wildi told me that the amazing lighting effects could only be installed inside the structures when the new hollow versions for the US tour were created. He worked with Michael Tait to create the effects. Michael had been dissatisfied with the exterior lighting on the UK tour.

Adam also told me that the transport arrangements for the scenery – and the rest of the kit – were also very different in the UK to North America. Band manager Brian Lane hired a set of removal vans (called moving vans in the US) that may have been owned by his brother or cousin and blankets were used to cushion the interiors. As Adam put it, " ... they were not very rock and roll." However, Tait used the initial UK tour to come to terms with the transportation requirements. It was all new to every member of the team.

> "Mike [Tait] was a bit slow to come on board with the scenery ... he wasn't sure whether it was going to catch on. He wasn't sure whether it was the right thing ... it didn't fit into his modus operandi ... it wasn't modular and it didn't fold up into a case and it didn't ... conform to his technical notions."
>
> Adam Wildi, Yes Music Podcast, 2025

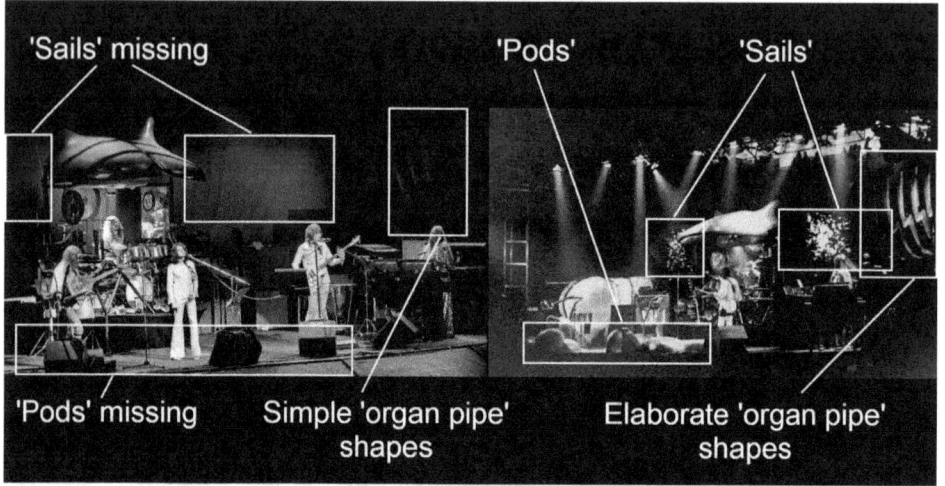

Left – the first night at The Rainbow, 20th November 1973, photo by Barry Plummer, right – 25th February 1974 Montreal Forum concert, photo courtesy of David Cohn

The image above right shows the full, rebuilt stage set in use in February 1974 at the Montreal Forum. The 'organ pipes' have a much more elaborate 'zig-zag' pattern than in the left-hand photo at the Rainbow the previous year. There are no 'sails' at the sides of Alan White's drum setup at The Rainbow whereas they can be seen in the Montreal shot, with starburst patterns projected onto them. Several different images were projected onto these sails at different points in the concerts – see chapter 16. Adam Wildi remembers the 'wings':

> "I think Gennaro reminded me about the insane butterfly wings we had on the drum setup ... with a mad Frenchman operating a series of projectors. It was completely weird ... I don't mean to demean him, but he didn't have a clue about ... touring or anything like that. He'd never been on a tour. He'd never been out of France. So he was quite out of his deck.
>
> But periodically we did have these projections in these wings. And really that first American *Topographic Oceans Tour*, it was a big deal because it was early days for audio visual shows ... You know, only the Floyd and us were doing it at that point."
>
> Adam Wildi, Yes Music Podcast, 2025

Small 'pods', like moulded rocks were used at the front of the stage in North America. They don't appear at The Rainbow but Peter Greenwood remembers them when he attended the Manchester Free Trade Hall shows (see chapter 22). Yes author David Watkinson recalls at least one of these pods outside Roger Dean's house in Brighton decades ago (see below).

On the far left of the Canadian photo above is the illuminated fibreglass tunnel through which the band entered the stage. It doesn't appear in-shot on the UK photos I have seen, but Peter Greenwood remembers seeing it at the concert he attended in Manchester – see chapter 22.

A photo uploaded to Forgotten Yesterdays by DRZK[52] showing both sides of the 'organ pipes' behind Rick Wakeman's setup and one of the 'pods' at the front of the stage

Another aspect Peter Greenwood remembers well is the drum canopy above Alan White opening during 'Ritual' to reveal an even stranger, illuminated shape inside. The effect was often enhanced (and sometimes practically hidden) by copious amounts of dry ice. Sadly, there is no known professional footage of the *Tales Tour* but a recent compilation of all the crowd-shot 8mm home movie film of the tour is now on YouTube[53], so at least we can get a rough idea of what that scarab beetle-like construction looked like during the tumultuous climax of 'Ritual'. Home movie camera technology was fairly basic and the very dark halls didn't help, of course.

---

52 https://tormatobook.com/DRZK
53 https://tormatobook.com/8mmtales

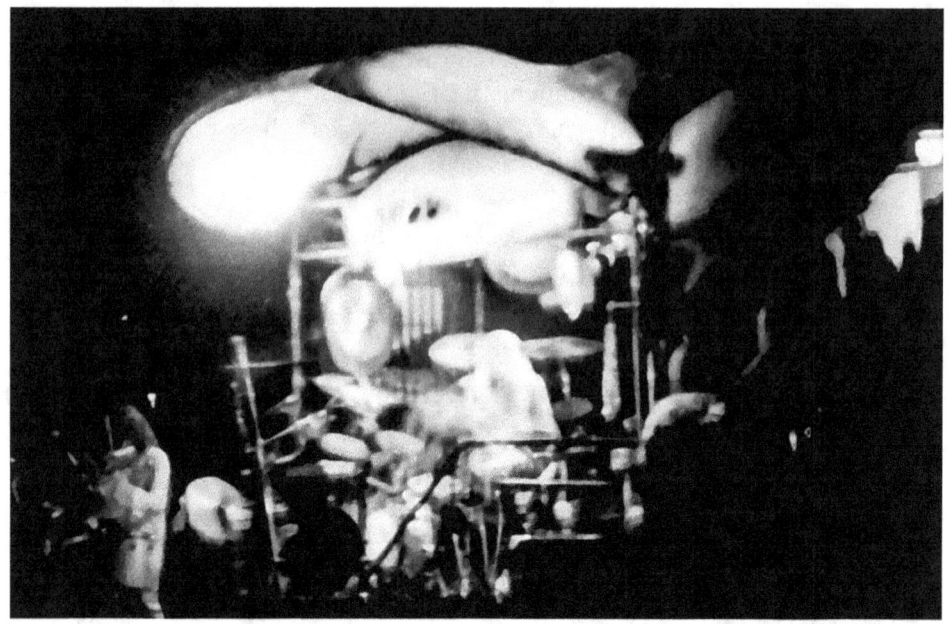

The canopy mid-opening, photo courtesy of David Cohn

"Roger had the idea of that shape and he said, 'oh, I want it to go like this', but he wouldn't know how to do that. So Martyn ... made that fibreglass stuff ... and then I made all the metal framework to hold it up and the mechanics to make it open and close."

Michael Tait, Yes Music Podcast, 2024

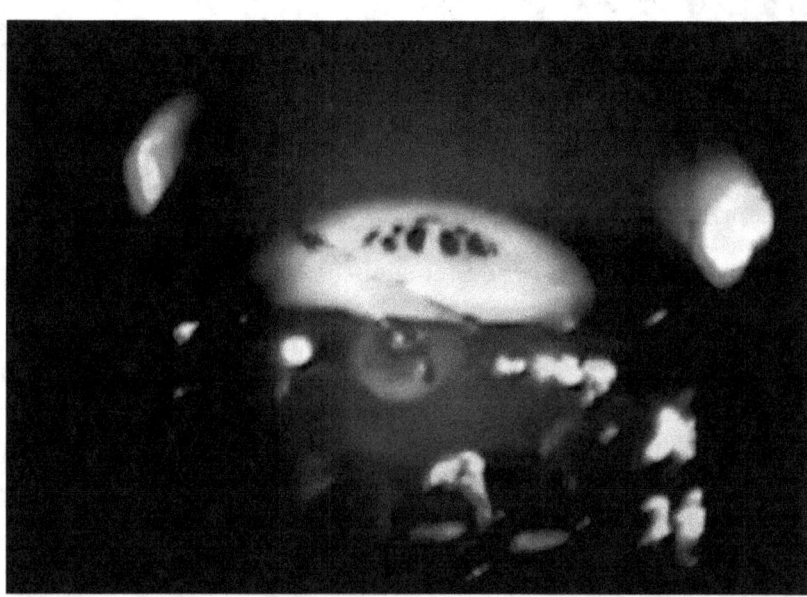

A rather blurry image of the canopy fully opened and illuminated, from the YouTube compilation of fan 8mm films of the *Tales Tour*, by Duke Albert

Professional footage does exist of 'Ritual' being played by the band, with Patrick Moraz replacing Rick Wakeman, on the 1974 *Relayer Tour* at the Queen's Park Rangers stadium. There is no way of proving this is the same drum canopy set up as was used on the *Tales Tour*, but perhaps it's reasonable to assume it is. Here we can see the beautifully painted underside of the canopy and the illuminated 'rock' beneath.

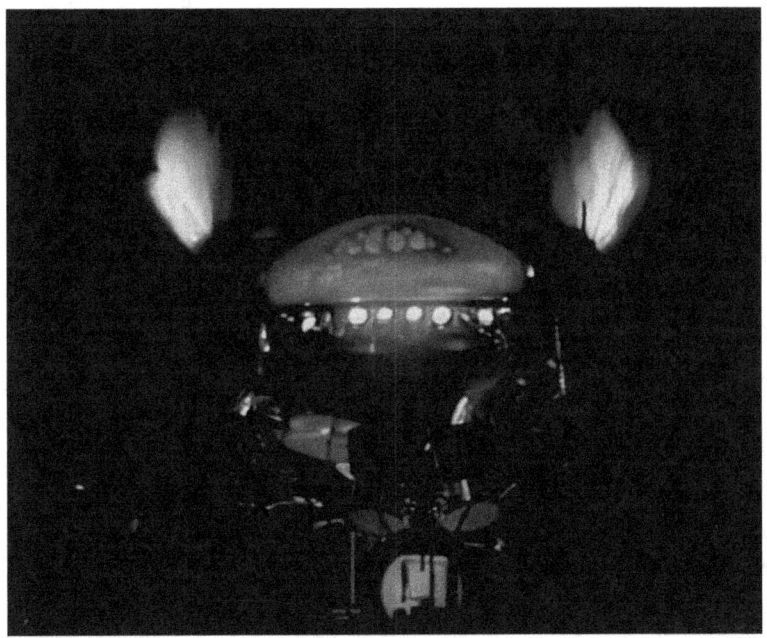

The drum canopy, a still from the Facebook video[54] of the 1974 *Relayer Tour* show at QPR by Bruno Samppa

You may be wondering what happened to the scenery after the tours were over. Yes author and expert David Watkinson recently reported on his quest to find out. It certainly hasn't been stored together:

" ... when I was living in Brighton in the 1980s [and remember] catching a glimpse of a front of stage light pod from the Tales From Topographic Oceans tour on the front lawn of Roger Dean's house, as it was then in Beaconsfield Villas. Just sitting there, larger than you think, dark green and a little worse for wear. It seems that storage was always an issue, so why not have it in the front garden?"

Yesworld.com article[55]

There have always been rumours that the scenery ended up 'in Alan White's lake' or 'somewhere in Wales' but, Dave reports, different parts of the iconic

---

54 https://tormatobook.com/facebookrelayer
55 https://tormatobook.com/davelost

Roger and Martyn Dean sets have turned up in London UK, Devon UK, Sussex UK and North America.

A number of different stage sets were reported to be in Chris Squire's garden when he lived at his dramatic house, New Pipers, in Virginia Waters, Surrey, UK. In addition, attendees at Alan White's wedding in Oxfordshire, UK in 1981 saw sets there. Subsequently, a dedicated Yes fan, Colin Ellaway, managed to persuade White and Squire to let him have a selection of Yes scenery. He put it all in his garden in Wales.

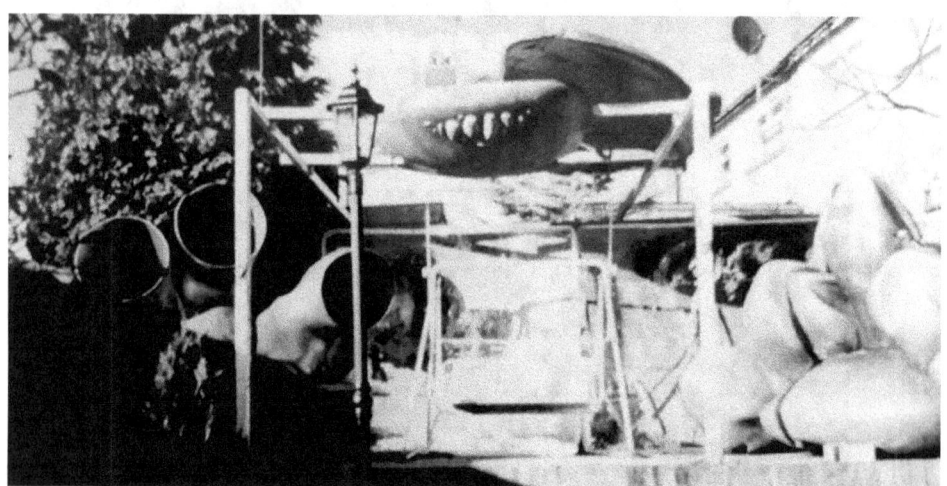

Parts of various Yes stage sets in Colin's garden circa. 1995, photo courtesy of Darren Allen/ David Watkinson Collection

The *Tales* elements in the photograph above appear to be the inner part of the drum canopy (mounted upside down) and one of the upper, 'beetle wing case' parts. In a post on one of the emerging social media platforms around 2001, Colin explained how he managed to illuminate the structures and create a magical atmosphere in his suburban garden. Interestingly, he refers to the drum canopy as consisting of 'lung fish' (the upper opening parts) and 'crab' (the lower part), complete with 'barnacles' that had fallen off and had to be re-attached. Unfortunately, he initially only had one of the 'lung fish' but claims that he went back to Alan White's house and eventually found its partner in the lake, in poor condition. Despite being told, "You must be mad," by Roger Dean, Colin treasured his stage set collection.

After a series of unexpected events, Colin had to leave his house and the whereabouts of the stage sets are now unknown. For more detail, see Dave's fascinating Yesworld.com article.

21 - THE SCENERY

Possibly the other 'lungfish' above the garden well, photo courtesy of Darren Allen/
Dave Watkinson Collection

22

TALES LIVE – A FAN'S VIEW

" ... they had the fibreglass tube ... that they walked through ... but Rick Wakeman came on, on my side of the stage and he got there first and then he's at the keyboards and then the guys came through the tunnel and he struck up with 'There's no business like show business' on the Hammond ... "

Peter Greenwood, Yes Music Podcast Episode 630

Pete playing with Alan White at the Cavern Club, Liverpool, photo courtesy of Peter Greenwood

In the early 1970s, Peter Greenwood was a regular concert-goer with his brother and friends in Manchester, North-West England. At the time, most pop and rock bands played at small venues such as universities, polytechnics and town halls. Pete was only a young teenager so had to rely on his older brother to help him get into the gigs he wanted to see. Amongst these were Yes concerts, beginning with 6th April 1971 on *The Yes Album Tour*, just a few days after the band had performed on the BBC's *Top of the Pops* weekly TV show. Sadly, the footage of that performance is lost. Yes played at Manchester's Free

Trade Hall on this tour, supported by Highly Inflammable, Lancaster and Jonathan Swift, all somewhat obscure bands today.

The Free Trade Hall in Manchester was an iconic venue where the pioneering Hallé Orchestra was based from 1858 until 1996, when it moved to another hall nearby. Its founder, Charles Hallé, was inspired by the belief that music should be for everyone and so his orchestra soon became central to culture and community in Manchester. The orchestra went on to perform premieres of music by great composers such as Berlioz, Elgar, Vaughan Williams and Mahler. After being requisitioned for the Second World War effort and then bombed, the Free Trade Hall was rebuilt and reopened in 1951. Pete remembers attending afternoon, illustrated concerts given by the Hallé Orchestra there under Sir John Barbirolli, as well as singing in choirs there when he was at the local Grammar School. Sadly, the Free Trade Hall was demolished in 2002 after the Hallé orchestra left and all that remains is the façade, now used as the entrance to a modern hotel.

Pete believes the venue held approximately 2,500 attendees in the 1970s. In common with a lot of northern cities like Leeds and Liverpool, Manchester had very little space for venues when the Free Trade Hall was built in 1853, so it's not surprising that it was small.

The remaining façade of the Free Trade Hall, Manchester, photo by Bernt Rostad[56], under Creative Commons Attribution 2.0 Generic license[57]

---

56 https://tormatobook.com/bernt
57 https://tormatobook.com/CC2gen

22 - TALES LIVE - A FAN'S VIEW

In 1973, Pete returned to the Free Trade Hall to attend both nights of the *Tales from Topographic Oceans Tour* on 28th and 29th November. *Tales* was released in the UK on 7th December. As pointed out by Pete, the only way to hear new music at that time was on the radio, where DJs like BBC Radio 1's John Peel piqued music fans' interests by showcasing up-and-coming artists (including Yes in 1969), as well as more established ones. According to various reports, the young Radio Luxembourg DJ David 'Kid' Jensen was intending to play *Tales* on 8th November 1973, but the tapes he received were inexplicably blank. The story was repeated by Jon Anderson in later years. Two more broadcasts did take place in early November, including on BBC Radio 1 and Pete may have heard one of those.

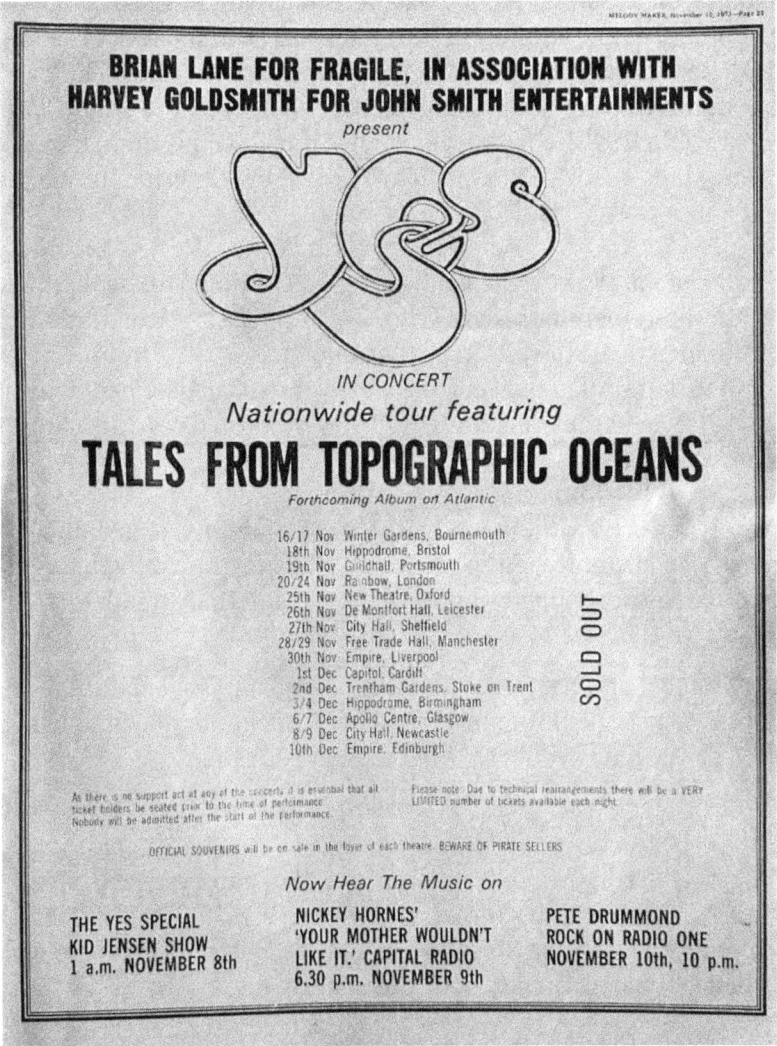

Advertisement from 10th November 1973 edition of *Melody Maker* including details of the radio broadcasts of *Tales*, photo author's collection

Nothing could have prepared him for what he was to hear and to witness at the Free Trade Hall, however.

> " ... when the lights started it was like, 'Oh my god, what's this?'"

Pete was on the front row and was puzzled by the little fibreglass pods over the bottom of the microphone stands, right in front of him. We know from Roger Dean (see chapter 21) that the stage set evolved over the tour with more elements being added but this does not appear to be consistent.

The Free Trade Hall boasted an impressive Wurlitzer pipe organ that was moved there from a cinema and Pete remembers a friend of his playing it, but the Roger Dean faux organ pipes above Rick Wakeman's keyboards made a powerful impression on him as well. Despite reading about the scenery in Melody Maker magazine, the visual effect of the pipes, the drum canopy, the microphone stand pods and the entrance tunnel made the whole scene seem 'otherworldly' to Pete. He had never seen a stage set this dramatic before, despite witnessing the early Pink Floyd live slideshow experiments and Emerson Lake and Palmer concerts.

Pete says the small stage at the venue seemed crammed full of equipment and scenery and he remembers vividly the lights pulsating around the pods and other stage elements. Despite the mind-blowing effects and electric atmosphere, uniformed staff kept everyone sitting down, as they had done at previous rock concerts in the Free Trade Hall – even those featuring bands like The Rolling Stones!

Pete had no idea if everything worked as it was intended to do but he certainly remembers the scarab-type top of the drum canopy opening up as the band played 'Ritual', as described by another Free Trade Hall attendee on Forgotten Yesterdays:

> "The two most abiding memories are of the drum solo in 'Ritual' and the drum cage rising into the air, and of Chris Squire playing the biggest acoustic bass guitar you have ever seen in your life."
>
> Geoff Horn on Forgotten Yesterdays[58]

Something that certainly didn't work as intended happened during the second song of the night, 'Heart of the Sunrise' from *Fragile*. Pete remembers Steve Howe running forward and his guitar lead flying out of its socket and whizzing past his head. The band had to start the song again.

Pete doesn't recall the quadraphonic sound system mentioned by Genarro Rippo (see chapter 20), so this may have been one of the occasions on which

---

58 https://tormatobook.com/geoffhorn

the venue was too small to accommodate it, but he does remember the excellent sound quality achieved by Yes. At other concerts he attended at the time, bands would often use what Pete refers to as 'souped-up guitar cabinets' as PA equipment whereas the sound from Yes' ex-Iron Butterfly system was crisp and clean. Just a few rows behind him, Pete could see Eddie Offord (and presumably also Genarro) at the live sound desk. After the show, Pete and about a dozen other fans gathered around the sound genius to compliment him on the quality of his work and to ask some questions. There were three reel-to-reel tape recorders set up as part of the system and Pete asked Eddie what they were for. He said one was to play the Stravinsky 'Firebird' opening music and one was to play in the 'incidental' music during 'Close to the Edge' and *Tales*. Apparently, they swapped from one to the other during the concert and changed the tapes, a bit like a cinema film projectionist would. Pete asked about the third tape recorder. Eddie responded that they were recording every show on the tour on that machine. He seemed to confirm that the band were hoping to put a live album together from the *Tales Tour* but, as we know, that never came about. Presumably, somewhere out there are dozens of reel-to-reel tapes of these concerts, including the ones Pete attended.

The widely-trailed music of *Tales* was introduced and explained by Jon Anderson and Pete recalls how quietly and respectfully the audience listened to all of it, including the softer parts.

> " ... as soon as you saw Steve getting his acoustic ready for 'Leaves of Green' ... you could hear a pin drop because people knew how good he was and wanted to hear what he was going to play."

Being a bass guitarist himself, Pete spent a lot of time watching Chris Squire and remembers him fiddling with his frock coat and seeming lost in deep concentration, ensuring his performance of this complex music was all it should be.

> " ... the concentration was pretty full-on, you could feel it coming off the band."

This included Rick Wakeman but, as the quotation at the beginning of this chapter reveals, he was still able to add some levity to proceedings. Apparently, Anderson's face was a picture. He didn't seem impressed by Wakeman's comic turn.

RABBIT HOLE TALES – CURRYGATE

Most Yes fans know the Rick Wakeman curry eating story and everyone probably has their own customised version of it they enjoy telling. In his book, *Grumpy Old Rock Star*, Rick recounts what he believes to be the real facts of the legend and (in contrast to some other stories in that book) it sounds pretty reliable to me.

The important aspect Wakeman clears up is that the incident sprang from a misunderstanding between him and his keyboard technician, not, as has been claimed since, from his own frustration with and disregard for his role in the band at the time.

The keyboard tech had to lie underneath Rick's Hammond organ during concerts because the setup was so complex and unreliable. He would be on-hand to fix anything that went wrong – as it often did. During a show at the Manchester Free Trade Hall, Rick thought the recumbent technician asked him if he wanted to go for a curry after the event. In fact, he was being asked if he wanted a curry right then! When asked what he wanted to order, Wakeman reeled off several items, assuming the tech was writing it down for later. In fact, half an hour later, during the next song, the aroma of fresh curry started to waft up from under the keyboards. Rick did indeed partake of the provided meal, but it wasn't his idea to eat during the performance.

Peter Greenwood was at both Manchester Free Trade Hall performances and does not recall the curry episode at all. Perhaps it wasn't quite as momentous at the time as it seems to have become since. Certainly, I don't think this story should be used to 'prove' Rick Wakeman's dissatisfaction with his role in the *Tales Tour* and in the band, as has been attempted by some commentators.

Pete playing with Yes tribute band Seyes at the Yes 50th Anniversary Fan Convention at the London Palladium in 2018, photo author's collection

23

TALES ON TOUR IN LATER YEARS

"'The Revealing Science of God' was one of many high points on the Topographic Drama tour when the band performed it in 2016. Jon Davison says his memories of that tour return to him on more of a deeply felt level, rather than a more visual, clearly defined type of memory playback. 'I've lately been reflecting on the fact that we have already performed much of Tales, but it all seems like a dream now,' he says. 'I reckon as the lofty nature of the music puts you in such a state, I don't really have any concrete memories of the experience. I get more emotional recollections.'"

The Gottlieb Bros.' tour book for *The Classic Tales of Yes Tour*, 2023

As noted in the previous chapter, since the *Tales Tour* of 1973–4, each side of the album has been performed in full, except side 3, 'The Ancient – Giants under the Sun'. The next Yes tour came surprisingly quickly in 1974, less than 7 months after the last *Tales Tour* concert. In the interim, Yes had lost Rick Wakeman, gained Patrick Moraz and recorded their next album, *Relayer*. They recorded this record at Chris Squire's house, New Pipers, using the equipment developed by Eddie Offord and operated by him and Gennaro Rippo. By anyone's standards, this was an amazing achievement.

On the *Tales Tour*, the band performed the whole of their previous album, *Close to the Edge*, and this pattern continued on the *Relayer Tour*, except that only one side of *Tales* was played – side 4, 'Ritual – Nous Sommes Du Soleil'. As the band's back catalogue expanded, clearly it would have been impossible to include all of their previous album this time and fans were no doubt keen to hear not only the already classic *Close to the Edge* material but also music from that latest, rather different album, *Relayer*. For me, 'Ritual' has always been a great live spectacle so it's unsurprising that this side was chosen to remain in the setlist for the next tour. It also meant that the animated stage setting could be used to accompany 'Ritual' again, with its moving drum canopy, dry ice and light show. In fact, the scenery for Patrick Moraz' keyboard station was re-designed in a more elaborate fashion than Rick Wakeman's. It can be seen lit up and moving in the *Relayer Tour* QPR video alongside what I think is Alan White's original *Tales*-era setup.

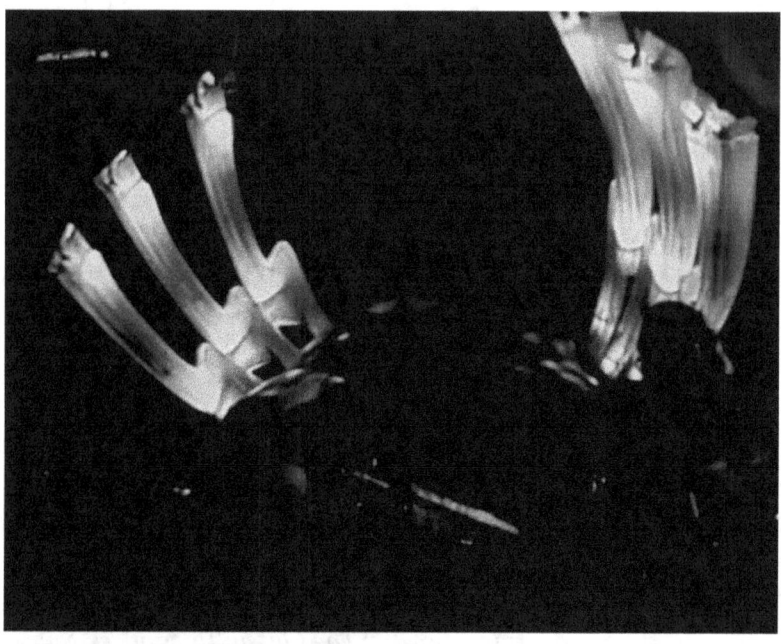

ABOVE: The rather more elaborate keyboard station developed for the *Relayer Tour*, a still from the Facebook video[59] of the 1974 *Relayer Tour* show at QPR by Bruno Samppa

LEFT: The Yes 50th Anniversary plaque in the basement of the former Lucky Horseshoe Café, London, photo author's collection

---

59 https://tormatobook.com/facebookrelayer

RABBIT HOLE TALES – TALES POSTER SUCCESS

Here is a lovely Rabbit Hole Tale from Yes fan, Ken Jonach:

I got back-stage passes for my girlfriend (now wife) and I at PNC Bank Arts Center in Holmdel, New Jersey on August 27, 2004. We had only known each other for short time, and she was still learning about Yes music and band members. After we briefly met the band for a picture, we were led into a much larger room with a sea of many, many more people. I handed Liz our 24x36 *Tales from Topographic Oceans* poster, and gave her the assignment to try to get it signed by the entire band, while I circulated separately. Jon was only able to stay for a short while, and when I looked for him a few minutes after we entered the room, he was gone.

I spotted Liz getting Alan White's autograph (he kissed her on the cheek for waiting patiently!). We both got Chris Squire's autograph at the same time and ended the evening having a really cool talk with Rick Wakeman about his *Return to the Centre of the Earth* album. Everyone in the band was really nice. When Liz unrolled the *Tales* poster to show me the autographs, she beamed and told me she got them all! As Jon had left before the other band members, I'll admit I had my doubts that she had indeed got all 5 autographs on the poster. As the stunning Roger Dean artwork on the *Tales from Topographic Oceans* poster was revealed, I saw the signatures of

The fully-signed poster, image courtesy of Ken Jonach

Alan, Chris, Steve, Rick... and Jon! Liz told me she happened to go to Jon Anderson first to get his autograph! It was a happy ending to a very memorable night!"

24

LIVE TALES BY GEOFF BAILIE

Prog Report stalwart Geoff Bailie kindly agreed to add his thoughts, research and insights on the whole area of *Tales'* live outings. Here is his absorbing take on the subject:

Live Tales
by
Geoff Bailie

As a reader of this book, I'm sure you will know the unusual, perhaps unique place, that *TFTO* has in the Yes canon. At the time of writing, Yes are touring the UK and are playing an 18-20 minute Tales medley featuring excerpts which have not been heard live for many years. But that was not always the way, as the *Tales* live timeline shows. Let's go on that journey.

The live debuts

We begin on 16 November 1973 in Bournemouth, England with the band embarking on their *Tales Tour*. The world of music and touring was very different then, and yet one must assume that the Yesfans of the day had no problem with a live show that featured (only) the band's last album, *Close To The Edge*, plus 'Roundabout', 'Heart of the Sunrise' and 80 or so minutes of music from the album that they would release 3 or 4 weeks later on 7 December 1973. Taking studio versions as a guide, that's 140 minutes of music, never mind between song chatter, of which 80 minutes was brand new to the ears of the listeners, unless they had tuned into BBC Radio's broadcast of the album on 1st November. Maybe some fans were astute enough to capture that broadcast on tape of some sort, to familiarise themselves, but my guess is that would have been very few.

I have to say that I admire Yes for doing this, but probably admire the audience members more! There aren't many reviews around from this first tour so it's hard to really know what the response was. I've listened to a few live shows from audience recordings from the era – this isn't like Bob Dylan going electric in 1966 where he was greeted with booing and cries of "Judas". By and large the audiences responded to the new material positively, in a similar way to which they respond to the rest of the music played. I wonder was there a sense of excitement at hearing something ahead of release? Remember back when Yes fans were open minded and excited by change? <wink!>

Yes in full flow, screenshot from 8mm film of the *Tales Tour* concert in Atlanta on 11th February 1974, courtesy of Ron Gerber Films and the Classic Rock Media Archive

Tales end...

So the band continued that tour playing the whole piece – but something had to give surely? Well after 44 full plays of all four sides, we had a casualty. The first shift was at the end of February 1974 and 'The Remembering' took a rest. It had 7 more plays during March 1974, before finally disappearing in Dallas on 25th. It didn't appear again until Patrick Moraz was in the band, and was part of the fluctuating early sets of the 1976 *Solo Albums Tour* on two occasions... but that was pretty much it until the excerpts included in the 2023/2024 medley. I suppose it's understandable that what is recognised as the most challenging part of the album (to play, to reproduce and maybe even to listen to!) should the first to be retired.

'The Remembering' did at least get another crack at a place in the set list in 1976, which unfortunately was not the case for 'The Ancient'. It did survive until the end of the *Topo Tour* but sadly made it no further. The Forgotten Yesterdays website tells us that 'The Ancient's 55 live appearances trump 'The Remembering's 35 but, of course, that's not the whole story – because of 'Leaves of Green'.

This little acoustic duet that is hidden in the chaos of The Ancient has lurked for many years, and appears with (on reviewing the stats) surprising frequency, whenever the Yes band includes Steve Howe and either Jon A or Jon D! Debuting in this reduced form at the Reading Festival in the UK in 1975, it popped up in 1976, 1977, 1979*, 1991, 1997*, 1998, 1999, 2000*, 2002*, 2010, 2011, 2012*, 2013, 2016*, 2017* and 2018* (appearing a significant number of times in the years marked *). At time of writing this "edit" has been played as many times as 'The Gates of Delirium', and if you factor in its inclusion as part of 'The Ancient' and the 2023/2024 *Tales* medley, it's close to being in the top 20 most performed YesSongs! (It's helped by the fact that some of those stats will include occasions where Steve has played it as part of his acoustic solo... which isn't technically 'Leaves of Green' in full!).

Next up is 'The Revealing'. A staple of the 1974 tour – how could a presentation of Tales open with anything else? Like 'The Ancient', it bowed out at the end of the 1974 tour and was completely absent until a surprising reappearance at the 1996 SLO shows that produced *Keys To Ascension*. I say surprising to reflect what I recall is my amazement at the time when, hearing that with Rick back in the band, 20+ minutes of the set being were given over to a song from an album he had spent many years saying he didn't enjoy! Rick spoke to the Notes From The Edge online fanzine about this at the time. Asked how he felt about playing 'The Revealing' at this show he said: "Actually of the four pieces as far as I'm concerned it's the most interesting piece to play and I didn't mind playing that ... the one thing I've accepted is that 'Revealing Science of God' and in fact the whole of *Topographic Oceans*, to a lot of people play an important part in their own personal Yes life. I certainly would not have played all four sides but I was happy to play the one side. I felt we actually played it better than we did on the original record." The 1996 performances are glorious and, as Rick says later in that interview, technology made the band much better equipped to play it.

Rick didn't remain in the band beyond those three shows in 1996, but 'The Revealing' outlasted him, and was a staple of the *Open Your Eyes* tour, brilliantly executed by Igor

> **A Revealing Story ...** I had the privilege of being able to attend the Yes 50th anniversary shows in the London Palladium. I went for the VIP experience and so had a fantastic seat in the first few rows. The gentleman beside me introduced himself as a French Yesfan who had made the trip to England especially for this show. I remember being blown away by the performance of 'The Revealing' this time – it's an exciting piece with many peaks and troughs. In one of the quieter movements I detected a strange noise and tried to figure what it was ... dodgy microphone ... PA issue ... ah ... no ... my French seat mate had fallen asleep and the peculiar sounds were him snoring!!! At least he woke for 'Nous Sommes Du Soleil' in his native tongue!

Khoroshev! It's funny really to think that of 250ish full performances of that song in Yes history, 70% of them were in 1996 or after! Rick was held to his 1996 expression of willingness to play it when he returned to the band, and the 2002 *Full Circle Tour* featured many performances. The track had another sabbatical until the *Topographic Drama* shows of 2016/17, with Davison, Sherwood and Downes plus Jay Schellen, and it carried on into the 2018 50th anniversary shows in Europe.

The performance 'Ritual'

I'm sure you'll realise that 'Ritual' is the most played *Topo* track in Yes live history. Like many of the songs from the album, its appearances have been sporadic and at times surprising. It lasted into the Moraz era, and was played at most of the *Relayer* shows and the *Solo Albums Tour* shows. As a result, it featured in the set list of the most attended YesShow of the 1970s, heard by the 100,000+ crowd at the JFK Stadium in Pennsylvania, PA. Its sabbatical commenced and after almost a quarter of a century it emerged as part of the *Masterworks Tour* of 2000, part of the 7 song set list, along with 'Leaves of Green'! Once again, Khoroshev showed he was up to the job of covering Wakeman's parts and adding his own spin on things. (I should say, set list research will often include the song as part of the *Open Your Eyes Tour* sets but of course this was really just Jon Anderson singing an excerpt of 'Nous Sommes …' with light backing.)

Having been reintroduced, 'Ritual' held its slot, and appeared in, perhaps, its finest incarnation during the *YesSymphonic Tour*. Supplemented by an orchestra, the track enjoyed glorious performances on this run of shows, and with full drama of the piece played out in the full sonic colours of the orchestra and band combination. I saw this tour in Dublin and, well, 'Close to the Edge', 'Gates', and 'Ritual' in one show with an orchestra – it was a mind blowing experience. Shout out also to Tom Brislin who made a brilliant contribution. In fact, I believe this makes 'Ritual' one of only six songs that each of Wakeman, Moraz, Khoroshev, Brislin and Downes have played live – am I right, fact fans? (The others are 'Starship Trooper', 'And You And I', 'Close to the Edge', 'I've Seen All Good People' and 'Roundabout'.) Another break and Rick and 'Ritual' were back in 2004 and a staple of the *35th Anniversary Tour*, brilliantly captured on *Songs for Tsongas*! 'Ritual' was back for the *Album Series* show along with 'The Revealing' in 2016/2017 and the 2018 *Yes50* shows.

The Live Albums

The first official live *Topo* track didn't arrive until 1980's *YesShows* when a 1976 version of 'Ritual' featuring Patrick Moraz was (unnecessarily?) split across side 3 and 4 of the album. But that isn't the earliest *Tales* live track that gained an official release. The 2016 reissue by the Panygeric label included –

on the Blu-ray Disc – a version of 'Ritual' from Zurich, Switzerland recorded in April 1974. We don't know anything much about the origins of this version – the booklet didn't reveal anything, but it does throw a few questions into the mix that I expect readers of this book would be interested in an answer to.

Are any more tracks available from this source? The show this recording is taken from was the penultimate show on the *Tales* touring schedule and therefore the penultimate show with Rick in band. Having toured this music for almost 6 months, I wonder was there a fear that it would go unrecorded and so a solution was put in place to record this show one way or another before the tour ended? The rough nature of the recording would suggest someone just ran the tape, and possibly that could have been instigated by Steve as it's a relatively guitar heavy mix. (I'm not suggesting any foul play – quite the reverse – i.e. if Steve had preserved a soundboard of, say, his monitor feed, then you'd expect the guitars to be up in the mix.)

Rick was back on the *Keys to Ascension* album, which captured one of the 3 performances of 'The Revealing' from his short stint back in 1996.

Finally, of semi-dubious origin, the *Yes Live In Philadelphia 1979* DVD also featured 'Leaves of Green' from 'The Ancient'.

The *Ladder Tour* 'Ritual' excerpt (all 59 seconds of it) appeared on the *House of Yes* album before the orchestral enhanced 28+ minute version featured on the *Symphonic Live* set. *Songs From Tsongas* caught 'Ritual' on that tour, the last tour on which it was played by its original writers and performers. Finally, the *Topographic Drama* live album brought together 'The Revealing', 'Leaves of Green' and 'Ritual' from the US tour. Here's hoping that the *Classic Tales of Yes Topo* medley is featured in a forthcoming release – who knows, by the time you read this, it may already have been!

TopoCovered Oceans

With the exception of specific Yes covers albums/tributes, Yes never were a band whose material received a significant amount of cover versions. I suppose that's understandable as the complexity of the music really didn't lend itself to easy reinterpretation, particularly when it comes to the songs from *Tales*! However, cover versions do exist if you allow me to slightly broaden the definition and include *Tales* tracks played by Yes members in a solo capacity.

The first such appearance is at what, for me, has always been an intriguing side bar in Yes history that is rarely mentioned or alluded to. July 1979 and the band have just completed the *Ten True Summers North American Tour*, which followed the *Tormato Tour*, on 30 June 1979. Less than three weeks later, Jon,

Rick and Steve all are performing at the world famous Montreux Jazz Festival in Switzerland... on the same day, the 19th July. Using the available unofficial recordings as guide, it appears that Rick and his regular solo band start the show with a selection of *Henry's Wives, Arthurian* excerpts and a bit of *Journey* plus a few other pieces. Jon is next up, but it would appear that Rick remains, joining him on some jams and improvisations and ... a version of 'Leaves of Green'! It sounds to me that Jon is on acoustic guitar and Rick is playing organ and keys. It's a nice if not very substantial version, and definitely lacks the classical guitar stylings of the artist who is taking the stage next, Steve Howe. Steve does join Jon and Rick on stage for some jamming before commencing his own solo set, but isn't featured on this song.

Of course, we know that Jon soon leaves the band, after the Paris sessions, records *Song of Seven* and is touring in his own right with a solo band by November 1980! That set list features a lot of solo songs, plus 'Future Times/Rejoice' and two Yes medleys which cover a number of songs each. Medley 2 features 'The Revealing', 'The Remembering' and 'Ritual', and it works very well. It's a brave move, at least through today's eyes.

Tales music began to appear in Jon's set lists when he set out in his truly solo shows from 2004 onwards. These regularly included a Piano Songs section where Jon accompanied himself on what I believe was a keyboard with some degree of pre-programming built in. As Jon cycled through chord patterns, he sang various song lyrics, and part of 'The Revealing' regularly featured – was it a version of 'The Revealing'... probably not, but it counts for these purposes. Contrast that with the regular inclusion of 'Nous Sommes du Soleil' on which Jon accompanied himself on acoustic guitar, giving a glimpse of how that song may have evolved originally. Shows in this format began in 2004 and were still happening 10 years later but the seismic shift came with the introduction of The Band Geeks.

A small diversion from those solo shows were the 2006, 2010 and 2011 Anderson/Wakeman shows. These shows were based around some new songs (which appear to be Jon adding vocals to Rick's piano improvisations) and some old favourites. In the early tours the same *Tales* moments ('Revealing' as part of the piano medley and 'Nous Sommes') featured in Jon's solo slots. In the 2011 shows, those evolved into a duet performance on acoustic guitar and piano which merged 'Nous Sommes' with 'Leaves of Green'. It's a nice version and always nice to hear Rick, in particular, adding a different spin to the *Tales* songs.

One notable performance of 'The Revealing' took place on a cruise liner as part of Progressive Nation at Sea in 2014. The first prog rock cruise kicked off with (solo) Jon as part of the lineup, but co-organiser and prog drummer extraordinaire Mike Portnoy (of Dream Theater, Neal Morse Band and a million other bands) managed to get Jon to agree to play with the band Transatlantic – a supergroup formed by Portnoy with Neal Morse (Spock's Beard, Flying Colors), Pete Trewawas from Marillion on bass and Roine Stolt from The Flower Kings on guitar. Despite their own notoriety, the band were delighted that their set to close the cruise would have a grand finale of being joined by Jon! You can imagine there must have been a certain... response when Jon's proposed set list included 'The Revealing', but a glimpse of some of the YouTube clips of this performance show that the band acquitted themselves extremely well. Portnoy has said when discussing the evening that it was a "really magical experience".

Anyway, on to The Bank Geeks... Starting life as a podcast, things evolved to the point where the musicians became a real YouTube band, with main man Richie Castellano at the heart of things. The Band Geeks' Yes covers regularly received kudos from Yes fandom and so when, in 2023, they hooked up with Jon Anderson for a short tour, many felt it was a match made in heaven! The first shows kicked off with a set list packed with Yes classics and playing 'Close To The Edge', 'Awaken' and 'Ritual' (oh, plus 8 other songs!) – breathtaking in the breadth of the set list, fans were hugely enthused by the musicianship and execution – and presumably so was Jon as he then hooked up with the band to record an album and tour some more! The Band Geeks' versions of 'Ritual' sizzle with energy and excitement, so the combination is perfect. It was a bit of a shame to learn that the JA/Band Geeks live album that came out in 2025 was from a later tour and so doesn't include 'Ritual'.

Asia Plays **Tales?**

In 1992, Steve Howe added some guitar to the *Aqua* album, the first release by the Geoff Downes/John Payne Asia line up. Steve then joined the band on some of their tour dates. The set list at those shows – and in some of the official bootlegs available on CD and streaming – does mention 'The Ancient'. While the prospect of the Payne-led Asia performing a track from *Tales* is intriguing, of course it's just an instrumental 'Leaves of Green' that Steve included in his solo spots during those shows. There's a pretty good audience version available on *Asia Live in Philadelphia* (also called *Live at the Stanley Theater* on some releases).

Steve's solo career as a touring artist really only kicked off in 1993/94, after the *Union* line up disbanded and he recorded *The Grand Scheme of Things* album. He toured completely solo, using occasional backing tracks and handling all of the vocals himself. Perhaps one of the most intriguing *Tales* versions, predating the 2023/24 medley is the 'Excerpts from Tales ...' that Howe played live and which appears on his *Not Necessarily Acoustic* album. It's a very clever abbreviation of the album's main themes played on nylon string guitar with Steve singing. He begins with the opening of 'The Revealing', into the main theme, before moving to a section of 'The Remembering', singing the first two verses, before switching to 'Leaves of Green' from 'The Ancient', again singing Jon's parts. Singing down an octave, Steve does a really great job with these songs, recognising that many of the ideas will have originated in Yes hotel rooms between Anderson and Howe and were presumably crafted on acoustic guitars. He neatly segues into 'Nous Sommes du Soleil' and again captures the essence of this complex music using one simple guitar and voice. If you haven't heard this one, it's definitely worth checking out.

The old favourite, 'Leaves of Green', appeared occasionally in the set lists of solo shows Steve played in Tokyo in 1995, a few times in 2000, once in Glasgow in 2004, a few times in the USA in 2006, and once in a show on the short *Homebrew 6* tour! Rarer than that, this tour also featured three solo performances of a section of 'The Remembering', similar to what was included in the 1993/94 medley, but a surprising inclusion, nevertheless. It also made a final appearance in the most recent solo Steve played at the Albany Empire in 2018!

And there must have been something in the air in 2018, because, in his solo piano show in Buenos Aires of all places, Rick played a Yes medley that began with an excerpt from 'Leaves of Green' before moving to 'Soon', 'The Meeting', 'And You And I' and 'Wonderous Stories'.

For the sake of completeness, and I haven't had the time or inclination to fully document it, excerpts from the bass solo from 'Ritual' have on occasion crop up in the Squire/White 'Whitefish' duet which was, in particular, a staple of the *90125*, *Big Generator* and *Union* tours. Largely based around 'The Fish', 'Tempus Fugit' and 'Soundchaser', on some occasions, I believe that moments from the 'Ritual' bass solo were slipped into the medley... but having scoured multiple versions of the track, I can't seem to find it! What I did find is that on the 1989 *Open Your Eyes Tour*, Alan White inserted a section of the 'Ritual' drum solo into the 'Whitefish' set, which may have been what prompted me!

One final mention should go to Circa: and the incredible 'Chronological Journey' track! For those of you who aren't familiar, on the first Circa: shows, the band, featuring Billy Sherwood, Tony Kaye, Alan White and Jimmy Haun played a 40 minute medley featuring excerpts of tracks from practically every Yes album recorded to that point in 2007. The *Topo* track that featured was an excerpt from 'Ritual' that allowed Billy to have a brief bass solo, and Alan to have a revisit of the drum solo from that track. It was a great moment to acknowledge this album and a foreshadowing of things to come!

Cover versions by others

I mentioned earlier, they are few and far between but they do exist …

'Revealing Science of God' by Adam Wakeman from Wonderous – A Tribute to Yes

This is a really interesting album with Adam on keys, with Rick's staple band members Lee Pomeroy on bass (and later to be member of ARW), Ant Glynne on guitar along with Richard Brook on drums. To begin such an album with 'Revealing' was a brave move. On vocals is Steve Overland, most famous as the singer of rock band FM. Steve is a great vocalist and I cannot fault his vocals on this challenging track. However, I am not convinced it fits with the style of the song – at times it's a bit like listening to Yes with Paul Rodgers or Rod Stewart on vocals which… isn't a thing! I should say that later in the album, Steve takes vocals on 'Owner of a Lonely Heart' altogether more successfully!

[Yes chronicler Henry Potts adds that De La Soul's 2004 piece, 'The Grind Date' samples 'Ritual' and Enigma's 1996's 'Morphing Thru Time' reportedly samples 'The Remembering'. Also, Mike Keneally (of Stanley Snail) quotes various Yes songs on his solo piece, 'Faithful Axe', including 'The Revealing Science of God'.]

Finally – Yes Covering Yes: The 2023/24 Tales Medley

While it had been publicised many times, lockdown/COVID-19 seemed to prevent the *Album Series Relayer* shows happening on so many occasions that the band decided to move on. With *Mirror to the Sky* recorded off the back of *The Quest*, I suspect that a *Relayer* tour would have overshadowed the new album/material. Thus, when the 2023 and 2024 *Classic Tales of Yes Tours* were launched, they were dressed in the artwork of the new album.

It seemed fitting that the 50th anniversary of *Tales* was acknowledged on the tour – having amply covered complete versions of 'The Revealing' and 'Ritual', plus 'Leaves of Green' in recent years, a repeat performance presumably didn't seem like a great idea… but then neither would covering 'The Remembering' and 'The Ancient' in full. In the 2023 American Tour Book, Jon Davison talks about the conundrum that the band has faced with *Tales* material – performing it in full would be, "at the expense of everything else you want to perform," or you ignore it. Howe seems to have been at the heart of the medley format and interviewed by Louder Sound called the arrangement, "my pride and joy at the moment". Interviewed by Ultimate Classic Rock he said, "In less than 20 minutes, you see four 20 minute tracks go rushing by you. It was great fun and I happen to like editing. I like working out how things can kind of fit together. It's been really delightful and lovely to play some of Side 2 again."

So, what's in there ... well I decided to complete some research to see exactly what is! My source is a YouTube video of the performance at Fox Performing Arts Center in Riverside, CA, dating from 4th November 2023. The version[60] I am using is posted by a YouTuber called "Steve" (how appropriate!) and lasts for 21 mins 24 secs. The medley has 13 sections in total, as follows:

0:00 – 0:35 – Steve's intro

0:35 – 2:27 – 'The Revealing' opening section "Dawn of the light…" covering verses 1,2,3 and 4 to "freedom of life everlasting". Drum break then jump cut to:

2:27 – 3:02 – The chorus section of 'Revealing' "What happened…" ending before the last "moment" to:

3:02 – 4:01 – the 10th verse section of 'Revealing' starting at "they move fast…" into the chorus of "Getting over overhanging trees…" then, skipping verse 11 we get to

4:01 – 4:25 – the instrumental section that precedes the "Skyline teacher" bridge section before a jump to:

4:25 – 5:09 – Part VI's chorus of "What happened …" through to "We must have waited all our lives…" without ending that section before shifting into:

5:09 – 5:54 – we are into 'The Remembering', and the third verse "I reach over…" into "Out in the city…" ending with a drum hit before:

5:54 – 7:21 – verse 5 of 'The Remembering' beginning with "Don the cap…" into verse 6 and the refrain ending "… to hold you" before a cymbal hit into…

7:21 – 8:05 – here the medley leaps to the "Relayer" section that follows Verse 8 and its chorus. The line about "sail the futile ears…" is omitted presumably to tighten up the section. The segue instrumental into verse 9 is then played, until…

[Interlude: What's very clever about this medley is how it makes use of reprises/refrains that are in the original pieces to make leaps across the songs. The Relayer section above is a good example of this because in the original piece, the section at Part 7 above goes straight into an earlier Relayer section, which has different lyrics. So, this jump skips 2 verses (Verse 7 "Like a dreamer…" and verse 8 "Things are all in colours") plus the repeat of the refrain "We will reach…".]

8:05 – 8:59 – Instead of going into verse 9, we skip to verse 10 "Ours entrance we surely…" through to the end. Steve takes a stool towards the end to jump into…

---

60 https://tormatobook.com/steveyoutube

8:59 – 13:37 – 'The Ancient' gets represented, perhaps not surprisingly, but possibly a bit disappointingly, by 'Leaves of Green'. The band leave the stage apart from Steve, with Jon and then Billy rejoining for the vocal section. What's slightly different here is that as Jon and Billy sing the wordless section, Steve is relieved of his guitar and gets up from his stool, with Geoff filling the final parts on piano, so that they can make a swift transition to...

13:37 – 15:50 The opening instrumental section of 'Ritual' begins this final section of the piece, with Side 4 receiving the largest chunk of time in the medley. It's effectively an abbreviated version of the first 4 minutes of 'Ritual' reducing it to 2 minutes with the removal of a few sections and repeats.

15:50 – 17:52 – With a nod between Jon and Steve we jump straight to the first "verse" of 'Ritual' from "Open doors...", through to the section where "Fight" is repeated three times. This then jumps to what follows the three times repeat of "the source", "Sent as we sing...". These jumps are very seamless, and are quite clever, condensing this part of the track from around 12 minutes to two – of course leaving out many elements, but yet it feels like a well-shaped section.

17:52 – 20:30 – We move to the main 'Nous Sommes Du Soleil' section starting at "Hold me...". It doesn't follow into the full musical ending of the piece, but brings things in at around about 20 minutes.

I know that this piece divided fan opinion (imagine that happening in Yes world). While I didn't get to see it live myself, I think it is a very good representation of the piece, if you take it for what it is. Because of the amount of *Tales* the recent Yes line ups have played, it is not 'bursting with unplayed in years' material – in fact, the parts from 'The Remembering' (2/3 minutes of the piece) are the only thing that hasn't been played, but I imagine from a band perspective this was largely like learning a new 20 minute epic and it definitely was worth the effort.

Here's what Steve told us on the Yes Music Podcast about the shortened version of *Tales*:

> "... I think this is a valid edit that we did because it does manage to portray many of the key parts of *Tales*. You certainly can't say that it *is Tales* in its true sense. No, it would have to be at least twice as long. But there again, then you get into 'why bother?' ... Part of the idea of doing it was to play it live, you know, whether or not ... WMG [Warner Music Group who now own the Yes back catalogue] ever think of adding this to the *Tales* box set, you know, as an alternative, which I don't think is a bad idea ... so it is another way of telling the story. And that's why I like it."

The fan reactions I have collected are mixed:

" ... I very much liked the idea of giving flavours of all 4 sides within an overall concert of many tracks from across their career. However, as I know the pieces so well, it did feel jarring when I was anticipating the next phrase or movement within a piece and it suddenly shifted to the next piece! It was definitely a case of leaving the listener (i.e. me) wanting more."

Simon Mara

"The performance is a pale copy, an emasculated version of music that deserves to be understood as a whole. It panders to those who blindly follow Rick's 'padding' comments without any effort to understand the structure of the pieces and how they fit together. The same people happily listen to rock songs which are verse/chorus/verse/chorus/solo/verse/chorus –repeat or fade. Now that is padding. How would lovers of classical music and literature react to the best bits of Mahler/Bruckner/Beethoven being cobbled together to make 'lite' versions or making a précis of a Jane Austen, or a Tolstoy novel."

David Perry

"I was at the Manchester show last year when they performed the Tales medley. It was beautiful and I wanted it to go on and on. I think it was put together very cleverly. Inevitably though, you want more. I wonder if, in future, they would consider performing, say, the whole of sides one and two. I know Steve has said that Jon Davison is particularly keen to perform side two. I'd certainly pay to see that!"

Pamela Firth

25

LIVE REVIEWS

" ... on most of that tour, I got better reviews than the band did. That tells you something. But the music, you know, eventually the kids got the music and it might have taken a few years, but eventually it was all accepted. But in the beginning, it really wasn't."

Michael Tait, Yes Music Podcast, 2024

Concert reviews of the *Tales Tour* were divided in a similar way to reactions to the album itself. With *Tales* being such a large part of the live experience in 1973 and 1974, reviewers were able to give their views on the new music as well as the performances. Some of the reviewers had not heard the album before attending the concert, of course, and this certainly contributed to their reactions – positive or negative.

Caroline Churcher had certainly not heard *Tales* before attending one of the two Bournemouth Winter Gardens dates on the tour. These were the first two dates on the UK tour and so the first 2 times *Tales* had been performed, on 16th and 17th November 1973. The album was released in the UK on 7th December. Perhaps she had a pre-release copy but it doesn't sound like it from her review:

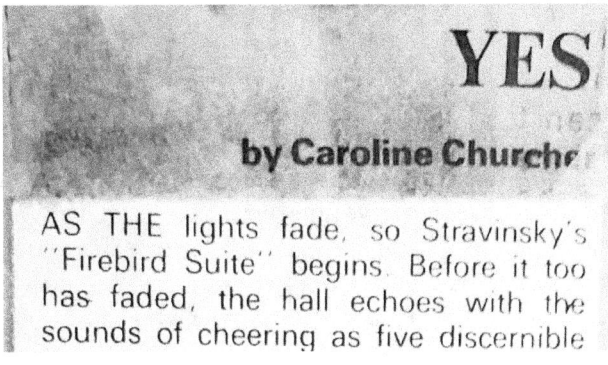

figures appear in the darkness on stage. And for the next three hours, the Winter Gardens at Bournemouth resounds to the music of Yes.

Verging on the classical, they devoted the first half of the concert to their best album to date "Close to the Edge". The album is great, but to hear it live is like hearing it for the first time.

But if that was good, the second half was quite exceptional.

Far from resting on their laurels, Yes have composed a symphony so unique that it will be no easy task to surpass it. "Tales from Topographic Oceans" (Jon Anderson's brainchild) is immaculate, and their performance was spellbinding. The intensity with which they executed the four movement work transferred itself to the audience, and after eighty minutes of music, Yes received well deserved appreciation. They did "Roundabout" for a loudly entreated encore. Special mention must go to Roger Dean for his incredible stage set, and Mike Tait for superb lighting.

Definitely "Concert of the Year" for me.

Caroline Churcher's review of the first or second time *Tales* was performed live, courtesy of David Watkinson Collection

As a direct contrast, the reviewer for the *UK Sounds* magazine, Steve Peacock's experience of the music at the specially-arranged press concert at The Rainbow Theatre (see chapter 20) goes under the heading 'Yes: Close to boredom' (see p.333):

" ... my response was fairly negative (I was bored stiff)," says Peacock, but he concedes that he should listen again before forming a proper impression. He also admits that *Close to the Edge* isn't his favourite Yes album and its rendition on this occasion seemed 'flat'. Perhaps a theme is emerging among the high profile UK rock journalists of the day. The direction of Yes post *Fragile* does not seem to have appealed to them, if Chris Welch (see chapter 19) and Peacock are typical. " ... [*Tales*] seemed so closely woven and densely textured that it had completely enslaved the musicians. I could feel no spark of personality coming through the music ... "

December 1, 1973

Yes: Close to boredom

YES — ESPECIALLY in more recent times — have never been a band to make music that you hear once and wander away whistling: so, to unveil a new 80 minute work in the very immediate surroundings of a Rainbow concert is a chancy business.

Steve Peacock writing in *Sounds* magazine following one of the concerts at The Rainbow Theatre, courtesy of David Watkinson Collection

So, 'concert of the year' for one reviewer and 'I was bored stiff' from the other.

Here are some fan reactions from the Forgotten Yesterdays website by concert-goers who attended Yes shows following the release of the album:

> "It was a great concert and parts are still engraved in my mind. The audience reaction to TFTO section was a bit muted, in my recollection, it was only recently released and was a challenge if you had not listened to the LP beforehand (luckily I had owned this for 2 days)."
>
> 'Apr71' recalling the 10th December 1973 concert at the Empire Theatre, Edinburgh

> "[The audience] sounded kinda bored during the *Close To The Edge* material! (especially during the 'I get up I get down' part on CTTE itself) and went nuts during the *Tales* part. In fact when Anderson announced that they were going to play the entire *Tales* album people started screaming like a bunch of drunk rednecks that were just told the next song was 'Freebird'. ;-)"
>
> Pete Whipple describing his experience at the 9th February 1974 concert at the Tampa Stadium, Florida

"We were very familiar with *Tales* after its release that fall, and were really impressed at how well it was performed. The musicianship was almost unfathomable to me. I had never witnessed guys who could play this well."

> Mark Brown reflects on his trip to the Georgia Tech Coliseum in Atlanta, Georgia on 11th February, 1974

" ... I was in heaven – not only was I getting to hear the entire album live (I had received it for Christmas and so had had seven weeks to learn it) but I was sitting about ten chairs from Eddie Offord; once he got the sound locked in to his satisfaction, it was like I was wearing headphones (to the extent that Rick let out one piercing sustained note that seemed to enter my left ear and exit my right)."

> Jeff Smith recounting his experiences at Baltimore Civic Centre, Maryland on 13th February, 1974

"I am one of the lucky (unlucky??) ones who saw them the day after Tales was released. It was a very silent audience in Newcastle, even at that time Rick looked bored, and had to be encouraged by Jon to play "something fun" for the audience – a police siren.....The crowd were pretty deflated at the end and the band knew it, Jon said for the encore they would play something that we could all dance and singalong too!! (Roundabout)...but the general comments on leaving were 'what was that all about??'"

> Steven English reflecting on his live *Tales* experiences on 8th or 9th December 1973 at Newcastle City Hall, UK

Regardless of the reaction to *Tales*, there was time to celebrate its sales (see facing page):

RABBIT HOLE TALES – TIME TRAVELLER?

You may have wondered about the sweatshirt worn by Claude Nobs in the photo above. He appears to be promoting a recorded music format that didn't exist in 1974. The first commercial Compact Disc was produced in 1980. However, despite the temptation to jump to a conspiracy theory conclusion, the logo on his shirt actually refers to the Compatible Discrete 4 format, introduced in 1972. It was a short-lived quadraphonic system for vinyl records, used by Atlantic amongst other labels. As Eddie Offord mentioned (see chapter 19), *Tales* was originally supposed to be released in quadraphonic format following the stereo version and a lot of the concerts on the *Tales Tour* used a quadraphonic sound system.

25 – LIVE REVIEWS

A PARTY FOR THE YES. Atlantic Records group is hosted during stay in Zurich, where they received gold record for "Yessongs" and "Tales from Topographic Oceans." From left are Allan White, Eddy Offerd (sound engineer), John Anderson, Hans-Ueli Hasler, WEA promotion manager, Claude Nobs (European coordinator), Chris Squire, kneeling.

Billboard Magazine from April 1974, courtesy of Doug Curran

A quadraphonic vinyl version of *Tales* would have been amazing. It is surely the perfect album to enjoy in a surround sound experience and maybe the Steven Wilson Dolby Surround Sound remix gives us a taste of what could have been done. I wonder if one of the reasons it didn't originally receive the quadraphonic treatment was because of the CD-4's reputation for being very difficult to set up on consumer equipment.

> "When played on a regular stereo, these discs sound normal (hence compatible), but to hear the quad separation, the signal must be demodulated. If setup correctly, it is a viable format that outperforms matrixed recordings and can still be enjoyed today. If it's setup poorly, it can sound brittle and distorted earning the name 'sandpaper quad'."
>
> 'Tab' on 4channelsound.com[61]

> "BTW, remember CD-4? That was a real joke. The Shibata styli wore out quickly, and the HF FM component on the LP wore out too, so one got "sandpaper" quad very quickly. The first dozen or so playthroughs were glorious, then garbage set in. This was because the

---

[61] https://tormatobook.com/tab

cartridge compliance wasn't high enough to follow the high-velocity ultrasonic track precisely, and wore out the HF info there fast. Then, the CD-4 matrix that was supposed to extract the four discrete channels couldn't reconstitute it accurately. That problem never affected the phase matrices SQ and QS, but they traded discreteness for durability."

Helge Skjeveland on 4channelsound.com

26
TOUR BOOKS/PROGRAMMES

Unofficial programme from UK *Tales Tour*, 1973, uploaded to Forgotten Yesterdays by Brian Neeson

Despite Roger Dean's best intentions, unofficial programmes were still created and presumably sold outside venues on the 1973 UK *Tales Tour*. Assuming this one is typical, the quality was pretty basic.

By contrast, the official Souvenir Programme was beautifully produced (see p.338). The simple, black cover was die cut to reveal the iconic Yes logo on the first page within, creating a dramatic effect. It's interesting to note the original Roger Dean *Fragile* logo on the first page.

Six pages out of the interior twelve are filled with photographs of the band (see p.338). Intriguingly, every band member apart from Chris Squire is given two different photos. Perhaps Chris was too late for the official photo session. His repeated shot was taken in the garden of his New Pipers home and

Tales from Topographic Oceans - Yes album Listening Guide

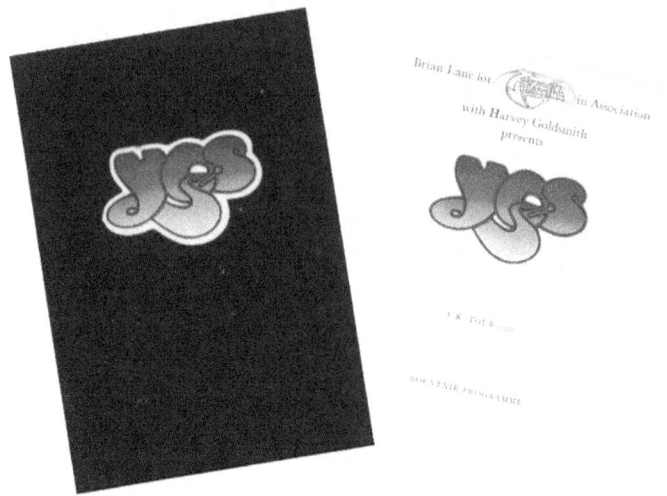

Official Souvenir Programme for the 1973 UK *Tales Tour*, uploaded to Forgotten Yesterdays by Steven Sullivan

perhaps the appearance of a halo is deliberate, who knows? In the larger Rick Wakeman photo, he looks a little upset.

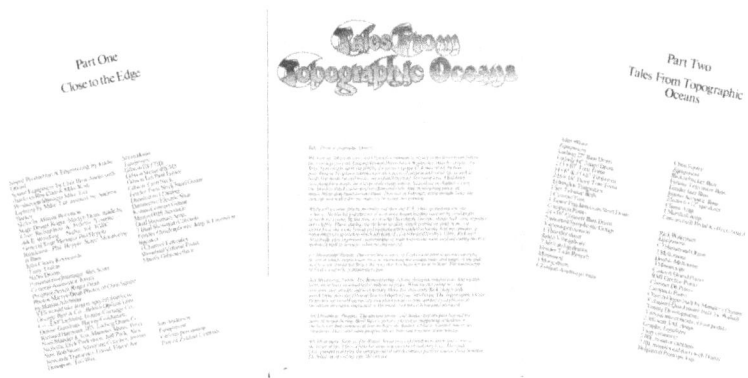

The three pages dedicated to text feature the Jon Anderson explanation of Tales and extensive equipment lists. A little like a classical concert, *Close to the Edge* is described as Part One and *Tales* as Part Two.

There is space for a full-colour reproduction of Roger Dean's cover painting and typography and the final page displays, perhaps surprisingly, an advertisement for

Wakeman's forthcoming concert in January 1974 with the London Symphony Orchestra. This was the legendary event that was recorded and released as the live album, *Journey to the Centre of the Earth*. Strangely, the advert doesn't mention what music will be performed but it's no wonder Rick's mind wasn't fully on the *Tales Tour*. The UK *Tales Tour* ended on 10th December 1973, Rick's Concert was on 18th January 1974 and the US *Tales Tour* began on 7th February.

The final unusual and ground-breaking feature of the UK programme was the inclusion of a sheet of stickers. As you can imagine, complete sticker sheets are now rare and worth a considerable sum. This example is courtesy of the David Watkinson Collection, as displayed in Dave's mini exhibition at Trading Boundaries in 2025 (see chapter 18).

When the time came for the North American *Tales Tour*, the accompanying tour book was significantly more lavish than the UK one had been. There was no sticker sheet, however, and the front cover lacked the die-cut aperture. The Roger Dean page was included, this time on a black background but, inexplicably, with the cover painting printed the wrong way round. I'm sure Roger Dean was not impressed:

26 - TOUR BOOKS/PROGRAMMES

Uploaded to Forgotten Yesterdays[62] by Steven Sullivan

With the benefit of a UK tour already completed, live photos could be included. These are credited to Martyn Dean. These are all interesting and characterful images, if mostly dark.

The most interesting photo appears in the middle double spread of the publication (see p.342):

---

62 https://tormatobook.com/talesbooks

While it's not clear where the other shots were taken, this image is definitely from one of the concerts at The Rainbow Theatre, London (see chapter 20). Many of the features identified in previous chapters can be seen here, including:

- The Mander 2-manual portable pipe organ being played by Rick Wakeman (chapter 5)
- The original scenery designs (chapter 21)
- Chris Squire's Guild Jetstar II short scale fretless bass on its stand (chapter 8)
- Chris Squire's Dewtron Mr Bassman bass pedals (chapter 8)
- Steve Howe's Danelectro Dane/Hawk A2N12 on its stand (chapter 7)
- The Michael Tait-designed guitar tree (chapter 20)
- Tympani – just visible (chapter 6)
- Slanted orchestra pit cover (chapter 20)

The rest of the tour book is taken up with text. There are similar kit lists to the UK version (although not split up between *Close to the Edge* and *Tales*), crew and equipment credits and two extensive pieces of writing. The first is by author Donald Lehmkuhl. His name may be familiar to you because he wrote the introduction to Roger Dean's book *Views* and one of his poems was used on the sleeve of Yes' next album, *Relayer*. Roger and Martyn Dean also collaborated with Lehmkuhl on a remarkable book, *The Flights of Icarus*, released in 1977.

The writing here seems to me to be a kind of earth and life creation story, weaving all sorts of scientific, historical and philosophical elements together, a little like Jon Anderson has done through the decades. Its theme seems close to what Anderson was trying to convey with *Tales*, so it is highly appropriate, if rather unusual, to see this essay in the *Tales* tour book. You can read the whole text on Forgotten Yesterdays but it ends, appropriately, with the words, "You and earth and history are one." I wonder how many Yes fans sat and read this before their chosen *Tales* concert. It must have set the mood effectively if they did.

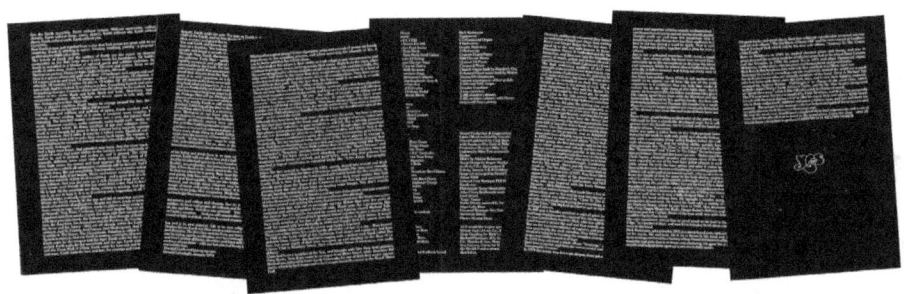

The other rather more traditional piece is by Chris Welch. Although he didn't have hugely positive things to say about *Tales* in his *Melody Maker* review, he knew the band intimately and presents here a biography of Yes from its conception in 1968. He praises the band's continual progress, from their beginnings playing tiny venues and culminating in *Tales*. Each current member is given a glowing write-up (and it's good to see a mention of Oliver Wakeman – presumably his first Yes 'credit'!) and the technical crew are mentioned warmly, especially Eddie Offord. Welch ends by saying, "Enjoy the show ... after all, it took them a long time to get here!" Looking back from the viewpoint of 2025, 1968 to 1974 doesn't seem that long.

Finally, there is a page with the locations of the *Tales Tour*. Once again, the enormous scale of the operation is brought home by this map and the details of the dates of the concerts beneath (see p.344):

As a tribute to the 1973 UK programme, the Gottlieb Bros. used the same die-cut approach for the front cover of their magnificent 2023 tour book for the *Classic Tales of Yes Tour*, photos Forgotten Yesterdays (see p.345, left) and author's collection (right).

Tales from Topographic Oceans - Yes album Listening Guide

AMERICAN TOUR 1974 PROGRAM

Part One
Close to the Edge
Part Two
Tales From Topographic Oceans

FEBRUARY

Thurs 7	Univ. of Florida	GAINSVILLE	
Fri 8	Miami Stadium	FLORIDA	
Sat 9	Tampa Stadium	FLORIDA	
Sun 10	Univ. of South Carolina	COLUMBIA	
Mon 11	Georgia Tech	ATLANTA	
Tues 12	Civic Centre	ROANOKE, VIRGINIA	
Wed 13	Civic Centre	BALTIMORE, MARYLAND	
Thurs 14	Nassau Coliseum	HEMPSTEAD, LI, NEW YORK	
Fri 15	New Haven Coliseum	CONNECTICUT	
Sat 16	Spectrum	PHILADELPHIA, P.A.	
Sun 17	DAY OFF		
Mon 18	Madison Sq. Gdns.	NEW YORK	
Tues 19	DAY OFF		
Wed 20	Madison Sq. Gdns.	NEW YORK	
Thurs 21	Civic Arena	PITTSBURG, P.A.	
Fri 22	Maple Leaf Gdns.	TORONTO, ONTARIO, CANADA	
Sat 23	Broome County Arena	BINGHAMPTON, NEW YORK	
Sun 24	Cornell Univ.	ITHACA, NEW YORK	
Mon 25	Forum	MONTREAL, QUEBEC, CANADA	
Tues 26	Boston Gdns.	BOSTON, MASSACHUSETTS	
Wed 27	Cobo Hall	DETROIT, MICHIGAN	
Thurs 28			

MARCH

Fri 1	Hershey Arena	HERSHEY, P.A.	
Sat 2	Convention Centre	LOUISVILLE, KENTUCKY	
Sun 3	Cincinnati Gdns.	CINCINNATI, OHIO	
Mon 4	DAY OFF		
Tues 5	Met Sports Centre	MINNEAPOLIS, MINNESOTA	
Wed 6	Amphitheatre	CHICAGO, ILLINOIS	
Thurs 7			
Fri 8	Kiel Auditorium	ST. LOUIS, MISSOURI	
Sat 9			
Sun 10	Civic Convention Centre	MEMPHIS, TENNESSEE	
Mon 11	Fairgrounds Arena	OKLAHOMA CITY, OKLAHOMA	
Tues 12	DAY OFF		
Wed 13	Univ. of New Mexico	ALBUQUERQUE, NEW MEXICO	
Thurs 14	DAY OFF		
Fri 15	Winterland	SAN FRANCISCO, CALIF.	
Sat 16			
Sun 17	Memorial Auditorium	SACRAMENTO, CALIF.	
Mon 18	Los Angeles Forum	L.A. CALIF.	
Tues 19	Arena	LONG BEACH, CALIF.	
Wed 20	Selland Arena	FRESNO, CALIF.	
Thurs 21	San Diego Sports Arena	SAN DIEGO, CALIF.	

27 CONCERT MEMORABILIA

With almost 80 shows across 3 legs, there was plenty of opportunity for creating and selling merchandise at and around the *Tales Tour*, in addition to the official and unofficial tour books/programmes. Despite Roger Dean's hope of coordinating all the visual aspects of the tour, there certainly seems to be a lot of variation in collections around the world. For example, the lovely, bright St. Louis T-shirt in Dave Watkinson's collection below doesn't feel very official, despite its use of the Roger Dean logo. The other T-shirt pictured is probably more official and issued to crew by management:

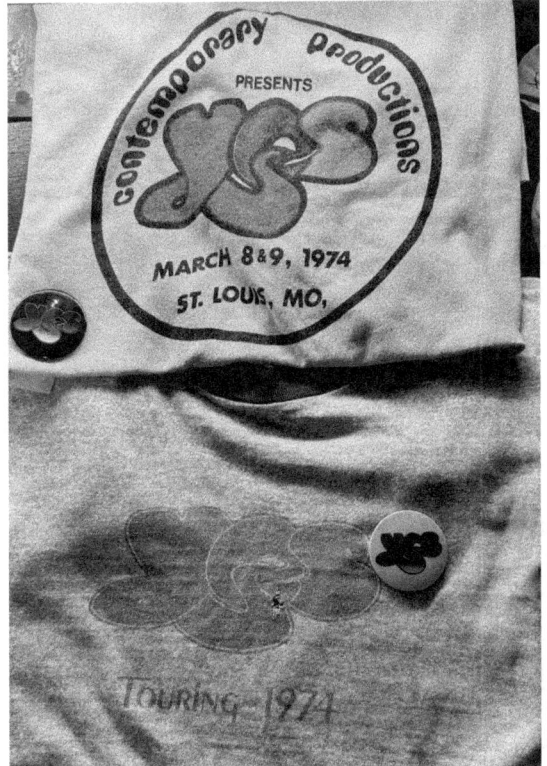

2 T-shirts and 2 badges (pins) from the *North American Tales Tour*, courtesy of David Watkinson Collection

Although it's difficult to know for sure, it's likely that the UK T-shirt below (see p.348) is an official one and the Miami Stadium version is a locally-produced unofficial item:

Many of the venues visited by Yes on the *Tales Tour* produced their own flyers and posters. Sometimes these used the Roger Dean *Tales* artwork without permission and sometimes they even delved back into historic Yes iconography. The *Fragile* cover and Yes logo were used on this poster from Cook Convention Center in Memphis, Tennessee:

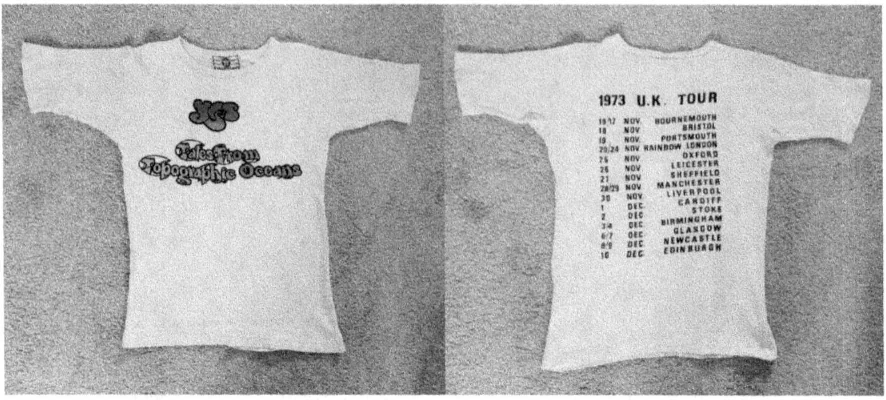

Above, UK *Tales Tour* T-shirt, courtesy of The Clive Ayer Collection, photo by Clive Ayer, below, T-shirt from Miami 1974 uploaded by Tonya to Forgotten Yesterdays

Handbill from Cook Convention Center, Memphis, courtesy of David Watkinson Collection

Some concert promoters opted for a basic approach – it's unclear whether this poster's use of the Roger Dean logo – or Atlantic's logo for that matter – were officially sanctioned see p.349):

One of the rare official publications was this balloon leaflet. I assume this was handed out at the concerts that featured this most unusual advertising gimmick (See chapter 18).

27 – CONCERT MEMORABILIA

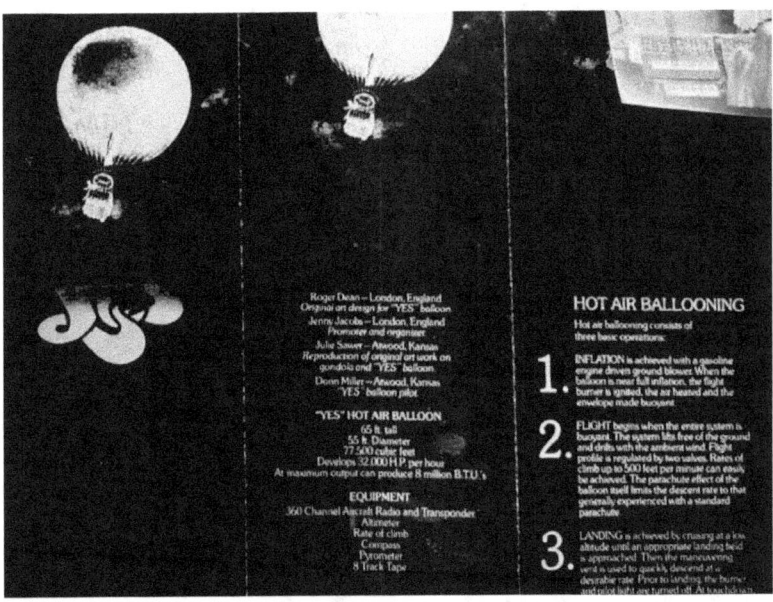

Advert for the final *Tales Tour* show at Palazzo Di Palaeur Dello Sport in Rome, courtesy of David Watkinson Collection

Hot air balloon leaflet, courtesy of David Watkinson Collection

Another interesting interpretation of the *Tales* artwork was produced for the 21st April concert in Zurich below left, while the same concert is used to tie in album promotion, below right. Unusually, the Yes balloon appears as does a double album collection of *Yes* and *Time and a Word*, released by Atlantic in Europe in 1973.

Concert posters from Zurich, courtesy of The Clive Ayer Collection, photo by Clive Ayer

PART 8 - EPILOGUE

28

EPILOGUE

As soon as the *Tales* tour finished, Rick Wakeman left the band. He could have been on his way even sooner. Yes were, once again, on the lookout for a replacement. As Sid says, it wasn't *Tales* that fractured Yes at that point, it was much more likely to have been the burgeoning solo career of Rick Wakeman. With the success of *The Six Wives of Henry VIII*, Wakeman had the opportunity to be in sole charge of his own musical destiny, rather than having to do battle with the inevitable factions within Yes. Rick didn't like a lot of the music on *Tales* but if he hadn't had the 'lifeboat' of a solo career, maybe he would have ended up staying. The band played huge venues on the *Tales* tour and life on the road playing music he didn't like finally convinced him it was time to go. I asked Rick to explain his view on the situation from the viewpoint of 2025 and he kindly replied:

> "Quite simply I was unhappy with the direction Yes were taking and Yes has always been a give and take band as far as I was concerned. The direction it was taking was not one where I felt truly able to "give" and I was getting little in return. Yes had always rehearsed meticulously before going into the studio and would be 75% prepared before the first recordings were made. 25% was added in the studio where the music progressed to its final stages. I loved this way of working and to me *Fragile* and then *Close to the Edge* epitomised this way of producing the best of Yes music. With *Topographic Oceans* we had four pieces of varying length. We were also governed by how much music you could fit on one vinyl side. The four pieces were all short of required length. Truth is that if CDs had been around there would never have been a problem but because it was vinyl we had to get around 18 minutes of music for each side. So we ended up "jamming" in the studio and using what I considered to be substandard writing and a lot of musical padding. This upset me greatly but I had no support from any of the others and so I felt it best I handed in my notice. The management convinced me to stay, saying that during the upcoming European tour I might be

able to find a way of enjoying the music. I tried but I didn't and toward the end of the tour called a meeting where I announced I was leaving. I was persuaded by the management to not make an announcement until they had found a replacement, which I happily agreed to as, in spite of what had happened musically, I still loved Yes dearly.

I actually officially left on May 18th 1974. I remember it well for two reasons. One, it was my birthday and two, *Journey to the Centre of the Earth* had just given A&M Records its first number one album in the UK. A day of very mixed feelings.

I still think there are some beautiful melodies and great playing on *Tales*, but still maintain it would have made a great hour long CD, but you couldn't fit an hour onto a vinyl album and not all the pieces would be the same length. All too late now and a lot of water has gone under the bridge.

As it turned out I personally know I made the right decision as, when *Relayer* came out, I realised I would have had nothing to contribute at all. But then *Going for the One* came along and the Yes musical smile came back to my face."

Wakeman Splits From Yes!

Rick Wakeman: The thought of playing 'Topographic Oceans' through another American tour, coupled with the smashing success of his own 'Journey' LP was enough to persuade Rick it was time to go solo permanently.

Rick Wakeman has said farewell to YES. Speculation about a possible departure has been in the air for quite some time now—ever since he began recording and performing as a solo artist.

A spokesman for Wakeman and Yes said that his departure was amicable and by mutual agreement. The official explanation is that he intends to pursue a solo career, although, as yet, his future plans are uncertain. At present Wakeman is taking a thorough rest in a cottage in Cornwall and Yes are officially on holiday. There is no news yet regarding a replacement for Wakeman in Yes, although it is stressed that there is no question of the band breaking up. All are expected back into London shortly, and Yes will begin rehearsing for a new album.

News of the departure of Rick Wakeman, UK publication unknown, courtesy of David Watkinson Collection

For me, *Tales from Topographic Oceans* is an endlessly fascinating work. Listening closely to the four sides of music has given me a renewed appreciation for the skill and seemingly boundless ingenuity of arrangement, production, recording and musical performance. There are so many layers of detail that I seem to hear new and surprising elements each time.

As I have tried to convey in this book, the path taken to complete the album was difficult and time-consuming. The initial reaction could have wrecked Yes' career but perhaps Jon Anderson and Steve Howe's determination to create something on a scale never seen before, to push the band's music much further than even *Close to the Edge* had gone is the best definition of progressive rock that has ever existed.

It's no surprise, then, that the band attracted so many technical innovators who went on to define every conceivable aspect of live music. Without *Tales* I'm not sure this could have happened and maybe the 'topography' of the modern musical spectacular – recorded and live – would be very different today without it.

ACKNOWLEDGEMENTS

In addition to the Executive Producers mentioned at the beginning, I'd like to thank the following people for their help in writing this book:

Martyn J Adelman, Jon Anderson, Clive Ayer, Elayne Barre, Geoff Bailie, Chris Berry, Simon Barrow, Joe Cass, Sharon Chevin, Jeffrey Crecelius, Doug Curran, Chris Dale, Jon Davison, Freya Dean, Roger Dean, Derek Dearden, Paul Denham, Geoff Downes, Steven English, Margaret Evans, Miguel Falcão, Preston Michael Frazier, Rachel Hadaway, Michael Handerhan, Tony Harris, Laurens Van Houten, Steve Howe, Karen Jackman, Paul Jeynes, Mark Jones, Mark Anthony K, Emma Leach, Bill Martin, John Martin, Geoffery Mason, Philip Mason, Sean McCarthy, James McQuinn, Paulina Mennen, Charlotte Mulryne, Edward Mulryne, Sarah Mulryne, William Mulryne, Stewart Munro, Frank Natale, Michael O'Connor, Ray Palmer, Ian Peacock, Thomas Perkins, Henry Potts, Phil Rathe, Raymond Riethmeier, Gennaro Rippo, Jean Ristori, Peter Robinson, Steve Rogers, Jay Schellen, Laura Shenton, Billy Sherwood, Dan Shinder, Stephen Shinder, Sid Smith, Steven Sullivan, Paul Sutin, Michael Tait, Bob Vandiver, Oliver Wakeman, Rick Wakeman, David Watkinson, Chris Welch, Frank White, Alan White (R.I.P.), Adam Wildi, Steven Wilson, Joey Wise.

www.ingramcontent.com/pod-product-compliance
Lightning Source LLC
Chambersburg PA
CBHW071228070526
44583CB00017B/2097